OFFSHORE SAILING

OFFSHORE SAILING

200 ESSENTIAL PASSAGEMAKING TIPS

BILL SEIFERT

with Daniel Spurr

International Marine / McGraw-Hill

Camden, Maine • New York • Chicago • San Francisco • Lisbon • London • Madrid
Mexico City • Milan • New Delhi • San Juan • Seoul • Singapore • Sydney • Toronto

International Marine
A Division of The McGraw-Hill Companies

10 9 8 7 6 5 4

Copyright © 2002 International Marine

All rights reserved. The publisher takes no responsibility for the use of any of the materials or methods described in this book, nor for the products thereof. The name "International Marine" and the International Marine logo are trademarks of The McGraw-Hill Companies. Printed in the United States of America.

Library of Congress Cataloging-in-Publication Data
Seifert, Bill.
   Offshore sailing : 200 essential passagemaking tips / Bill Seifert with Daniel Spurr.
      p.   cm.
   ISBN 0-07-137424-8 (alk. paper)
   1. Sailing. I. Spurr, Daniel, 1947– II. Title.
GV811.S39 2002
797.1´24—dc21   2001003449

Questions regarding the content of this book
   should be addressed to
International Marine
P.O. Box 220
Camden, ME 04843
www.internationalmarine.com

Questions regarding the ordering of this book
   should be addressed to
The McGraw-Hill Companies
Customer Service Department
P.O. Box 547
Blacklick, OH 43004
Retail customers: 1-800-262-4729
Bookstores: 1-800-722-4726

This book is printed on 70# Citation by R.R. Donnelley
Design by Carol Gillette
Page layout by Deborah Evans and Matt Watier
Production management by Janet Robbins
Line art by Jim Sollers
All photographs by the author unless otherwise indicated
Edited by Jonathan Eaton and Jane Crosen

Notice to Readers

The information in this book is predicated on the personal and professional experience of the authors. Sources are listed for informational purposes only. While the information is accurate to the best of our knowledge, the authors and publisher disclaim any warranty as to this book or any statements herein. Statements or descriptions are informational only, and not made or given as a warranty in any way.

   Outfitting, repairing, sailing, and maneuvering any boat can involve exposure to dangerous situations and substances. Offshore sailing, by its nature, entails unique hazards and challenges, and sailing outside the limits of previous personal experience is particularly hazardous. Neither this nor any other book can protect a sailor from the failure to exercise common sense, good judgment, and appropriate care at all times while working on or sailing a boat. Do not rely on this book as a substitute for proper seamanship, which includes the habit of mind known as "forehandedness" or anticipation. Think ahead of the boat, imagine what could happen and how you would respond, and be safe out there.

Metric equivalents are in appendix 9, beginning on page 231.

CONTENTS

CHAPTER 4.
Electronic and Electrical Equipment

CHAPTER 5.
Engine, Mechanical, and Plumbing Systems

CHAPTER 6. *At Sea*

CHAPTER 7. *Galley Tips*

APPENDICES
1. *Boat Selection*

I've been in the management of sailboat building companies almost all my adult life, generally in the position of project engineering new models, and working with owners on semicustom yacht production.

I started sailing before I was born. On July 4, 1945, six days before my birth, my mother was getting off the family boat when I must have kicked at the wrong time, because we both went swimming.

By August, I was back on board, usually napping in a big life preserver under the foredeck. I could steer a boat long before riding a bicycle. My family had a boat on the south shore of Lake Erie, which generally has prevailing winds from the north. My parents would beat out in the morning, then get the boat pointed to shore and give me the tiller while they napped.

I started sailing offshore at age fourteen, crewing with George White on *Gaudeamus*, a 36-foot Dutch-built varnished mahogany sloop, which we later converted to a yawl. George was a brilliant, multitalented man who taught me a lot about boats and their systems. I raced with him for ten years, until he was appointed Architect of the Capitol and moved to Washington, D.C.

When I graduated from college, everybody wanted the gray flannel suit job. I got mine with a division of Litton Industries that made large computer-controlled machine tools. Management had tried having the engineering department write operation and programming manuals, but results were comprehensible only to other engineers. When the service department took over the manuals, they had a lot of information on how to fix machines, but nothing about how to work them. The company finally decided to hire somebody who knew as much about their products as their customers, that is, nothing, and picked me.

I went around the company asking thousands of questions, and about every hundredth one would elicit the response, "Yes, I can see why you are asking that." Customers liked my manuals, and I was moving up the corporate ladder until the company announced one year that management's Christmas "bonus" would be a 10 percent pay cut.

I looked for a part-time job to supplement my reversing salary. I was hired by Douglass and McLeod Plastics Corporation one Wednesday to be project engineer on a new model, the Tartan 26. Friday of the same week, the company burned to the ground, including every scrap of paper. Charlie Britton decided to rebuild under the name Tartan Marine Company, and pursue the Tartan 26, so I worked in temporary quarters, approaching the creation of a new model the way a machine tool would be built, with proper engineering documentation. Knowing the cost of a new model preproduction was a new experience in the boatbuilding business, and by June, Charlie convinced me to give up the world of the three-piece suit for a full-time career in boatbuilding.

I bought a Tartan 26 and ripped the back left pocket out of all the shorts I owned by hooking the cleat I had carefully positioned on a drawing, at the proper 10-degree angle from the winch.

The next engineering project was the Tartan 46/48, followed by the very popular Tartan 41/44, which helped Tartan grow from $2 million to $10 million in annual sales.

I was also good at listening to and dealing with customers, and pretty soon all calls beginning with "I've got a question" were coming to my office. Ample feedback from customers gave me an understanding of how people use (and abuse) their boats.

I also was half of the Tartan Factory Racing Team. I cooked, Charlie steered, and we logged a lot of miles on bigger Tartans in the SORC, Bermuda, and Mackinac Races. At the same time I owned and raced a succession of smaller Tartans, buying a very basic boat and tricking them out with the help of my father.

In 1980, I moved to Rhode Island as Materials Manager of TPI, and helped the company get computerized. At our max, TPI built thirty-two boats a week in twelve models—J-boats, Freedom Yachts, Alden, and others. Everett Pearson is always on the cusp of technology, and I learned a lot about modern materials.

Alden Yachts eventually was split off as an operating entity, and I ended up as new boat project manager, interfacing between custom yacht customers and the shop. On the side, I also looked after a 76-foot aluminum ketch, owned by the owner of Alden, a man to whom perfection was a requisite. Unfortunately, the luxury tax of 1991 reduced a three-year backlog to one boat to build, and the company did not need an expensive project manager. I was laid off, which may have been the best thing that ever happened to me.

Customers had my home phone number and started calling.

"Last year the yard messed up my boat when they launched it. Any chance you could come and direct them so it does not get screwed up again?"

This led to my little yacht management company looking after boats all over the world. We do commissioning and decommissioning, deliveries, upgrades, routine maintenance . . . whatever the owner wants. This work has forced me to keep learning about boat products, tools, techniques, and best of all, takes me to sea for thousands of miles each year.

A request to prepare instructions on safety gear for the Marion–Bermuda Race Seminar was the beginning of this book. Other topics have been covered at the request of cruisers who have asked, "What would you do about . . . ?"

The Offshore Racing Council (ORC) is the international body that establishes equipment requirements, and to a small extent, yacht design (e.g., cockpit volume), for participating yachts. A small pamphlet describing ORC rules is available, for cruisers as well as racers, from U.S. Sailing (see contact information in appendix 7). In it you'll find good advice such as the need to restrain batteries, make companionway dropboards lockable from inside and outside, and prevent floorboards in the cabin sole from turning into deadly projectiles in the event of a knockdown. Books and magazines tell you the same thing, but seldom if ever show you precisely how.

This book does.

As you read, remember that no boat is ever perfect, nor any "to-do" list ever finished. Priorities are, in no particular order:

- Keep water outside the boat.

- Keep the rig in the boat.

- Keep the keel on and hull and deck intact.

- Be able to control the vessel's direction.

- Keep the crew on board.

- Know where you are and where you're going.

- Have enough experience or crew with experience that passages are pleasant, not terrifying.

If you can do these seven things, the rest—with a little effort—will generally take care of themselves.

Fair winds, following seas, and may your autopilot last until you get there.

Bill Seifert
Warren, Rhode Island

ACKNOWLEDGMENTS

This book would not have been possible without help from cruisers I have met all over the world. Some have read draft copies and offered suggestions. All have generously shared their experiences, problems, and triumphs.

Dan Spurr, former editor of *Practical Sailor*, took a rather ragged assembly of thoughts and turned it into what you now read. I mostly wrote the manuscript on airplanes coming and going to boats, or on the 4 to 8 A.M. watch offshore. Neither venue is conducive to coherent thinking, and Dan has done a yeoman's job. I'm sorry he's moved away to the mountains, but am glad he has agreed to continue to do the occasional ocean voyage with me.

Okay, you've decided you want to take off and go cruising. Just get the boat ready, sell the house and cars, kick out the kids, and head off to paradise. Fulfilling this dream is never easy. Things never go smoothly. Projects never get done on time. Everything always takes twice as long as expected and costs more.

I have seen a lot of cruising dreams abandoned because people forged ahead without adequate exposure to offshore conditions. Before even thinking about taking off, make a passage with someone else. Get beaten up offshore where you do not have the added responsibility of being the skipper—or of protecting *your* dream.

After you have a boat, take it out and get to know how it likes weather, if you will need bigger or smaller sails, how the vessel works at a 25-degree angle of heel. If possible, put some extra weight on board—sandbags or whatever—to approximate the extra displacement of equipment and stores for a long passage. Does the boat bog down and not move in light winds? Will she heave-to in heavy air? Have you accurately measured fuel consumption at various RPM?

As you are preparing your vessel, take a break now and then between projects, stow the tools, and go out for an overnight sail. You will gain confidence and get positive feedback that all the effort is worthwhile. You may come back in with more projects on the list—that's normal and proves the trip was not time wasted.

I have built and managed boats for people with vastly different levels of experience: business executives who can manage corporations but do not have a clue about how to provision for a trip; doctors who have to be chided to buy first-aid supplies; lawyers intimidated by customs paperwork; electrical engineers who have never crimped a terminal on a wire. But they all learned, and generally enjoyed themselves. Satisfaction derived is usually directly proportional to the amount of work done by the owner. A person who only admires work done by a yard misses the personal pride of being able to say, "I did that." This is much more gratifying than saying, "I paid for that."

And pay you will either way, but much less if you do a job yourself. As a bonus you'll have an intimate, firsthand knowledge of where and how, say, the inverter was installed. This knowledge will be most useful when the inverter stops working and there is no one else to fix it but you. "You know, I was never too confident of the crimp on that two-aught ring terminal."

If you have a lot of work to do (and what boat doesn't?), and money is a concern, make a budget before you dive in too deep. Generally, the upgrade budget has a lot to do with when you can actually quit work and go. Price safety gear early on. A new life raft, 406 MHz EPIRB, personal strobes, inflatable life vests, and man-overboard module can set you back eight grand in a heartbeat. Be sure to deduct essential safety gear from the amount you have to spend on upgrades.

Establishing priorities on what to do before going offshore depends on a lot of factors. Make a plan with job lists, and think about the order in which they will be done. If, for example, the boat is hauled, this is the time to do hull repairs or add through-hulls. You can't do these jobs after launching. In freezing temperatures, one has difficulty using resins, so these jobs must be put off. If the boat is not covered, and it is raining, one must work below. Fall back to plan B, and don't waste the day.

One mistake I see a lot of people making is uncovering a boat too early in the spring. The yachts I manage that are hauled in cold climates have winter covers with frameworks to allow crawling around on deck. I do all deck work—varnishing, cleaning, waxing, etc.—before removing the cover on the morning of launch day. If there is any sunshine, the deck gets nice and toasty under the cover. And if the guy next door power sands his bottom, my decks are not stained from dust. Also, having my van with tools and spare parts parked right next to the boat sure beats a long walk down a dock for one more $\frac{1}{4}'' \times 20$ nut.

Develop your job list while doing your own survey. It may be useful to systematically categorize them: rig and sails, deck, engine and drive train, safety gear, ground tackle, navigation, plumbing, and electrical. That's the approach I've taken in organizing this book.

I can't tell you in what order to perform all your jobs, but here are a few suggestions:

I like to get major projects out of the way first, especially those involving outside contractors, who probably will be late and make a mess. Why spend days oiling the teak coaming only to have a mechanic step on it with greasy boots?

A joke I tell customers is that my retirement job is going to involve hiring a minister and traveling all around the world performing marriage ceremonies for the *parents* of people who run boatyards.

In general, plumbing takes precedence over electrical work, as running hoses takes more room and requires straighter runs.

Removing through-bolted hardware can be a one-person job if a pair of Vise-Grip pliers will hold the nut, and the pliers are secured so they will not rotate and fall on anything fragile when the nut comes off. But because it is very difficult to hold a bolt head from rotating while screwing on a nut from down below, installing deck hardware is a two-person job.

When I'm working on a boat, I annotate the inevitably long work list:

L Jobs that must be done prior to launch.
R Jobs that can be done during inclement weather (I save these, literally, for a rainy day).
H Jobs for which I need help.
W Jobs that can be accomplished only in warm weather.
P Parts needed before work can be completed.

Plan your work, and then work your plan.

Now, let's get started.

CHAPTER 1

A SAFE DECK

When it was very hot aboard the 36-foot mahogany yawl *Gaudeamus*, the crew frequently would wear just bathing suits. The problem was a lack of pockets for things like cigarette lighters. Zippo makes a model with a bail for attaching a lanyard, and the crew's fashion was to wear one around the neck on a lanyard made from ⅛-inch nylon parachute cord.

One blistering August day we were making the final tack to cross the finish line. Somehow, one of the crew went overboard. He ended up in the water but hanging on to the toerail, so we were legal to finish. Because the maneuvering was very tight, we told him to stay put for the 30 seconds it would take us to cross the line, then we'd get him back on board.

I happened to look at him just as we crossed the line, and he was turning blue. Looking closer I could see the end of the lighter lanyard disappearing into his neck.

Fortunately, the knife I carried had a very blunt side opposite the sharp edge, which I was able to work into the skin on the side of his neck to cut the lanyard that was choking him. After he started breathing, he told us that the lanyard had wrapped around the genoa sheet during the tack and pulled him overboard.

This incident ended the wearing of neck lanyards on *Gaudeamus*, or any boat I sail on.

A good knife is just one of many safety tools and items of equipment that should be carried aboard the well-fitted offshore boat (see appendix 4, pages 204–5). But you can't bring a tool for every contingency; there is no substitute for learning to think on your feet.

The appendices will help your outfitting and provisioning. In any case, here are a number of installations and upgrades that ought to be done to keep the crew on board and water and thieves out.

CREW SAFETY

The well-being of your crew—very likely family and friends—is a strong theme in this book. When one thinks of offshore sailing, safety immediately comes to mind. In the pages that follow, we'll show you how to keep crew safe on board, rested, and well fed.

Jacklines and Cockpit Pad Eyes   TIP 1

Jacklines are ropes, wire, or webbing stretched between the bow and stern of a boat to which crew clip their safety harnesses when moving about on deck. Offshore, they should be left *rigged* (attached) in place, regardless of weather.

Jacklines made from flat nylon webbing are generally considered preferable to round wire, which will roll underfoot. The breaking strength requirement is a minimum of 5,000 pounds. The color

Jacklines made of flat polyester webbing don't roll underfoot like rope does, but they stretch more.

should be very bright so that they are visible both day and night. Quantum/Thurston Sailmakers in Bristol, Rhode Island (all contact information is in appendix 7), makes jacklines from "hot pink" webbing, which certainly meets the criterion for brightness. The drawback of colored jacklines is that they may bleed their dye on deck. To avoid this mess, soak them in a bucket of water before using.

The design I recommend is a continuous length with a loop sewn in at the bow, which is then shackled to the stemhead (see photo). The two aft legs tie off to the stern cleats the same way one would belay a line. With one continuous line, the sewing of the loop at the bow is not terribly critical. If using two separate jacklines, one for each side of the deck (sold by West Marine and others), the loop stitching must be protected from chafe with tape.

There are, as with most things nautical, differences of opinion regarding jacklines. In the 1998 Sydney–Hobart Race disaster, a number of sailors were critical of webbing because it stretched too much.

Others make an argument against belaying jacklines right at the stern, suggesting instead to terminate them a tether-length forward so that a person falling overboard won't be dragged behind the boat. In the 1999 Farallones Race off California, a J/29 crew member drowned while still tethered to the boat following a knockdown. After the boat righted, his partner could not stop the boat, which still made

A single continuous jackline shackled to the stem eliminates multiple fittings, and failure if stitching chafes.

The two aft ends of the jacklines are belayed to cleats.

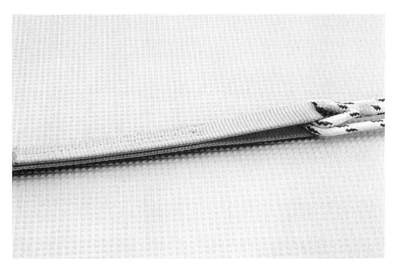

Stitching on jackline webbing must be heavy, UV-resistant, well executed, and covered to prevent chafe (not yet done on this jackline).

7 knots with all sheets released, and "towing" the crew-overboard.

John Neal, author and adventure–charter skipper, recommends rigging a rope lifeline from the stern pulpit to an Aladdin cleat 5 feet above the deck on the upper shroud, and then down to the bow pulpit; he says this is much easier to work with than jacklines on the deck. Others locate jacklines on centerline so a person simply can't fall over the side.

Boats also should have strong—5,000-pound minimum breaking strength—pad eyes close to the companionway so crew can hook in safety harness tethers before coming fully on deck. Because crew must also be able to move aft to positions in the cockpit, including the helm, additional pad eyes or jacklines are necessary. Where the cockpit configuration permits, rig a jackline on each side, beginning near the companionway and running far enough aft so that the helmsman can steer while clipped on.

If the cockpit layout does not permit continuous jacklines from the companionway to the helm, install pad eyes both port and starboard of the helm for the person steering to hook into, preferably with two tethers, one on each side.

I was hooked in with two tethers during the 1976 Bermuda Race when we took a wave over the deck that caught me square in the chest, knocking the wind out of me. The force of the wave hitting also bent the steering wheel, which I was holding onto with both hands.

That's sufficient force to knock a person overboard, despite his death grip on the wheel. (For data on actual wave forces, see Lashing Gear on Deck, tip 6, and Cockpit Speakers and Other Holes, tip 7.) When that happens, your safety tether and jacklines are all that stand between you and the deep blue sea.

Pad eyes outboard of the helm have another purpose, and that is lashing points for heaving-to. No pedestal brake is strong enough to hold the rudder stationary in storm conditions. Strong pad eyes to which the wheel can be lashed should be located exactly athwartships of the wheel, or the wheel can be lashed to permanent fore-and-aft jacklines in the cockpit footwell.

This rope jackline is stretched between two through-bolted pad eyes in the cockpit footwell.

Cockpit jacklines also can be used for tying off the steering wheel, though taking the lines to pad eyes results in less give.

Safety Harnesses   TIP 2

Safety harnesses must have a snap-shackle with a nonfouling lanyard on the release ring at the wearer's end. There have been numerous occasions while changing sails on the foredeck when I have stepped over the new sail so that I was on one side of it and my harness tether clipped to a jackline on the other, and nearly been pulled overboard when the sail was raised and it lifted my tether. By releasing the tether, I was able to stay on board. A carabiner hook cannot be released under load and is *not acceptable* for the wearer's end attachment.

Tethers with a loop (such as those made by Lirakis) can easily be retrofitted by passing the loop through the bail of a snapshackle and back over itself.

I make my own harness tethers with a Gibb #1079 carabiner hook with a locking mechanism at the boat end and a Gibb #773 snapshackle at the harness end. The line is 6 feet of ½-inch three-strand, which is easy to feel in the dark amongst a pile of braided running rigging. ORC (Offshore Racing Council) requirements limit the length of tethers to 2 meters (6 feet, 6 inches) because the farther one can fall, the greater the shock load. If it is rough, I use two tethers so I can snap onto one attachment point before releasing from another.

My personal preference in harnesses is the SOSpenders model 38AH-AR, which has a built-in automatic inflation collar providing 35 pounds of buoyancy and a whistle. SOSpenders offers an optional pouch, model ASP-1000, which holds a personal strobe, dye marker, and signal mirror. This equipment must be tied in with strings long enough so you can hold the strobe overhead, place the whistle in your mouth, and conveniently open the dye marker. Be sure to test the whistle in a swimming pool. Referee-type whistles barely sputter when full of water.

If you use an inflatable PFD, be sure to have spare rearming packs on board. My autoinflating harness has blown up at strange times, such as while standing in the galley drinking a cup of soup after coming off watch.

Manufacturers recommend that inflatable PFDs be manually inflated once a year and left inflated for 24 hours to check for air leaks. Use an air pump for this, as blowing up by mouth introduces moisture into the bladder.

Each crew should have a designated harness, preadjusted to size. Harnesses should be tight. A loose harness can break your ribs or dislocate a shoulder should you be thrown and come up short.

After dark, the standing watch order should require everybody on deck to wear a harness at all times, and clip in.

Never hook a harness tether to the lifelines. The force of someone getting washed overboard can break the lifeline or rip stanchions out of the deck. Never hook a harness tether to a pedestal guard, either. Pedestal guards are not very well secured, and if they should hold, the consequences may be equally dire: ripping out the entire steering pedestal.

A good safety tether uses a Gibb hook at the boat end and a center-jointed snapshackle at the harness end.

Knives   TIP 3

Each crew member should have a very sharp rigging knife, which is kept on his or her person at all times. I keep one in the pocket of my foul-weather gear for ready access when the knife in my pants pocket is under the foul-weather-gear pants.

Every boat should have a sharp knife affixed in the cockpit. Being able to cut away a sheet override if the boat is being held down by a sail taken aback can save the boat and the rig. The pedestal is a handy central location, but before mounting the scabbard be sure to test the knife for magnetism by moving it near the compass.

I also like to keep a knife by the mast. On boats with hydraulic or rigid boom vangs, taping the scabbard to the upper side of the vang works nicely. Otherwise, a sail tie can be used to secure the scabbard around the mast.

If the vessel has Kevlar or similar exotic lines, be sure to have a very sharp serrated knife available.

Cutting Lines Fouled
Underwater   TIP 4

Propellers and spade rudders sometimes pick up line in the water. Rather than dive under the boat with a knife in hand, affix the handle of a serrated knife (a bread knife works) to a boat hook with hose clamps. Hopefully, by hanging over the side (with a harness on) or getting in the dinghy, you can saw through the line, avoiding the dan-

Keep a knife handy to the cockpit, such as this skindiver's sheath model lashed to the steering pedestal. (Tip 3)

ger of being in the water under hull overhangs. Most lobster and crab pot warp is polypropylene, which may melt and fuse together when wrapped around a prop shaft, resulting in a lot of sawing.

SECURING THE DECK

Knots TIP 5

In addition to the mandatory bowline, be sure everybody knows how to tie a rolling hitch. I frequently use a rolling hitch around the genoa sheet, mostly to move the lead to the rail and forward when reaching, but occasionally to take pressure off the sheet when it gets overridden on the primary winch. When offshore, I keep a spare sheet in the cockpit to be used for moving sheet leads. An old rope that has lost its slippery feeling is best for tying a secure rolling hitch.

Lashing Gear on Deck TIP 6

At least a couple of times a year I see a boat coming in from a passage with mangled lifelines and stanchions. The crew is generally haggard, and the stories always run something like this:

"We got into heavy weather and the jerricans of extra fuel and/or water were washed overboard. After the storm, we were short on fuel/water and have had a miserable passage."

Even worse are the boats with sailboards attached to lifelines. These vessels are always missing stanchions, and the pulpits are frequently mangled as well.

Both wind and water can cause damage to gear on deck.

Seawater weighs 64 pounds per cubic foot. Assume the wave top of a small comber breaking on deck is 8 feet long, the breaking portion 4 feet wide, and only 1 foot high. We have 32 cubic feet × 64 pounds = 2,048 pounds, or a ton of water on deck. Now suppose the wave is traveling at 20 knots, and imagine the momentum that would generate.

You can afford to lose a sailboard but not survival gear such as a life raft or crew-overboard module. These should be lashed to through-bolted pad eyes with strong lines or webbing, and with a snap-shackle for quick release.

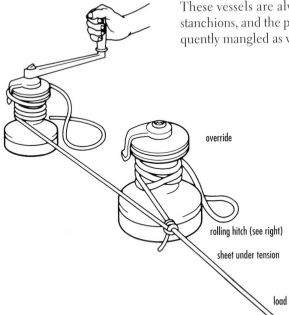

override

rolling hitch (see right)

sheet under tension

load

A short piece of line tied with a rolling hitch to a sheet override allows you to ease tension, but you'll probably need some mechanical advantage, such as another nearby winch. (Tip 5)

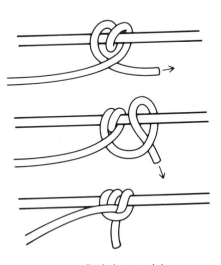

rolling hitch to create slack

Cockpit Speakers and Other Holes   TIP 7

Many owners whose boats have cockpit-mounted stereo speakers are totally unaware that they can admit seawater at the rate of almost 1,000 gallons per minute (GPM) if deluged by a 1-foot wave on deck.

Here's how to calculate the potential danger: $q = 3,600(a)(h)$ in which q is gallons per minute, a is the area of the hole in square feet, and h is the height of water over the hole in feet measured to the lowest part of the hole.

The calculation for 1,000 GPM is predicated on two speakers, each having a 5-inch-diameter hole. The area of a circle R is πR^2, the diameter is 5 inches or 0.417 feet, and the radius is half of the diameter, or 0.208 feet. So the math is

$$3600 \times 3.14\,(0.208 \times 0.208) \times 1 = 489\ \text{GPM, per speaker}$$

It is not uncommon to have more than a foot of water on deck. Seawater weighs 8.6 pounds per gallon, so one would get more than 4 tons of water below per minute with 1-foot-high waves washing through blown-out speaker cones.

Fortunately, it is relatively easy to install removable deck plates over existing speaker holes. ABI and Perko make chrome-plated, cast bronze deck plates with screw-in centers in 5- and 6-inch sizes. Beckson has plastic 4- and 6-inch screw-in deck plates.

I bolt the deck plate through the deck structure and a ¾-inch-thick plywood backing plate. Half-inch-long screws hold the speaker (generally without the decorative grille) to the backing plate behind the

Cockpit stereo speakers can let a lot of water enter the boat if blown out by a wave. Better to install them behind deck plates that can be covered in bad weather.

Beckson deck plates come in 4- and 6-inch sizes. ABI and Perko make bronze deck plates. The deck plate here has been removed so one can hear music from the speaker behind.

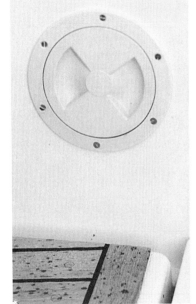

The deck plate is in place for water-tight integrity. (Tip 7)

fiberglass cockpit side. A black fiberglass window screen glued to the front of the backing plate makes an attractive speaker grille and will not corrode. With deck plates covering speaker apertures, one can enjoy music on good days while maintaining watertight integrity in heavy weather.

Easy to Flood TIP 8

When I inspect a boat that has old hose for underwater connections, it is easy to convince the owner to change hoses by telling him that a 1½-inch ID (inside diameter) toilet outlet hose 2 feet underwater will admit 88 GPM. Even a ¾-inch ID engine intake hose 3 feet submerged will admit 33 gallons per minute.

"But I have a 2,000-gallon-per-hour, 1½-inch power bilge pump," some say. "Why worry about a dinky ¾-inch hose?" People tend to forget that most electric bilge pumps are rated in gallons per hour (GPH) with no head (i.e., the height water must be pumped until it flows overboard, often 5 to 6 feet). A 2,000 GPH bilge pump pumps just 33 GPM with no head, same as the inflow from the ¾-inch hose in the example above.

To amplify the point further, in its June 2000 issue *Practical Sailor* tested twenty electric bilge pumps, including the Rule model 14A rated at 3,700 GPH at 0 feet of head. The manufacturer's rating for 5 feet of head was 2,800 GPH. Actual tests at 13.6 volts produced 2,400 GPH, and at 12.2 volts just 2,156 GPH, or 36 GPM.

A very good test of bilge pumping capacity is to remove the knotmeter impeller, make sure the bilge pump is turned on, and monitor bilge water level from this relatively small hole.

The lesson is that if a boat is taking on water, quick action is needed to stem the flow. If water is entering through a hole in the hull, the damaged area must be accessed immediately. Brutalized interior joinerwork can be repaired if the boat is saved; that's why an ax used to be standard equipment on offshore yachts. Nobody cares what the interior of a boat looks like at the bottom of the ocean. The preponderance of molded fiberglass interiors, however, makes it difficult to access all parts of the hull in a hurry.

Leaking Deck Hatches and Portlights TIP 9

Before replacing the gaskets on leaky hatches or portlights, take a little time to be sure the frame or lid has not been sprung during installation or warped by the vessel working. There is a very simple test to determine if an opening is flat. Tape a piece of thread at one corner of the opening. Tension the thread diagonally to the opposite corner and tape it in place. Repeat the process for the other diagonal to form an X with two lengths of thread under equal tension (elastic thread is especially helpful). If the two threads barely touch each other where they cross, then the opening is a flat plane. Space between the threads indicates the extent of distortion.

Leaks due to improper mounting are most prevalent on opening ports in cabin house sides. On most boats, cabin house sides have a gentle curve fore-and-aft. If the mounting fasteners are only on the outside, it is essential that the fore-and-aft middle fasteners, top and bottom,

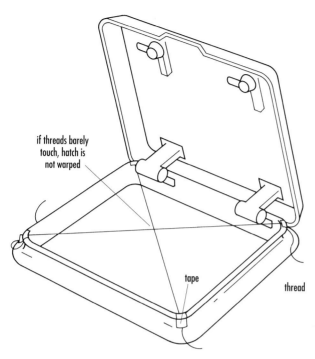

if threads barely
touch, hatch is
not warped

tape

thread

Test for hatch distortion by taping two threads diagonally across the top.
If they do not touch, you may have discovered why the hatch leaks. (Tip 9)

Toilet bumpers screwed into the forward corners of deck hatch frames
prevent sheets from snagging under
the lids and possibly ripping them
off. (Tip 10)

are screwed down first. Conversely, interior fastener installation should be started from the ends. Fasteners that go through both the inside and outside (commonly done with barrel nuts and bolts) are especially tricky. Use the cross-thread trick described above to check for warping. Watch for signs of distortion as the fasteners are snugged up.

I was once asked to help rebed the plastic glazing of a hatch just aft of the mast. This was on a boat that had just completed a rough passage made miserable by a leaking hatch. Suspecting a less obvious root cause of the problem, I told the owner that I would not help him with the hatch, but would take

a look at the interior support for his deck-stepped mast. We jacked up the deck, installed a ¾-inch spacer under the compression post below decks, and his leaking-hatch problem was solved.

Toilet Bumpers on Hatches　TIP 10

Yes, this sounds strange. Most metal frame deck hatch lids do not extend close enough to the deck to preclude a sheet from getting wedged under a corner of the hatch. The force of a sail on a sheet can easily rip the hatch lid off. An inexpensive preventive measure is to fill the gap

by mounting a round rubber toilet bumper either to the frame of the hatch or to the deck.

Toilet bumpers cushion seats from the bowl and are sold in hardware stores, but most come with carbon steel screws. Remove them and replace with stainless steel screws.

A lot of hatches have a fastener in the corners of the frame. It is simple to remove the screw and replace it with a longer one going through a toilet bumper. Even if the hatch gasket compresses, the toilet bumper rubber will give and not affect watertightness. The life of rubber toilet bumpers in the sun is about two years, so when you find the right size, buy spares.

Duct Tape on Deck Fills   TIP 11

I have learned the hard way to tape over fuel and water fill plates on deck before leaving on a passage. When the boat is heeled, the vent line on fuel or water tanks may not work well and the pump will create a partial vacuum in the tank. This vacuum pulls any water on deck through the gasket in the deck fill plates, contaminating the tank contents.

While the tape is out, I also tape closed the pelican hooks in the lifelines. I leave an inch of tape folded over on itself to make a tab to facilitate fast removal.

3M General Purpose Adhesive Cleaner works wonders to remove sticky tape residue. Buy a second can for home, or the can on the boat will migrate.

Duct tape does not hold well on wood. Acrylic sealing compounds (DAP is a popular brand) can be used on wood hatches as a temporary sealant on passages.

A brief aside on tape and metal cans: I always put a wrap of electrical tape around the bottom rim of any metal cans stored on board to prevent rust rings in storage lockers.

A plastic blast gate used on industrial vacuum systems makes a good closure for blower vents. (Tip 12)

Closure of Deck Blower Vents   TIP 12

When water shoots through the overhead into the cabin during heavy weather, it is relatively easy to remember to remove on-deck Dorade cowls and replace them with deck plates.

Easily forgotten are the openings for engine room blowers, which provide a 3- or 4-inch-diameter conduit for water directly to the engine. If the blower outlet cannot be reconfigured to use a vent that can be replaced with a deck plate, an inexpensive and convenient closure for blower vent lines is a plastic blast gate used in industrial vacuum systems. These have a manual slide closure. Suitable blast gates, with short collars at each end, can be purchased from Woodworker's Warehouse.

Vent hose is best secured with a few screws through the hose into the collar; a hose clamp, of course, also is used.

A smear of silicone sealer on the collars before shoving the hose on provides an airtight connection. Woodworker's Warehouse also sells heavy-duty vacuum hose with a vinyl reinforcement that is a vast improvement over the flimsy dryer vent hose with steel helix used on most boats. Because blower hose tends to collapse when making a sharp bend, I use Woodworker's Warehouse plastic elbows.

Regulatory standards do not require a blower for a diesel engine, but forced ventilation of an engine compartment will make your alternator happier, as its output is reduced as temperature goes up. Therefore, do not permanently close off ventilation to an engine to prevent water ingress.

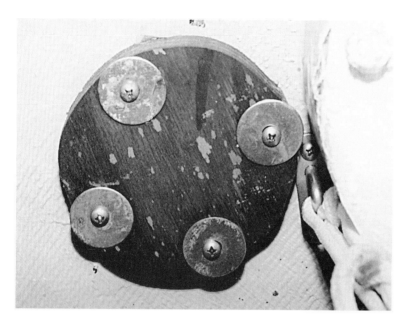

Windlasses with integral chain pipes present a waterproofing challenge. This scrap-plywood plate screws to the underside of the deck where the chain pipe is located. Foam tape on the top side seals out water coming down the pipe.

Closed-cell-foam tape on the upper side of the plywood seals the chain pipe.

Closure of Chain Pipes Built into Windlasses TIP 13

Many windlasses have an integral chain pipe that does a decent job of striping chain from the gypsy and directing it below decks. Unfortunately, they leak. One way I have found to keep these fittings water-tight is to remove the chain and screw a wood cap to the underside of the deck covering the hole (see top photo). The upper surface of the cap is covered with closed-cell foam to make a tight seal (see bottom photo).

On boats that make frequent offshore passages, I replace the screws with hanger bolts, screwed and epoxied into the underside of the deck. (Hanger bolts have no head; one half has machine screw threads and the other end has wood screw threads.) The cap has clearance holes for the machine screw portion of the hanger bolts; I use wing nuts. Jamestown Distributors sells stainless steel hanger bolts and wing nuts. Plumber's test plugs that expand when a wing nut is turned will work on smooth bore holes.

Bedding Deck Hardware   TIP 14

There is a tendency to overtighten deck hardware, squeezing out all the bedding compound. For any metal hardware, use a polysulfide compound (such as Life Calk by BoatLife or 3M 101) or a low-adhesive polyurethane (3M 4200). Silicone compounds do not adhere well to metal, but must be used on some plastics such as Lexan, which polysulfides attack. On cored decks, drill oversize holes through the upper skin and the core. Fill these holes with epoxy resin mixed with a high-density filler. Force the epoxy in with a putty knife. After the epoxy has hardened, drill the right size fastener holes through the epoxy fill.

Be sure to work bedding compound into the threads of fasteners. Bolts should be forced through the deck without turning, and held stationary while the nuts are tightened below decks. Allowing the bolts to rotate may twist out the bedding compound. Always use as large a backing plate as possible (¼-inch-thick aluminum, or ⅜-inch solid fiberglass) to spread loads.

To ensure that backing plates spread the load, they should be installed with a solid filler between the backing plate and its mounting surface. The ideal filler is epoxy mixed with a high-strength filler, such as West System #404. But even good old automotive body putty, such as Bondo, is better than a compressible filler.

If the chainplates leak, take the time to remove their mounting bolts to check for rot in the bulkheads or knees to which they are attached. Remove chainplates to check for crevice corrosion, as happens to stainless steel in an anaerobic environment. Be sure the deck core around chainplates is scraped out to a clearance of about ½ inch and that the void is filled with epoxy and filler. (See also tip 65.)

I like to bed chainplates in two stages. First I bed the chainplate to the deck, which is done with polysulfide filled to just under the top level of the deck. After this hardens, I bed the chainplate covers with a hybrid compound such as BoatLife Life Seal that does not form a strong permanent bond.

For more information on installing deck hardware, see appendix 1, pages 175–77.

Anchors on Bow Rollers   TIP 15

Remove anchors from bow rollers for offshore passagemaking. The force of the bow burying in a wave will dislodge even the most securely pinned and lashed anchor.

Before dropping the end of anchor chain down the hawsehole, tie a small piece of line to it so you can find it again. On occasions when I have forgotten this, I have spent a miserable hour sorting through chain that has shifted during a passage.

All-Chain Anchor Rodes   TIP 16

Anchor chain should be secured to the boat so that you don't lose the bitter end overboard. Some people shackle the end to a through-bolted pad eye below decks in the anchor locker, but this can be difficult to undo in an emergency.

It is better to splice a piece of rope to the bitter end of the chain and tie the rope to a pad eye in the chain locker. The rope should be long enough to reach from the pad eye to the deck through the windlass chain pipe. If and when it is necessary to get rid of the anchor rode (generally when another vessel has dragged down on you and has fouled your chain), it is expedient to run the chain to its end and then cut the rope on deck rather crawling into the chain locker and trying to undo a shackle that could be under a lot of pressure.

I also paint the last 20 feet or so of chain with Day-Glo orange paint so I know when I'm coming to the end. To mark length on chain rodes, paint 3-foot lengths every 25 feet or so. Shorter markings are not visible when the chain is whizzing out. Jim Buoy makes a neat self-unraveling anchor marker buoy that is handy to deploy if an anchor must be abandoned.

Cleat Guards TIP 17

Just as autopilots have an affinity for heading the boat toward lobster pots, sheets love to wrap themselves around cleats. This always happens to me when I'm alone on deck and tacking in the middle of the night. It is easy to make wooden chocks that fit under the horns of cleats to prevent sheets and other loose lines from accidentally belaying themselves. Shock cord holds the two chocks together (see top photos). I affix wide nylon webbing over the top of the chock, which is a snug fit to the top of the cleat horn. You can also make fancy cleat protectors with recesses in the wood for the horns (see bottom photos).

To keep lines from snagging on deck cleats, and to eliminate them as toe stubbers, a pair of teak blocks connected with shock cord renders them harmless. This set uses polyester webbing over the horns.

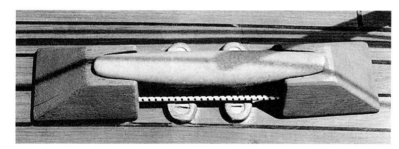

More elegant cleat guards can be made from solid blocks of teak.

Supports for Cockpit Structures   TIP 18

The standard fastening methods for dodger and bimini frame components are prone to failure when these structures are grabbed or fallen against by crew members. Replace the standard set-screws, rivets, or self-tapping screws with through-bolts. Cobalt drill bits in a slow-turning power (or even hand) drill cut stainless very nicely. Use an aircraft lock nut (Nylok, acorn) on the bolt, and then cut off excess thread with a carbide hacksaw blade and file smooth.

While the drill is out, drill drain holes in all deck socket fittings. Without drains, sockets or stanchion bases will fill with water, which puts hydrostatic pressure on the bedding and expedites leakage. The photo at far right shows rusting on deck under a socket base without a drain hole.

Instead of Allen screws, drill stanchions and dodger tubing for through-bolts. While you're at it, water collecting inside stanchion or pulpit bases can cause corrosion. Drill drain holes with a cobalt bit.

Rust on deck from socket without drain hole.

WAVE HEIGHTS

Estimating the height of waves is difficult. This table gives a basis for making an educated guess at a given wave height, based on wind speed, fetch, and how many hours the wind has been blowing in that direction. For example, if the wind has been blowing 20 knots over a fetch of 50 miles for 8 hours, expect wave heights to be about 6 feet.

Wind in Knots	Fetch											
	10 Miles		20 Miles		50 Miles		100 Miles		300 Miles		500 Miles	
	feet	hours	feet	hours	feet	hours	feet	hours	feet	hours	feet	hours
10	2.0	3.0	2.0	3.0	2.0	3.0	2.0	3.0	2.0	3.0	2.0	3.0
15	2.0	2.2	2.5	4.0	4.0	8.5	4.5	14.5	5.0	35.0	5.0	35.0
20	3.5	2.2	4.0	3.5	6.0	8.0	8.0	12.4	9.0	30.0	9.0	30.0
30	5.5	1.7	6.5	3.5	10.0	6.0	13.5	10.0	17.0	24.0	18.0	35.0
40	7.0	1.5	9.0	2.5	15.0	5.0	20.0	9.0	27.0	20.0	30.0	30.0
50	9.0	1.4	11.0	2.3	19.0	4.5	26.0	8.0	37.0	18.0	44.0	26.0
75	14.0	1.3	18.0	2.0	27.0	3.7	35.0	6.0	55.0	14.0	55.0	20.0
100	19.0	1.0	26.0	1.7	37.0	3.3	48.0	5.5	75.0	12.0	85.0	18.0

YACHT DEFENSE STRATEGY

While it does not get much press coverage, yachts are boarded by thieves both on the high seas and in harbors. Plan ahead what you will do in either situation. Because the choice of carrying firearms is strongly debated, I will not get into the fray.

At close range, a flare pistol is a very effective weapon. As a minimum, carry a can of pepper spray mounted with Velcro close to the companionway, and perhaps an additional one close to the owner's in-port bunk.

A relatively easy wiring job is to add a switch for the spreader lights at the owner's in-port bunk. Being able to illuminate the deck without getting out of bed brings some peace of mind when you hear those strange sounds in the night.

On the high seas, never head toward smoke. A common ploy of modern pirates is to start an oily fire in a barrel on board, then plunder those who come to help.

One time, on the way back from Bermuda, I picked up a large radar target closing fast from astern. Naturally, it was the middle of the night. I looked aft, and could not see any navigation lights, so I made a 20-degree change in course. Radar indicated that the pursuing vessel also deviated to follow. I tried calling the ship on the VHF radio, but received no reply. Growing concerned, I called the U.S. Coast Guard Portsmouth (Virginia) Communication station on the single-sideband radio (SSB) to report the situation. My call was immediately answered by a voice with an Amerian accent telling me they were on a coast guard cutter 1.5 miles astern of us.

To determine if he was really an American, I asked who was the best hitter the Yankees ever had.

The voice from the cutter replied, "Babe Ruth. Heave-to for a boarding."

I answered that while I appreciated his knowledge of baseball, there was no way I was going to heave-to for a boarding party from an unlit ship pursuing us. I also pointed out that seas were running about 15 feet, and I would hold them responsible for any damage to our vessel. This cooled them a little bit, and after I gave them a lot of information about our boat, the cutter decided not to board us. I watched on radar as they changed course and steamed away, still unlit.

In thinking about the incident later, I believe I was prudent to deny boarding and only change course 20 degrees. If the vessel had been hostile and I had turned 90 degrees, the distance between us would have decreased.

Although it's difficult to stop a determined burglar from gaining access to the interior of your vessel, there are a few simple measures that will deter casual access. Also see Securing the Cabin in chapter 3 for additional safety measures that can be taken.

Clean Your Combination Lock   TIP 19

When most of us open up a boat, we leave combination locks showing the opening numbers (this popular type of lock made by Sesame and others has numbers on the tumblers that must be aligned in the correct sequence in order to open). The numbers weather in this configuration, and are easy to spot as each tumbler is rotated. Cleaning the numbers on the lock with metal polish makes them all look the same.

Replace Fasteners in Companionway Stiles   TIP 20

Most boats have stiles made of wood or metal that are mounted alongside the horizontal sliding companionway hatch and on which the hatch rides. These stiles have exposed screws holding them down. It is easy for a thief to gain access to the boat interior by simply unscrewing the stiles.

On a lot of boats it is not easy to replace the screws with bolts locked with two nuts. You'll have to drill holes through the deck. However,

Combination locks often are left with the opening combo numbers exposed to the weather, making it easy for thieves to identify them by rolling the tumblers until they find the weathered numbers. (Tip 19)

if you can, use two nuts tightened against one another on the threaded bolt end inside the cabin. This ensures that turning the bolt head on deck won't loosen the nut.

Another possibly easier solution: "tamper-proof" stainless steel screws with unusual heads are available from industrial supply houses. These fasteners are most commonly used on lavatory panels in commercial installations. More readily available are square-drive screws, available in bronze and stainless steel. Two sources are McFeely's Square Drive Screws and Jamestown Distributors.

Replace Hatch Hinge Pins   TIP 21

Some deck hatches, and all hatches with a reversible opening feature, have easy-to-remove hinge pins. This is an invitation to thieves. If the hinged side of the hatch does not have dogs (screw-down knobs, handles, or levers to tighten the hatch), it is easy to pull the hinge pins, which provides sufficient leverage to break the securing mechanism on the opposite side of the hatch. Bicycle-type locks with a long rod are good replacement hinge pins.

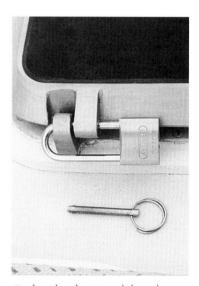

Replace hatch pins with bicycle-type locks. (Tip 21)

Square-drive screws make it more difficult for thieves to break into a companionway hatch. (Tip 20)

Dinghy ID   TIP 22

Do not put the boat's name on the dinghy. Thieves might steal your dinghy from a wharf and take it to your boat, as they will know you are ashore. None of your neighbors in the anchorage would think it strange to have the dinghy alongside a boat of the same name, or that equipment is being off-loaded.

Come up with some cute name if you want to identify your dinghy, or preferably use your vessel documentation number. The documentation number makes it easy to establish "proof of ownership" to officials in foreign countries. Also, the documentation number on the dinghy may enable you to talk your way out of having to separately register the dinghy in foreign ports.

I make dinghy security painters from old lifelines, with a large Nico-pressed loop at each end. The painter starts at the motor where the wire is put around the motor's carrying handle and through the loop in one end. The wire then runs forward through the dinghy bow eye and is padlocked to the dock. I have never had a tender secured in this fashion stolen or come up missing, as there is always a more easily appropriated dinghy nearby.

This dinghy has a nice protective cover to retard UV attack, but it has its mother vessel's name imprinted on it—a sure invitation to theft! (Tip 22)

Test-Fire Flares   TIP 23

Flares are for drawing attention to yourself when you're in trouble. The boat doesn't have to be sinking to merit the use of a flare. An attack or threat of attack certainly would be a good reason as well.

Everyone carries flares, but most people have never used one. It is worth the price of a flare to do a test firing. Check with your local U.S. Coast Guard station, which may advise you to test on land. Local Coast Guard Auxiliary Flotillas sometimes arrange practice firings. And there is always the Fourth of July, when flare launchings seem to go unnoticed (pity the poor soul whose boat is really sinking on this holiday!).

Be sure your test flare is identical to the brand on board, as firing procedures vary. An emergency is not the time to try understanding the terse firing instructions.

MISCELLANEA

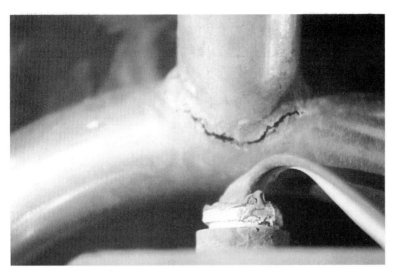

Metal corrosion is a constant problem on boats. A weld on the underside of this bow pulpit cracked wide open. When much more of the weld is broken, it will create a serious safety hazard. **TIP 24**

All windows or portlights larger than about 2 square feet should have storm shutters that can be fitted either before the passage or at least with the onset of nasty weather. Unlike plywood or metal shutters, these clear polycarbonate shutters allow light through, but the fasteners need to be fitted with larger washers. When mounting anything made of polycarbonate, remember that the material will expand and contract as much as 5 percent from changes in ambient temperature. Always make fastener holes oversize to allow for this, or cracks will develop. And remember that it is the windows on the leeward side of the boat that are more at risk. See also the Windows section, with drawing, on pages 186–87. **TIP 26**

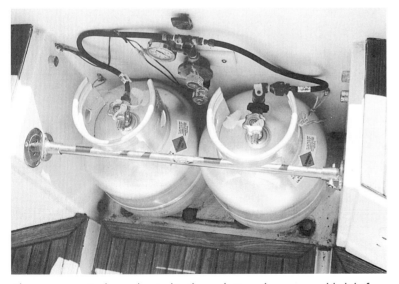

These propane tanks are located in the cockpit, under a removable lid. If the cockpit should fill with water, the tanks will float, possibly straining the hoses and leaking gas. As a precaution, a bar was fitted across the locker to restrain the tanks. **TIP 25**

Making oval chain pipes watertight. Even with copious application of duct tape, oval chain pipes can only be made partially watertight (**photo 1**). There is an easy way to convert an oval hole to a round one: Use the correct size hole saw for the 4-inch deck plate, and cut a scrap piece of ¾-inch plywood; save the plug cutout. Use two screws to hold the plug in place over the oval hole (**photo 2**). The plug becomes an internal mandrel to guide the hole saw for the cut. The partially completed round hole saw cut is visible in **photo 3**. Coat the edges of the deck core with epoxy to seal it and prevent water seepage (**photo 4**). Screw the chain pipe into the deck plate (**photo 5**). ABI also makes this ventilator, which screws into the same deck plate to air out the forepeak in harbor (**photo 6**).

TIP 27

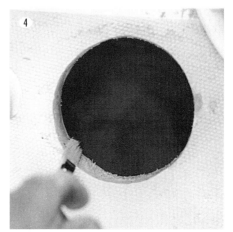

Sheet winches are too often used for securing docklines. While they may be plenty strong in the direction of sheet pull (fore-and-aft), they may not be so strong when pulled from other angles. On this boat, strain on the winch pulled the entire cockpit coaming free.

TIP 28

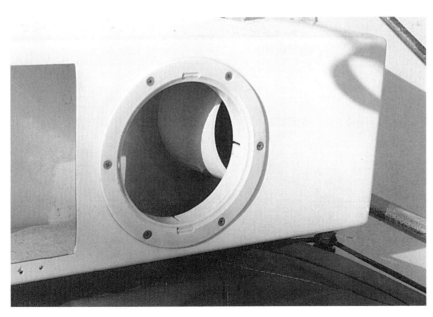

The owner of this boat wondered why water was leaking into the cabin through the supposedly waterproof Dorade vent. The answer was easy to see once the vent was removed. The builder had placed the through-deck pipe so that the edge of it lay directly underneath the vent, rather than offset several inches.

TIP 29

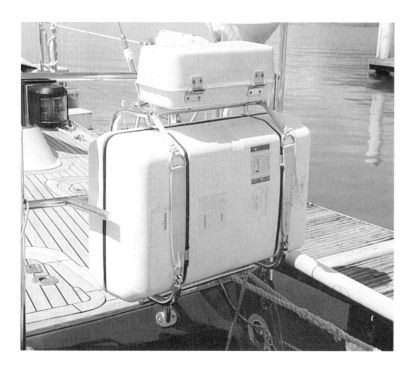

The life raft must be stowed where it can be easily and safely deployed—preferably from the cockpit, as a boat that has suffered a holing from a collision usually sinks bow-first. Also, the cockpit offers more protection. If there is room, mounting the life raft in or near the cockpit is convenient. On this center-cockpit boat, however, the raft is mounted on a custom stern pulpit where it is easily deployed but vulnerable to breaking seas. It is well lashed in place, but will require a knife to free. Better to use snapshackles or some other fastener that doesn't require tools to free it.   **TIP 30**

CHAPTER 2
RIG AND SAILS

Of all the things you don't want to have happen at sea, rig failure is near the top of the list . . . right after sinking and losing the keel or rudder. A dismasting is a sudden and terrifying experience. The rig seems to come down in slow motion. Things get quiet, then the rolling starts. The boat will lie beam to the seas, and without the inertia of her rig she will roll gunwale to gunwale.

Resist the temptation to start the engine to bring the boat into the wind. There is a strong likelihood that some rigging will foul the prop, and then you will have no propulsion. If the spar has just folded over, secure it to keep it from completely snapping off. A broken-off mast pounding on the hull must be quickly disposed of, and methods to do this are discussed later in this chapter.

A majority of rig failures can be prevented by careful inspection. Start by always going aloft before a passage.

Check spreader attachment to the mast. Shake the outboard end as hard as you can and watch the spreader bases for movement. One time I was up a recently repainted rig on an Alden 54. Shaking the spreaders pulled off a mast bracket. Trying to tighten the fasteners in other brackets revealed that some of them were stripped. And we were about to embark on a 1,500-mile passage!

Inspect clevis and cotter pins. I have found undersized clevis pins with heads barely larger than tang holes.

Rod Stephens, brother of Olin Stephens and part of the famous Sparkman & Stephens design house, used to be a bug about cotter pins. He insisted that the legs be trimmed so that they only protruded half a clevis pin diameter past the pin, and that the legs spread just 10 degrees each. He carried a wedge cut to 20 degrees with a line down the middle.

On a visit to the Tartan Marine yard in Grand River, Ohio, when he was sixty-eight, Rod went up the mast of my own Tartan 33 hand-over-hand. He came down smiling and said, "Nice job commissioning, young man."

"Thank you, Mr. Stephens," I replied, and pulled out of my pocket my copy of his wedge.

Rod was right. I find that cotter pins bent to his specification always stay in, yet can be readily removed (see Cotter Pins in Clevis Pins, tip 45). Be sure cotter pins are the largest diameter that will fit in a clevis pin hole—not just what a rigger happens to have in his pocket.

Despite commissioning by a big-name yard affiliated with a builder, I insisted on going up the rig of a recently commissioned Alden 50. We had just sailed the boat from the yard about 30 miles, all, fortunately, on the same tack. Upon going aloft, I found a clevis pin missing a cotter pin and a long cotter pin sticking out so far it would have ripped the genoa had we tacked. Before this boat went across the Atlantic, I disassembled her rod rigging terminals to inspect the cold heading of the rod. (Rod rigging is not heated when the head, which fits into a special socket or slot in the mast, is formed.) A V-1 (lower panel of an upper shroud) had a bad crack in the cold head. I took the shroud to a rigging shop where we attempted to put another head on the rod. After three reheadings failed to produce a crack-free head, we

The rigger at a well-known yard told the owner there was nothing wrong with the angle his upper spreaders made to the mast, when in truth, any angle other than bisecting the stay places dangerous stress on the spreader and its mount on the mast.

concluded that the alloy in this particular piece of rod must have been defective, so we replaced it.

Other experiences with rod have led to the recommendation in this chapter that standing rigging be wire with mechanical connections. While #316 stainless is more corrosion-resistant than #304, it is only 85 percent as strong. Increasing wire diameter frequently increases the diameter of clevis pins in terminal fittings as well, resulting in incompatibility. Drilling out the tang or chainplate to accommodate a larger clevis pin may leave insufficient metal around the hole to exceed the breaking strength of the wire.

The next boat from the same yard had the upper spreaders at a downward angle, not an upward angle bisecting the cap shroud (see photo). The owner questioned the yard and was told that the mast was "fine." Spreaders under any load other than straight compression will fail, as they are not designed to withstand bending.

There is no substitute for personal inspection of any work, regardless of the alleged competence of the contractor.

Sails also need careful inspection and testing. As a Marion–Bermuda Race inspector, I insist that the required storm trysail be hoisted as a part of the inspection process. I've lost count of the ones with wrong or missing fittings that could not possibly have been set if needed.

Wind force increases with the square of its velocity (see Roller Furling, tip 36). A sail that is difficult to manhandle in 25 knots will be impossible in 50 knots when the force is *four times* as great.

The rig and sails are your primary means of propulsion, so don't be tight-fisted when it comes to your investment in them. If your sails are growing thin and baggy, a new sail is more important than an electronic color chartplotter.

Lastly, a good deal of one's enjoyment—or annoyance—with sailing of any kind is directly related to sail handling systems. Sails should be easy to reef. A preventer should be set up with minimum fuss. Storm sails should be ready to go. Generally speaking, systems that are already in place (or nearly so) are more likely to be used than those buried in a sail locker.

RUNNING RIGGING

Boom Preventer   TIP 31

Accidental jibes are a major cause of injury and gear failure. A pre-rigged preventer system is easy to install and use. I am particularly sensitive to the use of preventers, as I was on board a boat when an accidental jibe knocked the owner overboard and he was never recovered.

Rigging a preventer by shackling a boom vang tackle to the rail is a bad practice. When the outboard end of the boom goes underwater, the boom pivots on the mid-boom tackle, which either damages the gooseneck, bends the boom, or breaks the vang. The 1993 Marion–Bermuda Race was mostly 30 knots downwind, and twelve boats damaged goosenecks or booms.

The purpose of a boom vang is to hold the boom down, not out. A line from the end of the boom running to a strong block at the

PREVENTER SIZING

Boat Length, ft.	Double-Braid Dacron, in. (diameter)	Minimum Breaking Load for Hardware, lb.
to 28	⅜	4,900
28 to 35	⁷⁄₁₆	6,600
35 to 44	½	8,500
44 to 50	⁹⁄₁₆	11,500
50 to 60	⅝	14,600

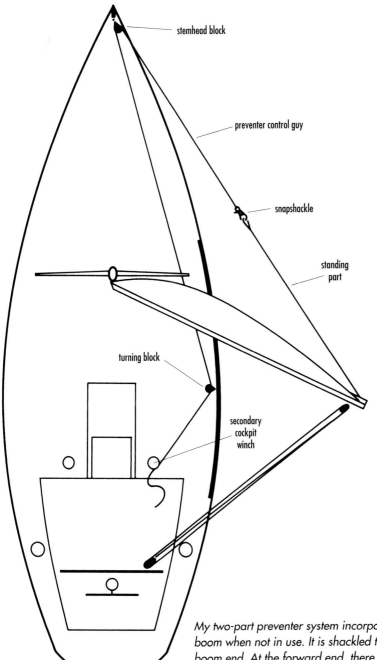

stemhead block

preverter control guy

snapshackle

standing part

turning block

secondary cockpit winch

stemhead and then back to the cockpit puts the least stress on the boom, and is easily controlled. See the Preventer Sizing table, page 27. The block at the stem should be two times stronger than the rope's breaking strength.

Because it is dangerous to rig a preventer to the boom end while underway (risk of jibe, crew hanging out over lifelines, etc.), it's a much better idea to have a permanently rigged preventer system (see illustration). I make up preventers in two parts. The permanent part is shackled to a pad eye through-bolted at the after end of the boom (top photo, opposite) and led forward along the boom when not in use. The forward end can be tied off at a cleat near the gooseneck (bottom photo, opposite). Splice a stainless steel thimble in the end. Boats with mid-boom sheeting require two preventer lines, one on either side of the boom, in order to not interfere with the mainsheet. Boats with end-boom sheeting need only one, shackled to the underside of the boom.

The second part of this preventer system is a long line with a snapshackle at one end. The line should lead from a cockpit winch forward to a block at the bow (possibly shackled to the stem fitting, as in the right photo, opposite), and then aft where the snapshackle can be

My two-part preventer system incorporates a standing part stored along the boom when not in use. It is shackled through a stainless steel thimble to the boom end. At the forward end, there is another stainless steel thimble for shackling it to the preventer control guy. The guy is led forward to a block at the stemhead and then aft to a secondary cockpit winch.

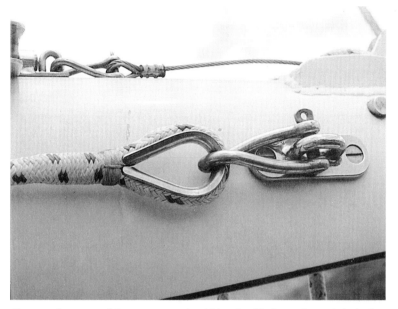

The standing part of the preventer should be shackled to a through-bolted pad eye at the aft end of the boom. Remove the end cap to fasten washers and nuts to the machine screws.

fastened to the thimble on the boom part of the preventer.

This system is easy to rig. What's more, it's simple to trim the boom because the control end is in the cockpit where the mechanical advantage of a winch is available.

Many times I've been knocked down while jibing with the main sheeted in tight, as the mainsheet doesn't run out quickly through multiple blocks. Consequently, when I now jibe in heavy air I don't haul the mainsheet in, but rather try to spin the boat quickly on top of a wave, backwind the main, and then ease the boom across by paying out the preventer line from the cockpit.

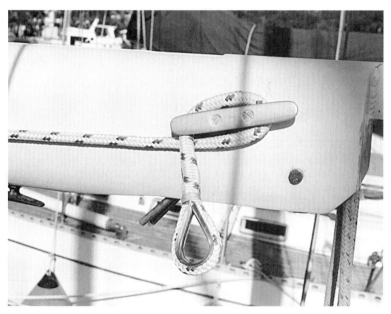

The forward end of the preventer's standing part should have a stainless steel thimble in the splice; it can be tied off to a simple cleat when not in use.

A strong block at the stemhead is used to turn the control guy aft. On many boats, the block can be shackled to a spare hole in the vertical stem plate, aft of the headstay attachment.

Spinnaker Halyard TIP 32

The spinnaker halyard is useful for more than hoisting chutes. Because of its location forward of the mast truck, it also can be used for retrieving a crew overboard or for hauling a crew up the mast in a bosun's chair.

If your boat has a powered anchor windlass (electric or hydraulic), be sure the spinnaker halyard is long enough to reach it. You'll need pad eyes on deck to attach a block so you can lead the halyard tail to the windlass. If the spinnaker halyard is internal (inside the mast), be sure the pad eye is positioned so the lead is fair coming out of the mast exit. I also like to be able to run the spinnaker halyard back to a primary genoa sheet winch in the cockpit, which is always the most powerful winch on board.

In a crew-overboard situation, one can leave the Lifesling line attached aft, pull in as much slack as possible, cleat it off, and then clip the spinnaker halyard over the line. By taking up on the halyard, the person will come aboard about amidships. This is faster and much easier than rigging a tackle off the main boom. (See also Crew Overboard, tip 180.)

When taking a person aloft, try to lead the halyard fair to a deck-mounted winch. Winches mounted on masts are tapped into thin aluminum and can pull off because the fasteners securing the winch are tapped into the mast wall. In general, the rule of thumb for stainless fasteners into aluminum is that the aluminum thickness must be one-and-a-half times the fastener diameter for a tapped hole to achieve strength equal to that of the machine screw. Because most mast walls are $\frac{1}{8}$ to $\frac{3}{16}$ inch thick, a tapped hole has very few threads, with a resultant loss of strength.

This is why I do not like to go aloft on a halyard running to a mast-mounted winch. When there is no alternative, I use a second halyard. After I'm about 10 feet off deck, I ask that the second halyard be made off by tying a clove hitch around the mast under the gooseneck.

Never trust a cleat mounted on a mast. Cleats usually have only two fasteners, where a winch usually has five. A powered windlass or a large-power-ratio cockpit winch certainly makes the job of hoisting a person aloft easier, in addition to safer.

Also, do not trust snapshackles — use screw-pin shackles or a bowline to belay a halyard to a bosun's chair.

During one race aboard my Tartan 30 we got to the leeward mark and no amount of pulling could get the spinnaker down. I finally had to go up the mast, and found the rope splice had jammed in the halyard block. I told the crew to keep the boat moving as fast as possible on a broad reach, and opened the snapshackle. The spinnaker floated down the headstay and made two piles on deck! A neat but time-consuming takedown.

Although I didn't get too bruised on this occasion, the movement of the boat can really throw around a person up the mast, whether in just a harness or sitting in a bosun's chair.

When going aloft at sea with a mainsail set, and a tight tether around the mast is therefore not feasible, I like to wear a padded life jacket with a safety harness outside. I clip a carabiner hook around a spare halyard and to the harness attachment point to hold me close to the mast. In rough conditions I wish for a football helmet with a face guard.

In addition to getting a person aloft easily, the spinnaker halyard/windlass or primary winch rig is a convenient way to hoist a dinghy aboard.

Right Side Up TIP 33

I had to go up the mast of an Alden 46 in a bosun's chair to replace the Windex (see tip 59). I put the spinnaker halyard through a snatchblock on the rail and through a fairlead so that it led back to a cockpit winch. I paid particular attention so that the block ended up right in line with the halyard's exit from the mast. For more information on halyards, see Running Rigging in appendix 1, page 188.

To ease the load on the winch while ascending, I put my feet on the lower spreaders and stood up. When I had reached my full height, and resumed sitting in the chair, I fell several feet. I looked down to see an empty, mangled snatchblock and the halyard leading directly from the mast exit to the cockpit winch.

There was only one other person on board—the crew member grinding the winch. I managed to hoist myself up hand over hand and stand on the spreaders again. While a new snatchblock was shackled to the rail, I diagnosed what had happened. I had hooked up the snatchblock with the opening side up. The slack from my standing on the spreader had moved the halyard to the latch part of the snatchblock and popped it open.

Now I am very careful that a snatchblock is always used with the latch mechanism down so that slack in the line will not open the block.

Masthead Sheave Arrangement   TIP 34

The most common masthead arrangement is two sheaves forward on the same axle and two sheaves aft. If the halyards are external (outside the mast), the main halyard generally is led over the two starboard sheaves and the jib halyard led over the port sheaves.

If the main halyard is internal, however, and there are halyard winches or turning blocks mounted on the mast, use the aft starboard sheave for an internal main halyard exiting on the starboard side (see illustration). Use the forward starboard sheave for an internal jib halyard exiting on the port side of mast.

Because roller furling is popular, I mount a stopper (rope clutch) on the mast for the internal jib halyard, in line between the exit box

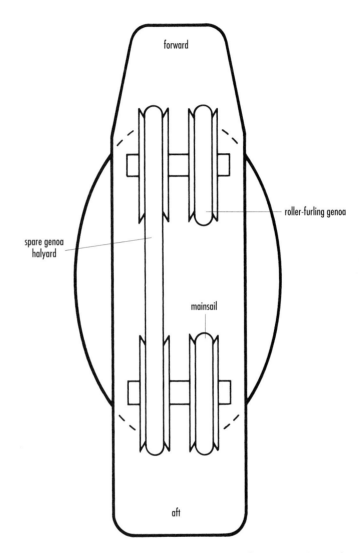

view looking down at top of mast

forward

roller-furling genoa

spare genoa halyard

mainsail

aft

The typical masthead configuration has two sheaves forward and two aft. The spare genoa halyard (left) runs over both sheaves on the port side and runs externally to a winch on the mast. In an emergency, the bitter end can be used for a main halyard. In less dire circumstances, it can be used to lift the outboard end of a passarelle (Mediterranean-style gangway bridging the stern to the quay; see page 199). The starboard forward sheave (right) is used for the roller-furling genoa's internal halyard. The starboard aft sheave is used for the mainsail's internal halyard.

and winch. This is because the sail is seldom dropped, meaning that the halyard can be secured and forgotten until season's end. It certainly doesn't need to be left wrapped around a winch, eliminating that winch for other purposes.

The port side sheaves are used for an external spare jib halyard, which is led over both the forward and aft sheaves. This external halyard can be used as a main halyard if needed, either by re-reeving, to put the shackle on the aft end, or if needed quickly, by tying a shackle onto the bitter end.

For long passages, I prefer to keep the spinnaker halyard external. Dacron double braid is my preferred cordage for spinnaker halyards, as it acts as a shock absorber when the spinnaker fills. Because a spinnaker halyard is almost always working a little, having it external eliminates chafe on mast entrance and exit boxes.

If winch placement necessitates an internal spinnaker halyard, consider making the top few feet wire, with the splice at least 3 feet down from the mast top entrance. Wire will handle chafe much better than rope. Eventually, 7×19 stainless steel wire will develop meathooks. Galvanized wire does not have this problem, but rusts quickly.

Mainsheet Blocks TIP 35

I see many boats with mainsheet tackles that tend to twist, causing chafe and inhibiting free movement. This is easy to cure. Any blocks attached to the boom should not swivel. Some blocks have small set-screws that can be tightened to stop swiveling. For blocks without this feature, a seizing of Monel wire or even a large plastic cable tie prevents rotation (see photo).

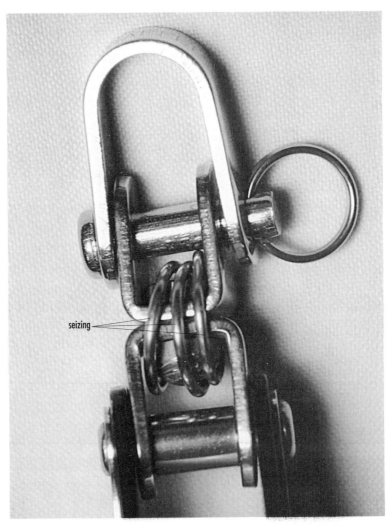

seizing

Mainsheet tackle, especially in midboom sheeting, has a habit of twisting, due to swiveling of the blocks attached to the boom. If the block doesn't have a locking feature, you can stop the swiveling with a seizing of Monel wire or a plastic cable tie. (Tip 35)

Roller Furling   TIP 36

Modern roller-furling systems with low friction bearings work very well to reduce sail. The bad news is that when partially furled (reefed) they transmit a large percentage of the sheet load to the furling. Frequently check your furling line for chafe, and carry a spare.

The formula for computing genoa sheet loading is

$$\text{sheet load in lb.} = 0.00431 \times \text{sail area in sq. ft.} \times (\text{wind velocity in knots})^2$$

Because the wind velocity is squared, the force on a sheet goes up exponentially with wind strength. Even though you may reduce sail area as the wind comes on to blow, the force on the sheet remains constant or can even increase.

In the accompanying table are the calculated sheet loads for several headsails on an Alden 44.

Note that the maximum load occurs with the #4 genoa, which is 64 percent smaller than the 150 percent genoa. Modern high-tech lines such as Technora-Spectra blends have great strength for small diameters and will wrap up on the furl-ing drum. New England Ropes' (see appendix 7) $\frac{5}{16}$-inch T-900 has a breaking strength of 7,300 pounds; 10 mm (just over $\frac{3}{8}$ in.) is 11,800 pounds; and $\frac{7}{16}$-inch is 14,300 pounds. The highest load in the table is for the #4—2,627 pounds. Because the working load should be 20 percent of breaking strength, we'll use this number to determine sheet size: 2,627 pounds ÷ 0.2 = 13,135 pounds. Technora-Spectra genoa sheets should therefore be $\frac{7}{16}$-inch, because its 14,300-pound breaking strength exceeds the 13,135-pound load.

I might be tempted to go down to 10 mm for the furling line.

Running Backstays   TIP 37

When a staysail is set on a cutter or double-headsail rig, the windward running backstay must be tensioned to keep the mast in column. Because runners are frequently parked close to the shrouds when not in use, one must leave the cockpit and go forward to bring them aft when they are needed.

When tacking, the leeward run-ner must be released and the wind-ward runner tensioned, requiring trips forward on both sides of the boat. Because the staysail is fre-quently used in heavy weather, trips on deck are neither fun nor safe. I make runners self-retracting with a

Going forward in bad weather to pull lazy running backstays out of the way during tacks is neither safe nor fun. Shock cord can be used to make the runners self-retracting. It is run through a small block attached to the lower shroud turnbuckle. (Tip 37)

ALDEN 44 SHEET LOADS (TIP 36)

Headsail	Sail Area, sq. ft.	Maximum Wind, knots	Sheet Load, lb.
150%	847	18	1,183
#3	495	30	1,920
#4	301	45	2,627
storm jib	160	60	2,483

After turning through the small block, the ⁵⁄₁₆- or ³⁄₈-inch shock cord then runs up the mast to a lower shroud tang. (Tip 37)

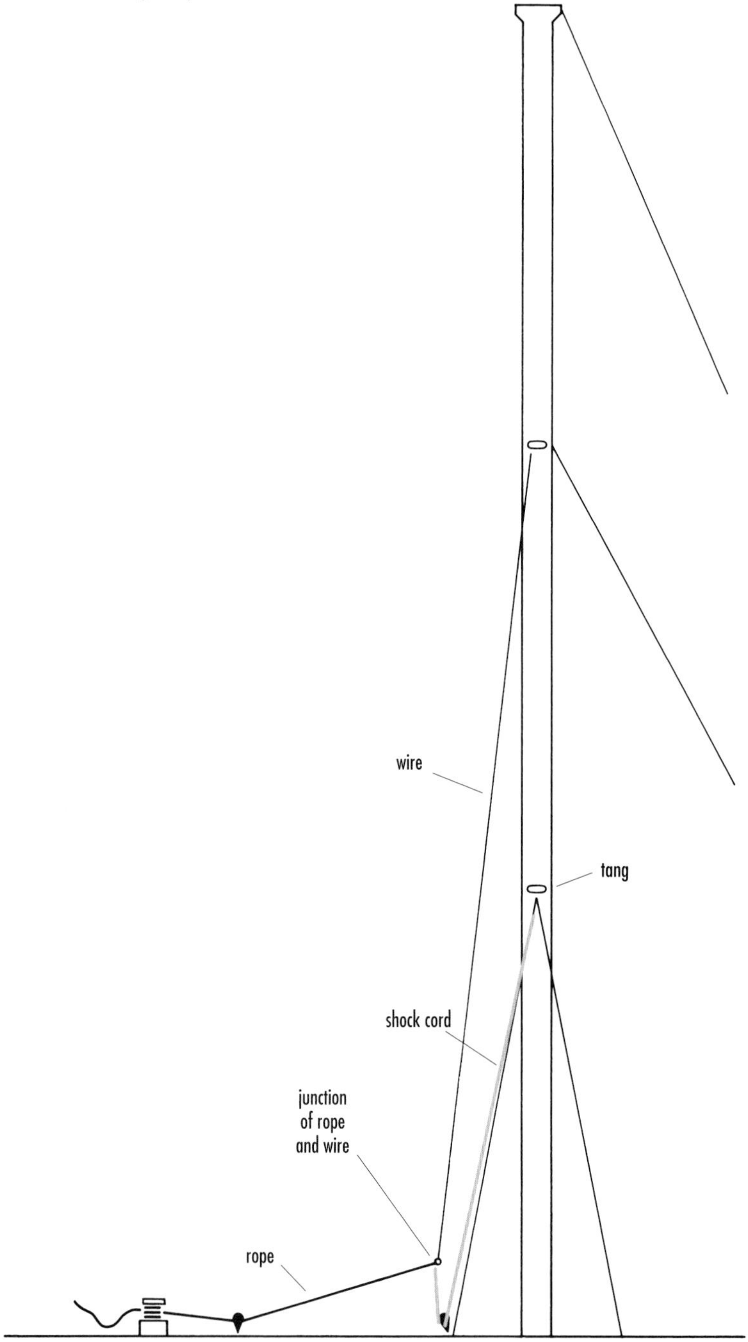

wire

tang

shock cord

junction
of rope
and wire

rope

Perhaps the slickest arrangement is a one-piece running backstay of low-stretch, high-strength rope leading through a block aft on deck, then to a winch. A small block is tied to the end of a length of shock cord to make the runner self-retracting. (Tip 37)

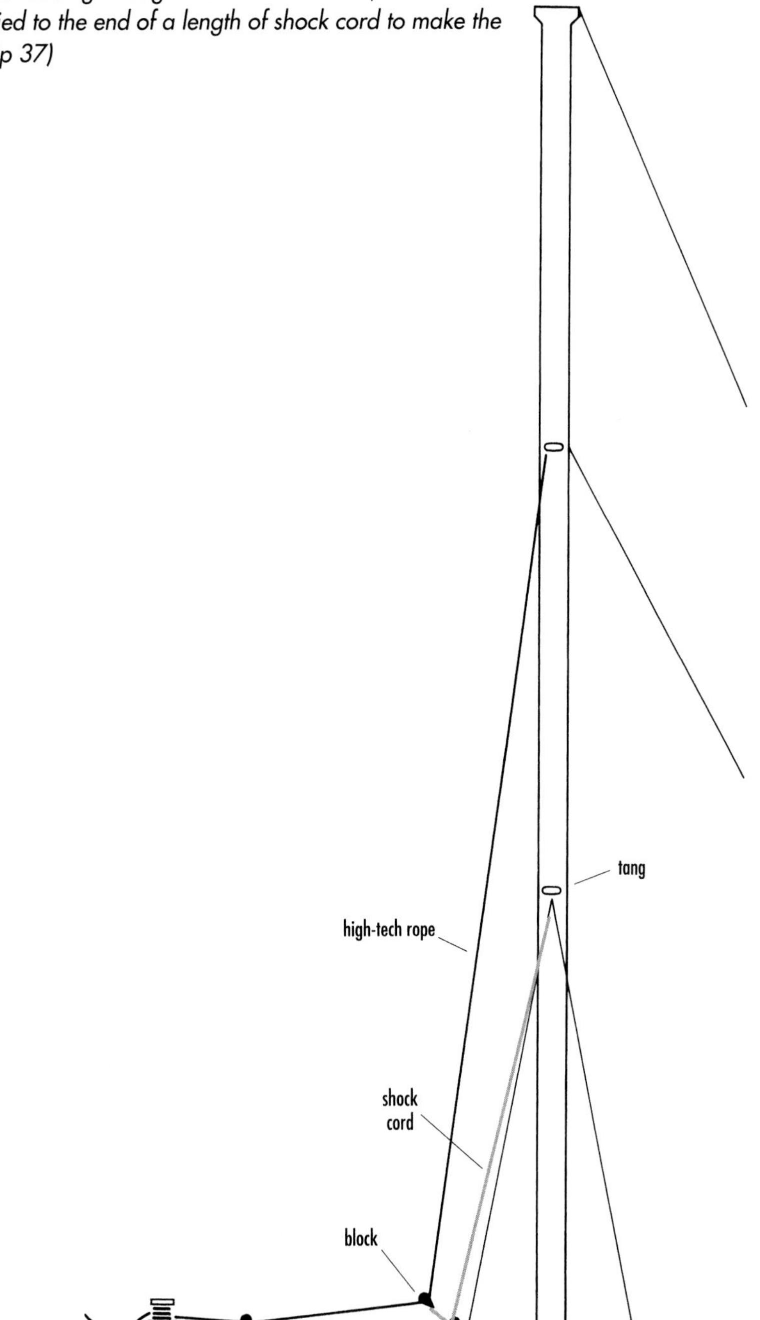

tang

high-tech rope

shock cord

block

piece of shock cord, so the tail can stay in the cockpit at all times and be tensioned by the windward secondary cockpit winch, which is seldom in use.

I attach one end of $\frac{5}{16}$- or $\frac{3}{8}$-inch shock cord to the junction of the runner's upper wire part and lower rope tail. The shock cord runs through a small block lashed to the base of the shrouds, and then up the mast where the bitter end is secured to a lower shroud tang. Small-diameter Kevlar rope works well for securing both the block at the base of the shroud and the bitter end of the shock cord at the tang. When the runner's tail is tensioned, the shock cord stretches.

It is even neater to make the running backstay entirely of high-tech rope such as Spectra or Kevlar. With no rope-to-wire join to jam in a sheave, you can lead the runner through a small block attached to the lower end of the shock cord (see illustration page 35) for pulling forward to the shrouds when not in use.

The shock cord is tied to the junction of the running backstay's upper wire portion and lower rope portion with thimble and spliced eye. (Tip 37)

Securing a Halyard Tail

TIP 38

Rod Stephens insisted that halyards be coiled in such a way that they can be quickly freed when it's necessary to drop a sail in a hurry. Here's a good method.

Step 1. Starting with the bitter end, coil the halyard, trying to avoid overlapping loops.

Step 2. When the coil is 3 to 4 feet from the mast, bring the halyard halfway down the coil and hold it in place while rolling most of the remaining halyard around the coil by rotating the coil, *not* wrapping the halyard over the end. This prevents kinks.

Step 3. When a foot or so of halyard remains, bring a loop through the coil.

Step 4. Hang the loop over the halyard cleat. To let the halyard run, grab the bottom of the coil. Pull upward to disengage the loop on the cleat and pull outward to unwrap the turns around the coil.

Whipping Lines   TIP 39

Marlinspike skills (and please don't call it *macramé!*) seem to be in danger of going the way of navigation expertise.

Although I admit that a GPS beats a sextant, and that the marvelous synthetic lines available to sailors beat manila, I'm not ready to accept a rope end dipped in some can of goo as superior to a good whipping.

Step 1 shows a triangular needle, threaded with waxed line, starting six passes through the rope. These stitches anchor the cover to the core of braided line and prevent the untwisting of three-strand. The needle end is then cut flush, leaving the working end as the roll of seizing line.

Complete the wraps in *step 2*. There should be enough of them to make the length of the whipping equal to the diameter of the line. Note the half hitch taken under the last turn, which is pulled very tight to lock it in place.

Step 3 shows the beginning of the linear lock-up stitches, which keep the turns from slipping. I do three stitches, leaving the bitter end at the long part of the line. In *step 4*, bury the end with six to eight through-stitches; this will further anchor parts of the line. Note the vertical passes (two visible) that hold the whipping in place.

It is common to permit that part of the cover beyond the whipping to fray. I prefer, however, to thoroughly melt the cover to the core with a hotknife, making a slightly

tapered cone shape to facilitate pushing line through stoppers.

A sewn whipping of this kind, with sharply tightened turns, has a narrower diameter than the unwhipped line, and so should last a long time. And unlike a rope end dipped in goo, a whipping like this is ever so nice to look at.

Reel Out Spools   TIP 40

When removing anything from a spool, such as rope, always rotate the spool to remove the contents; pulling rope off the end of a spool causes hockles (kinks).

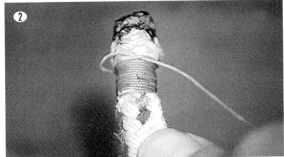
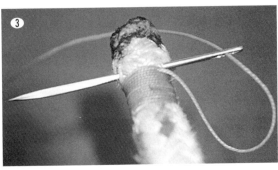

Tip 39

STANDING RIGGING

Magnaflux Test Kit   TIP 41

This sounds like an exotic piece of equipment, but is actually just a set of aerosol cans whose contents may save your mast. Magnaflux is but one brand name; there are other similar kits, such as Weld-Shield's NDT Fault Check Penetrant.

The first of the Magnaflux cans is a cleaner that is sprayed on the wire terminals of standing rigging. Next is a red dye. Be sure not to spray the dye on anything you do not want red for a long time. Let the dye soak in for a few minutes, and then wipe it off the surface. The third can is called developer and is similar to white paint.

After spraying all three on, the dye retained by any cracks in the fitting will be visible. Longitudinal cracks should not be longer than the wire diameter. Any circumferential cracks are immediate grounds for replacement.

Welding supply stores sell Magnaflux test kits for less than $40, which will do all the terminals on a 45-foot boat. It's cheap insurance both for the rig and for your peace of mind.

Bolt or Wire Cutters   TIP 42

Most boats carry cutters but their owners have never used them. I have been dismasted twice and found the only device that easily cuts standing rigging on a bouncing deck is hydraulically actuated jaw cutters—very expensive. Take your cutters to a rigger and try to cut a scrap of the same-diameter wire or rod as your standing rigging. Chances are you will end up with a handy tool to keep at home. Instead of trying to sever standing rigging in an emergency, make the attachment points easy to remove. An easy way to do this is described in Cotter Pins in Clevis Pins, tip 45.

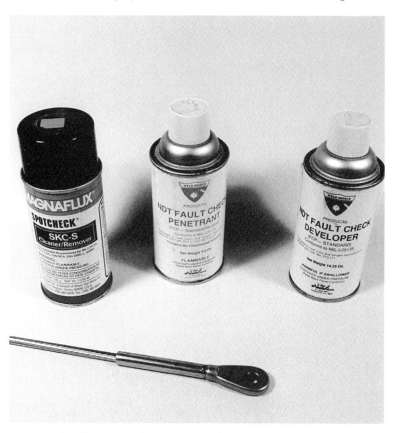

A Magnaflux kit consists of several aerosol spray cans whose contents, once applied to metal rigging (such as swaged eyes and turnbuckles), render any hairline cracks visible to the naked eye. (Tip 41)

Turnbuckles   TIP 43

On most yachts I manage, the usual bent cotter pins to keep turnbuckles from unscrewing have been replaced with round-head machine screws tapped into the cotter pin hole (see photo). The machine screws do not have to be wrapped with rigging tape to prevent ripping sails or people. I use a larger-than-normal pilot drill for the tap and a machine screw length equal to the diameter of the turnbuckle screw.

Machine screws are quick and easy to remove for standing rigging adjustment. In a dismasting, fully unscrewing the turnbuckle is the neatest way to disconnect rigging, provided the turnbuckle has not been bent. Always generously lubricate the turnbuckle threads. Excess lubricant can be cleaned off exposed threads, but a full load of lube on engaged threads permits adjustment years later. Note that WD-40 is not a lubricant. In fact, it works very nicely to *remove* lubricants. Super Lube grease or anhydrous lanolin will work if you do not have molybdenum disulfide grease handy.

Never tension a turnbuckle that is under load. If it is not convenient to take the boat for a sail to adjust shrouds on the leeward side, heel the vessel at the dock by running a spinnaker halyard to a fixed object and tension it to induce at least a 5-degree angle of

machine screw

The cotter pins through the studs in this turnbuckle have been replaced with round-head machine screws. The studs have been tapped and threaded. The round-head screws don't require tape (which is bad for stainless steel) and are faster to remove in the event of a dismasting.

heel. By sighting up the mast with the vessel inclined, you can come very close to proper tuning of the upper and lower shrouds. It is easy to release the spinnaker halyard tension, make adjustments, and then re-tension to check the effect.

See also the Turnbuckles section in appendix 1, page 187.

Tape on Turnbuckles TIP 44

Another reason to avoid tape on turnbuckles is oxygen deprivation–induced crevice corrosion, to which stainless steel is very susceptible. Just as prop shafts generally break right at the stuffing box, wire often breaks where it enters a terminal. Turnbuckles and rigging parts experience accelerated corrosion when air is removed from the surface of the metal. In December 1997, two turnbuckles parted on boats I was working on, both caused by corrosion under tape (see photo).

As a race inspector, I sometimes ask skippers to remove tape on turnbuckles to allow for a close inspection, and recommend that it not be reinstalled. This, of course, means that vinyl covers on shrouds and lifelines, as well as spreader tip boots, also are potential troublemakers.

Cotter Pins in Clevis Pins TIP 45

The "yachty" look of cotter pin legs bent around a clevis pin in curlicues makes removal very difficult. Most cotter pins are too long. Rod Stephens, as mentioned earlier, always admonished me to cut cotter pins to one-and-a-half times the diameter of the clevis pin. Each leg is only spread 10 degrees (see photo page 42). A small dab of silicone over the short, spread cotter pin legs prevents ripping sails, gashing toes, etc. I take the time to round cotter pin leg ends with a

When deprived of oxygen, stainless steel is susceptible to crevice corrosion. Over time, the consequences can be disastrous. Therefore, the practice of taping stainless steel turnbuckles and other hardware should be avoided as much as possible. Routine inspection revealed the dramatic fracture in the body of this turnbuckle. For want of a minute's job, the whole rig might have been lost. (Tip 44)

file, which facilitates installation and helps prevent ripping sails.

On turnbuckles that do not exert a lot of side force on the cotter pins (such as shrouds), the normal stainless steel cotter pins may be replaced with brass, which makes them easier to drive out in an emergency such as a dismasting.

Clevis pin heads should be oriented on the side of the chainplate having the *least* clearance to a fixed object (like the cabin house side). In a dismasting, the ship's small 4-pound sledgehammer and a drift punch can be used to drive out the clevis pins. If brass cotter pins are used, they will probably shear, saving time. Try this on your boat— the price of one cotter pin is worth it. Both the sledge and drift punch should have wrist lanyards, as they are likely to be used with waves washing over the deck. Headstay and backstay attachments are likely to be side-loaded, so stainless cotter pins should be used, cut, rounded, and spread 20 degrees.

Contrary to what one might think, a sailboat without a mast rolls much faster and has a lot more uncomfortable motion without the damping effect from the inertia of the rig. Soon after a dismasting, suggest to your crew that they take anti-nausea medication, because once the adrenaline rush wears off, seasickness is likely to set in.

Cotter pins should not be bent around clevis pins in curlicues, as it takes far too long to remove them. Rod Stephens was adamant that the angle of the legs be spread no more than 10 degrees each. (Tip 45)

SAILS

For offshore passagemaking, I like a double-headsail rig with both jib/genoa and staysail roller furling. This eliminates almost all sail changes on the foredeck in heavy weather. When a partially rolled-up genoa is too much, just furl it completely and unfurl the staysail.

People tend to want too much overlap in headsails. A good offshore genoa has a high clew so it will not scoop in waves (see illustration). Since genoa overlap is measured from the clew to the luff (known as the LP, a line perpendicular from the luff to the clew), a high-clew 120 or 130 percent genoa will have an overlap above the clew equal to a deck-sweeping 150 percent. The only sail area lost is a triangle at the bottom of the sail, which is frequently in the lee of the hull and deck when heeled.

The downside to a cutter rig is the necessity for running backstays to counter the forward pull of the staysail stay. If tails on the runner tackles are long enough, the leeward runner can be eased off during a tack and then secured after everything else is done. Running backstays can be exotic rope, such as Kevlar or Spectra, running through a large-diameter sheave block and then to a secondary place even when tacking in heavy weather.

The staysail should not be on a boom. Generally, the genoa tracks can be extended forward as a sheeting point for the staysail, or short lengths of track added on deck to provide correct sheeting angles. When I order sails, I always make a rough deck plan, noting the location of existing track, and tell the sailmaker to make the sail to fit the tracks. That way, if the sail does not fit, the sailmaker must recut on his nickel.

While the ORC (Offshore Racing Council) rules require a storm trysail, I would put the cost of one toward a spare mainsail. Hoisting a storm trysail is a difficult job. Even if the separate storm trysail track comes down to deck level, the sail must pass mast-mounted winches and the boom. Because a storm trysail sheets independently from the boom, a flogging clew can cause injury to people or deck structures (see tip 56).

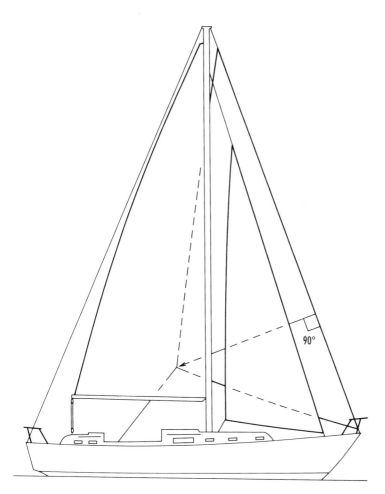

90°

Deck-sweeping genoas are undesirable offshore, as they have a tendency to scoop water as the boat heels. A high-clew genoa of around 110 to 120 percent provides adequate overlap of the mainsail.

winch. This rig has the advantage of no block and tackles to bang about. For other ideas on how to make running backstays easier to manage, see tip 37.

Mainsails should have three reefs, with one reef (generally the second or middle) putting the headboard at the height of the staysail stay. The third (upper) reef should take at least 50 percent of the mainsail area.

On a cutter rig, it is very handy if the running backstays can be brought far enough aft so the boom doesn't hit them during a tack, and the third reef in the mainsail brings the leech of the sail below the running backstays. This allows both runners to be set up and stay in

Because storm sails are seldom used, the crew may forget how to set them. During a practice session, take photographs of the trysail for quick reference. I keep these photos taped to the underside of the chart table lid.

DESPEDIDA
STORM TRYSAIL DETAILS

NOTE:
Pennant on tack should be higher than in this photo so sail will clear rolled in mainsail.

Sheet leads to large snatch block on rail track then to primary winch

Storm Trysail and Storm Jib   TIP 46

Be sure to hoist storm sails and sail with them before embarking on a passage. The time to find out that you need a tack pennant on the bottom of the trysail is not when it is blowing 50+ knots. Remember that the storm trysail sheets to the deck, *not* the boom, and be sure that there is suitable hardware installed for sheeting the sail.

I like to have a sheet permanently affixed to the storm trysail to avoid having to rummage through a locker looking for one. I always take pictures of the storm sails set to record sheet positions, and keep the pictures in a clear envelope taped to the underside of the chart table lid (see photo).

It is easiest to hoist the storm trysail before taking the main down, which keeps the boat steady and reduces flailing of the loose-footed trysail. This, of course, requires a separate track on the mast.

Storing Spare Sails   TIP 47

I found a neat way to package and protect spare sails. A mid-cockpit Alden 50 got a new mainsail, and her owner wanted to keep the old one as a spare. Storage room, however, is very limited on the boat. I folded the old main as carefully as I could, but it still took up too much space. At the local life raft repacker's I noticed the staff putting a raft in a heavy plastic bag and then using a vacuum pump to suck out all the air. After the raft shrank, they heat-sealed the bag along the edges and trimmed off the extra bag. We had the same procedure performed on the spare mainsail, and now it is 16 inches long, 14 inches wide, 5 inches high, and protected from moisture and mildew.

Marking Sails   TIP 48

A few minutes with a waterproof marker can save a lot of time when you are changing sails on a dark and stormy night. For hanked-on sails, I draw an arrow pointing up at each hank. For boats with furling sails or boats equipped with racing luff extrusions such as Tuff Luff, I mark the luff tape on the sail with an arrow at about 2-foot intervals. Write "Head," "Tack," and "Clew" on each sail in the appropriate corner. On the head and tack, identify the sail itself—like "130 percent Yankee."

Measuring Sails   TIP 49

Having all the measurements recorded for each sail can be very handy in case you have to order replacements. For genoas, measure luff length, leech length, and LP (greatest distance from the clew to the luff).

On mainsails, in addition to luff and foot dimensions, measure the cutback at the tack (distance from mast to tack pin) and cutback necessary for the outhaul.

Most sailmakers have a standard dimension sheet for recording all the information they need to make a sail. Stop by your sailmaker and pick up a few blank copies.

Sail Repair Materials   TIP 50

Every boat must be ready to make sail repairs at sea. Get the following supplies from a sailmaker:

- Roll of sticky-back Dacron sailcloth about 4 inches wide; it's handy for fixing small tears along seams. (For spare rigging parts, see Generic Safety and Spare Parts Inventory in appendix 4.)

- Six or more square yards of heavy Dacron sticky-back sailcloth; use it for larger repairs when the cloth is destroyed. It also works well for chafe patches

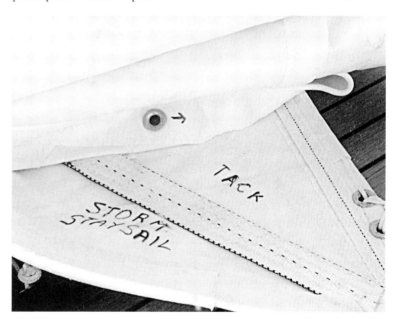

Labeling the key parts of a sail—tack, clew, head, as well as hanks and luff tape—with an indelible marker makes nighttime identification much easier. (Tip 48)

at spreader locations. Be sure to round the corners of any sticky-back sail repairs and apply them only to dry, salt-free sailcloth.

- Heavy webbing with which to replace a corner of a sail. I have made webbing repairs on pulled-out clews that have lasted thousands of miles.

- Stainless steel rings to replace a grommet with webbing and ring.

- A good supply of heavy sail needles and strong thread or nylon sail twine. A sewing palm also is handy, but a pair of pliers can be used if needed.

You should be able to make quick, effective repairs to sails. This kit includes sticky-back Dacron sailcloth in both strips and larger panels, webbing, stainless steel rings, needles, and palm. This repair kit from Quantum/Thurston has everything needed and costs less than $200. (Tip 50)

Mainsail Reefing **TIP 51**

Jiffy or slab reefing is great for quick sail reduction while day sailing or racing on a closed course. On long passages, however, chafe takes its toll, and reef lines part, often with disastrous results. Even if the main boom does not drop and damage the deck or crew, trying to re-reeve reef lines inside a boom is not an easy task. A few modifications help prevent chafe and result in easier reefing.

Most chafe occurs at cringles in the leech. A reef line passing over the small radius of a pressed-in cringle will chafe through in 24 to 48 hours of sloppy conditions. While adding a little weight and windage, small but stout blocks lashed to a cringle will greatly extend the life of reef lines. Modern Kevlar tape strapping is a strong and convenient material for the lashings. Unfortunately, rubber shell blocks are not made, at least as of this writing. On new sails, Quantum/Thurston Sailmakers uses Harken #1991 running backstay blocks with a piece of shock cord to keep the block from flopping around. For existing sails, you can use a Harken #1754 block, shown in the left photo next page.

It is difficult to pull a third reef down to the boom because of the angle the aft reef line makes to return to the aft end of the boom (see bottom photo). This problem is easily solved by leading the reefing line through a small block tied to the bitter end of the same reef line after a clove hitch is tied around the boom (see left photo next page). The reef line leads through this block, then back to the end of the boom. Initially, it takes a little bit of adjusting to get the block at the right height to clear the stacked up mainsail and to lead fair to the boom end.

On the mainsail luff, it is considerably easier to get a stainless steel ring around a tack hook than

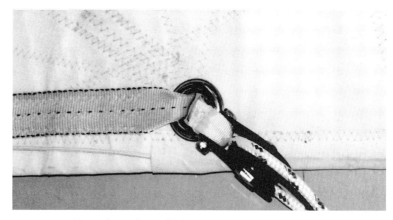

Reeving reef lines through small blocks lashed to the cringles reduces chafe and extends the life of the line. This is how Quantum/Thurston Sailmakers retrofits existing mainsails.

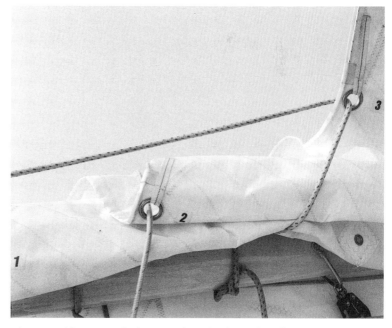

There is seldom enough downward angle of the aft reefing line.

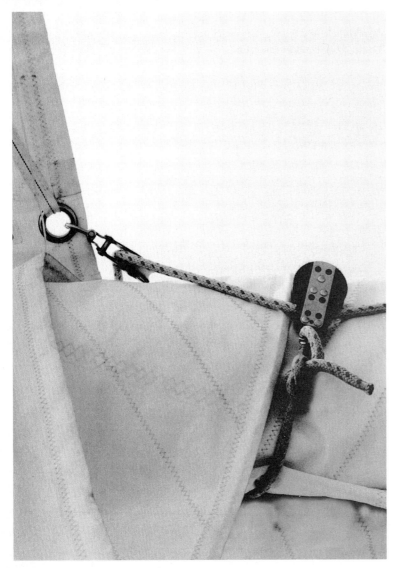

It's often difficult to force a reefing cringle over the tack hook at the gooseneck because the sail is hard to twist sideways. A solution is to sew stainless rings to a short length of webbing that runs through the grommet. The rings should be large enough to slip easily over the tack hook, and larger than the cringle so they can't pass through. (Tip 51)

To alter the angle, tie a small block to the end of a reef line led under the boom. (Tip 51)

a cringle in the sail. A small piece of webbing can be drawn through the cringle and a stainless ring sewn on each end, larger in diameter than the cringle so it can't pull through (photo, right).

Unguarded tack hooks (top photo, opposite) can snag the main as it is hoisted, resulting in rips. Having done this, I now make a guard for tack hooks with a piece of fuel line hose. For a snug fit, the

inside diameter should equal the diameter of the tack hook (bottom photo, opposite). A piece of string in the middle of the hose prevents it from getting lost. After the reefing ring is in place on the tack hook, slip on the hose to prevent the ring from disengaging.

The ability to reef quickly and

easily makes offshore passages more pleasant. Relieving weather helm by reefing the main reduces wear and power consumption on autopilots, and enables vane-type steering gear to operate efficiently.

A lot of boats try to take some reefing functions back to the cockpit. Unless everything is all in one place, it takes longer to put in a reef and requires more crew. This includes the system that uses one control line to pull down both the leech and luff for reefs, with blocks inside the boom. Unfortunately, this design is limited in the height of reef by the length of the boom. Using just one rope going first to the leech, then along (or in) the boom to the gooseneck, up to the reef point on the luff, then down to a fairlead and back to the cockpit does work, but the reefs obtained are less than ideal.

As much as I dislike getting out of the cockpit, I've found the fastest and simplest reefing system has leech reef lines led through stoppers to a winch mounted on the boom, on the same side of the boat as the main halyard winch. I drop the main halyard to a pre-marked point and belay it. Then I tension the leech reef line, hook the luff ring onto the gooseneck horn, slip the protective piece of hose back on, and re-tension the main halyard. My "personal best" time for this operation is 54 seconds . . . from leaving cockpit to returning. Even on the darkest and stormiest night, putting in a reef has never taken more than two or three minutes.

Tack hooks can snag and tear the mainsail when it is being hoisted. (Tip 51)

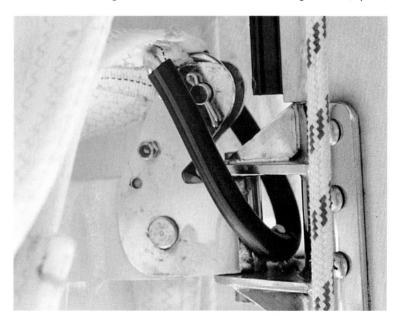

Tie the hose to the gooseneck so that each end of the fuel hose can be slipped over the hooks. (Tip 51)

OTHER TRICKS

Masthead Burgee TIP 52

With the proliferation of masthead-mounted devices, it has become difficult to hoist a proper burgee on a pigstick without getting it tangled. Here's a little trick I learned from David MacFarlane, whose father was captain for a prominent yachting family.

Before hoisting, tie a piece of light thread near the top of the flagstaff around the halyard. This will hold the staff vertical as it is hoisted. If the space at the masthead is small and the burgee large, bunch up the burgee and hold it tight to the staff with the thread. When the thread reaches the masthead flag halyard cheek block, a sharp tug will break the thread and shoot the staff vertically up past the masthead instruments.

To keep down noise and wear on the mast, I secure foam pipe insulation to the lower half of a pigstick with plastic electrical cable/wire ties (not illustrated).

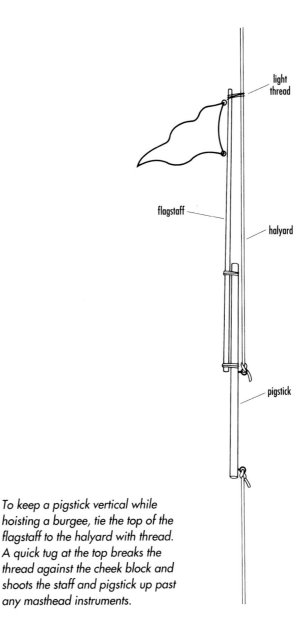

light
thread

flagstaff

halyard

pigstick

To keep a pigstick vertical while hoisting a burgee, tie the top of the flagstaff to the halyard with thread. A quick tug at the top breaks the thread against the cheek block and shoots the staff and pigstick up past any masthead instruments.

Spreader Flag Halyards

I make flag halyards as a continuous line, running through a block under the spreaders and another block near deck level (see photo). Shock cord run from the lower block to the deck maintains tension on the halyard. Snap eyes are secured to the halyard by passing a loop through the eye and over the backside of the snap (see inset). Flags of different sizes can be accommodated by moving the eye snap on the halyard, and more snaps can be added without un-rigging the halyard.

I make up flag halyards with a continuous line led between a block under the spreaders and another block tied to a length of shock cord to keep tension on the halyard. Notice how the halyard is run through the eye of the snap hook (inset).

Rigging a Radar Reflector Hoisted to a Spreader   TIP 54

According to tests conducted at the Stanford Research Institute and published in the September 1995 issue of *Practical Sailor*, the folding aluminum Davis Echomaster is as or more effective than more expensive, permanently mast-mounted reflectors. Such a reflector cannot be rigged on a simple up-and-down flag halyard, however, as it will chafe the halyard. The drawing shows the addition of a second block to keep the halyard away from the reflector. I use a piece of high-tech line to secure the ends of the halyard together in case the radar reflector fails.

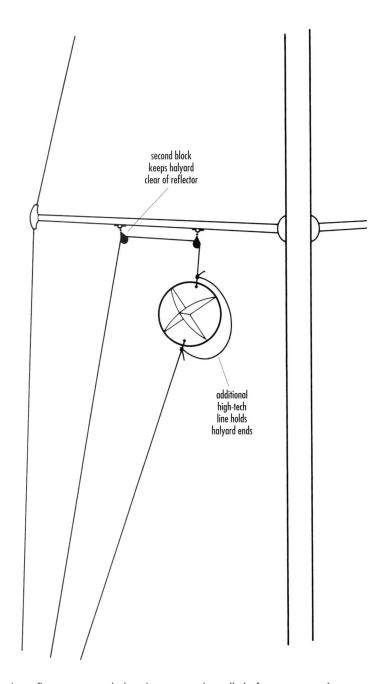

second block
keeps halyard
clear of reflector

additional
high-tech
line holds
halyard ends

Radar reflectors suspended under a spreader will chafe conventional up-and-down halyards. Screw a pair of blocks to the underside of the spreader so the continuous halyard doesn't touch the reflector.

Dissimilar Metals

TIP 55

During the fourth year of a seven-year circumnavigation, my friend Dan Dyer was tensioning the genoa halyard after a sail change when the mast-mounted halyard winch ripped off the mast and fell overboard. Failure was not due to the fasteners. The bronze winch base had been mounted directly on the aluminum mast, causing corrosion of the mast. Dan was left with a Barient #10-size hole in his mast.

I now specify dielectric insulation under all fittings attached to aluminum. The preferred material is 1/16-inch-thick UHMW (ul-tra high molecular weight poly-ethylene), but even a washer cut from a plastic milk jug is better than nothing. I like to make the spacer about 1/8 inch larger than the perimeter of the hardware to stop salt water from bridging the gap and causing corrosion. Anhydrous lanolin or other antiseize compound should be liberally applied to the threads.

A special problem exists with two-hole cleats used on spars. Salt eventually builds up inside the cleat where the fastener runs through it and bonds the fastener to the cleat. One solution is to wrap the portion of the fastener inside the cleat with electrical tape and apply an anti-seize compound.

Before leaving on an extended passage, it is worth the aggravation to remove all fasteners in aluminum and reinstall them with dielectric insulation and antiseize compound. An impact screwdriver helps loosen them. If that doesn't work, heating seized fasteners with a torch and then letting them cool will sometimes break the bond. One must be careful not to overheat aluminum. Most masts are made from #6061 alloy, heat-treated to a T-6 condition that gives an ultimate tensile strength of 45,000 psi. In the non-heat-treated condition, the same metal's tensile strength is just 18,000 psi.

Wherever stainless steel comes in contact with aluminum, corrosion will surely follow. Here, both the track and rivets are making the mast's paint peel. Insulate stainless from aluminum with thin plastic gaskets (even milk bottle material works) and use an antiseize compound such as Duralac on all fasteners.

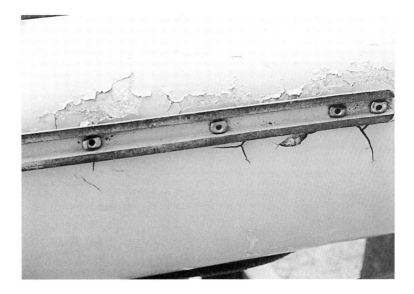

MISCELLANEA

Sheets should never be shackled to the clew of a sail because the hardware on a flapping sail can be a real widow-maker for some crew member. Instead, use a simple bowline, which is strong and relatively easy to untie even under a modest load. For less snag potential, be sure the tail ends up on the outside of the sail so it has less tendency to snag the babystay or fittings on the front of the mast. **TIP 56**

U-bolt cable clamps must be installed so the saddle is on the working end and the U-bolt is around the bitter end. To remember the correct way, use this mnemonic: Do not saddle a dead horse. **TIP 57**

If using a snapshackle for a halyard or, as shown here, on the upper bearing swivel of a furler, tape the snapshackle shut to prevent accidental opening. But because permanently taping stainless may lead to crevice corrosion, it is better to use screw-type shackles. **TIP 58**

The Windex masthead wind indicator came out about the same time as the Tartan 41. I thought they were great, and put one on the option sheet at our cost of $40. Nobody ordered them, so I added a light and upped the price fivefold, and the owner of every new boat requested one. **TIP 59**

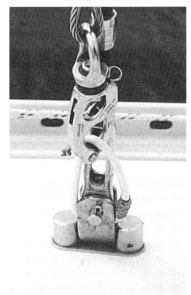

When reaching, it is sometimes desirable to move the sheet lead farther forward than the track allows. Here, a line with a large bowline tied around the sheet is used to pull the sheet down, which simulates a lead farther forward. When tacking, the genoa sheet will slip through the large bowline.

TIP 61

Rather than shackle unused halyards to lifelines or turnbuckle barrels, where they may be in the way or cause damage, a short length of wire, Nicopressed into a loop that runs through the turnbuckle fork, makes a convenient place to anchor halyards. Do not use an attachment point like this for anything highly loaded. **TIP 62**

For years I was annoyed by the clanking of running backstay tackle when secured to a genoa car as a storage position. Then it dawned on me that I could splice a rope quoit passed through the genoa car eye and secure the tackle to it, eliminating the noise. **TIP 60**

This is what happens when you are having difficulty furling the genoa and put the furling line on a power winch without first checking to see if the halyard is wrapped. **TIP 63**

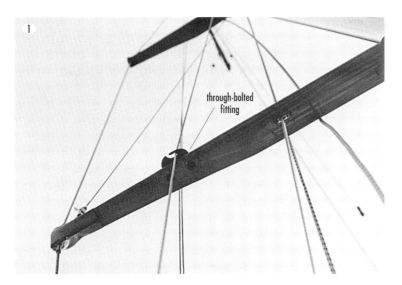

through-bolted
fitting

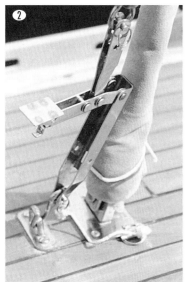

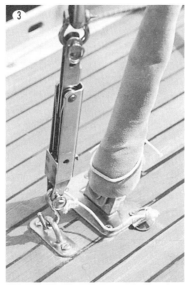

Stowing inner forestays. *Because inner forestays are longer than the distance between their attachment point on the mast and the base of the mast, stowing them so they are taut requires some ingenuity. One way is to through-bolt a fitting to a spreader that both captures the stay and keeps it from chafing on the spreader (1). Locate the proper spot on deck where the stay, with a small quick-release lever, reaches when it is closed. Install a pad eye, here just forward of a shroud (2). Hook the pad eye with the lever and close the lever to make the stay taut (3). A lashing also works in lieu of a small-boat quick-release lever.* **TIP 64**

A source of deck rot on many boats is where the chainplates pass through the deck. Because the rig is constantly working, it is difficult to keep this opening from leaking. When the rig is out of the boat, periodically remove the chainplate cover and recaulk. And once in a while, remove the chainplate entirely to check both the integrity of the knee or bulkhead to which it is bolted, and the chainplate itself. Note the slight elongation of the bolt holes in this chainplate—a sure sign of impending trouble! **TIP 65**

The mast on this boat broke right at an exit slot. The most heavily loaded places on a mast are generally where things attach—the gooseneck, spinnaker pole, spreaders and standing rigging, and of course, the partners at the deck.

I have developed my own standards for placement of mast exits. Paramount is that all exit holes have generously rounded corners, never sharp cuts that make a natural place for a tear to start. If I am installing a plate-type exit (such as Schaefer Marine part #34-49), I drill 5/16-inch holes in the upper two corners and one at the bottom, and then use a saber saw or router to cut the metal between the holes. Beeswax on a saber saw blade will stop aluminum from clogging the teeth. I make the lowest exit slot at least 4 feet above the gooseneck and stagger the exits at a minimum of 1-foot intervals on opposite sides of the mast, so there are 2 feet of vertical spacing between exits on the same side of the mast. I am also very careful that exits on the same side of the mast are not in alignment with each other vertically. **TIP 66**

site of break

When rigging fails and the boat is dismasted, the heel of the mast can jump the step and cause great interior damage. ORC rules require that it be secured. With a 1-inch-diameter stainless steel bolt going through heavy ears on the mast step and the mast, the heel of this stick isn't going anywhere.

TIP 67

  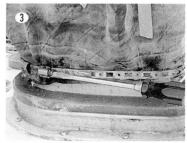

  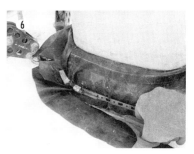

 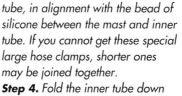

Watertight mast boot. On boats with through-deck-stepped spars, a watertight boot goes a long way in keeping the interior dry. Here's a reasonably watertight boot made from readily available materials.

Step 1. Wrap a piece of inner tube around the mast with a 2- to 4-inch overlap at the back of the mast. Tape it in place so the bottom of the cut tube is about 1 inch above the mast partners and chocking. Spartite poured-in-place mast chocking is used in this photo and is highly recommended.

Step 2. Liberally apply silicone sealer to the mast about ¾ inch above the lower edge of the inner tube, between the mast and inner tube.

Step 3. Install a large hose clamp around the lower edge of the inner tube, in alignment with the bead of silicone between the mast and inner tube. If you cannot get these special large hose clamps, shorter ones may be joined together.

Step 4. Fold the inner tube down over the hose clamp. Liberally apply silicone to the overlap area. If you want to make a super boot, use the glue from an inner tube patching kit instead of silicone to bond the overlap areas together.

Step 5. Apply a lot of silicone to the mast partners (not shown) and then install the lower hose clamp around the inner tube and partners. Boats not going far offshore, and which have their masts removed annually, may skip the silicone on the inside of the inner tube and partners.

Step 6. Trim off excess inner tube from mast partners.

Step 7. Apply additional bead of silicone at the top of the boot-to-mast juncture.

Note: Inner tube material is subject to sunlight degradation. I recommend placing a decorative canvas mast boot around the inner tube boot to act as a sunshield.

TIP 68

CHAPTER 3

INTERIOR MODIFICATIONS

While the wide-open spaces of lesser-priced yachts seduce potential buyers at boat shows, the astute shopper will find that the appearance of room is achieved by the lack of cabinets for storage, and generally too many berths. And to make them more appealing dockside, many modern boats are much beamier than designs of twenty years ago. Beamy boats, however, are often less safe than narrower hulls because of the greater distances between handholds or places to brace oneself in a seaway (see photo with Handholds, tip 69), not to mention pounding upwind.

A good offshore boat enables one to move about below with plenty of handholds. Similarly, the galley should be configured so that the chef can remain stationary with both hands free for pots, pans, and utensils. This is why U-shaped galleys are popular. With U-shaped, L-shaped, or sideboard-type galleys a strong strap, attached at both ends to through-bolted eyes, is essential for restraining the cook and giving him or her something to lean back against when the boat is heeled.

Much of this chapter deals with securing all the things—batteries, cabinet doors, floorboards—that in violent weather can cause serious injury to the crew or damage to the boat.

Sometimes you just want things to stay put; other times you want to lock things in or lock things out. In the case of companionways or seat lockers, the following anecdote illustrates the importance of having certain closures work both ways.

While preparing an Alden 46 for the Marion–Bermuda Race I

noticed that when I washed the boat, water leaked into the large cockpit seat locker. Because I knew that the problem would be worse offshore, especially if the locker was on the leeward side and the boat was taking spray or waves into the cockpit, I decided to add foam tape weather-stripping to seal the space between the underside of the lid and the lip around the hatch opening. Gaskets around the locker lip will not last long when abused by taking things in and out of the locker, so the place to install tape is the underside of the lid.

I started by taping the full perimeter, then hosed down the cockpit, still finding many leaks into the locker. On closer inspection, it was evident that the underside of the lid and the molded-in lip were not parallel to each other. I decided the only way to determine where to put more tape was to get inside the locker and look at the gap.

I climbed into the locker and started examining the tape. The side toward the hinges appeared tight, so tight that the locker lid was not closing all the way. I raised the lid with my head about 6 inches and then dropped it. When the lid fell, I heard a click.

I tried to open the lid, but it would not budge. I quickly surmised that the noise I heard was the exterior hasp mounted on the lid falling down and closing over its eye mounted on the cockpit footwell wall. I felt like a kid locked in an abandoned refrigerator. It was black as night, but at least I could breathe!

It was after 5 P.M. and the boat was out at the end of a dock, so I figured the odds of anybody hearing me hollering for help were slight. I felt around in my pockets and found a pair of pliers. With them I was able to unscrew the nuts on the back of the hatch hinge bolts and, with a lot of jiggling, work the hinges loose so I could escape.

From that day onward, I always mount hasps so the hinged portion is the lower half and stays open until folded up to engage the eye on the hatch lid. This also prevents people from using the hasp as a handle for opening the lid, which can distort it.

SECURING THE CABIN

Even high-quality boat manufacturers often do not provide adequately strong handholds and closures for doors, drawers, berth top locker bins, and removable cabin sole floorboards. Elbow or friction catches will let go when a locker's contents hit the door during a knockdown.

Handholds — TIP 69

It is essential that sturdy handrails be installed below decks to allow even the shortest crew to move throughout the interior always with another handhold within reach before releasing the last one—just like kids swinging from ring to ring on the school playground.

All interior woodwork that may be grabbed as the boat heels and lurches must be tested by the heaviest crew yanking as violently as possible. Any sign of movement must be corrected, as any weakness will always degrade. Unfortunately, the screw heads in interior joinerwork are often bunged for appearance's sake. To facilitate bung installation, counterbores for bungs are frequently deep, leaving little wood under the screw head. Further weakening occurs when flathead screws are used, as their chamfer is a natural starting place for wood splitting.

For passages, clearly identify for your crew any interior components that should not be used as handholds (think of the "No Step" signs on airplane wings). This is a good use for a label maker (see Labels, tip 87).

I once failed to point out which fiddles on a chart table were removable (see Place Fiddles, tip 78). During a 40-knot blow in the Gulf Stream, a crew member grabbed a removable fiddle, which came out in his hands, and he was thrown across the cabin, sustaining several broken ribs.

Foam pipe insulation is handy for padding bulkhead edges or other

The saloon of this O'Day 40 has full-length handholds on the overhead, plus two good sea berths, but they will require lee cloths (see Lee Cloths, tip 82). Floorboards must have a means of being secured, and the galley needs a strap to hold the chef in place. And what about all the loose stuff on shelves? (Tip 69)

places a body may be thrown against. At the conclusion of any rough passage, I can measure the height of the galley countertop rails by looking at the bruises on my hips.

On yachts without a bridge deck, I install companionway dropboards to the level of the seats, then pad the top with pipe insulation. Thin, stick-on foam weather-stripping installed in the side and lower perimeter channels, and between boards, improves the watertight integrity of companionway dropboards. It does not last long, however, so plan on replacing the stripping before each long passage.

Locking the Companionway   TIP 70

To fulfill the ORC regulation that requires that crew be able to open the companionway hatch and slides from both the inside and outside,

some years ago I designed a special fitting that is now standard equipment on J-boats. Many other boats can use it, too.

The fitting is a stainless steel socket that mounts on the companionway's sliding hatch. A fastpin locks one end of a tang to the socket. The other end of the tang passes through a slot in the drop-in weatherboard so an exterior lock can be put in place (see photo). The socket and fastpin are available from TPI as part numbers 10303 and 18005.

Another way to make a tang removable is to epoxy a threaded insert in place of an existing screw or bolt. Brass threaded inserts (see photo, next page) are available from Woodworker's Supply (see appendix 7).

With a threaded insert in the companionway, there are many ways of devising a readily removable bolt with which to hold the tang. One way is to screw a wing nut all the way onto a bolt, tight-

I use this companionway mock-up at seminars to show how the TPI socket and a fastpin can be used to secure the weatherboards, and to make the lock operable from inside and out. (Tip 70)

A brass threaded insert is an alternative to the TPI socket. (Tip 70)

ening the two together with tools to make an assembly that will not move under hand pressure. Secure the knob with a drop of Loctite.

Alternatively, use internally threaded plastic knobs from Woodworker's Supply. The part number for a 1⅛-inch outside diameter (OD) three-prong knob is #862-193.

Remotely Activated Lock   TIP 71

Exterior companionway hasps and hardware can be readily pried off with a crowbar. They also can be shin bangers. Key locks corrode and become unusable.

Here's a lock design by Alden Yachts in Rhode Island that uses mostly off-the-shelf components. It is tamperproof, keeps the mechanism inside, and also offers a measure of convenience by being remotely activated. Essentially, it is a bolt or plunger that travels back and forth, in and out of a hole, and is actuated by a push-pull cable (see photo).

The only custom-fabricated item is the lock plunger, which can be readily made from ½-inch-diameter round bar stock with a 10-32 hole tapped on one end and the other end rounded. Fairleads are stock Ronstan or can be fabricated from plastic or wood if required. The mechanism is actuated by a #33-C cable (the same as a marine throttle cable). These cables are available in 5- to 40-foot lengths, so the control handle can be mounted in just about any convenient location. A Teleflex clamp secures the outside jacket of the cable at the plunger end. The handle is from Morse, which can be mounted through a bulkhead. If a surface

Remote-controlled lock installed on the lazarette hatch of an Alden 50. (Tip 71)

mount is needed, add a Morse mounting bracket. Because a #33 cable provides 3 inches of travel, the plunger stroke can be long enough for positive engagement.

In some installations you may have to glass in a gusset to make the hole for the plunger. For deck hatches, a U-bolt can be used to capture the plunger (see photo).

This remote-activation lock has other applications. Commercial vessels are required to have a remote fuel shut-off outside the engine room; the same cable and handle are often used. The actuator end is a Teleflex clevis attached to the handle of a ball valve.

A U-bolt used in this Bomar hatch captures the remotely activated plunger rod (not shown) to prevent the hatch from being opened from outside.

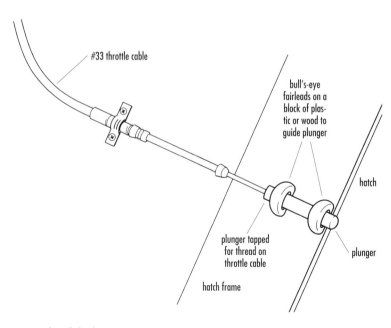

Remote hatch lock.

Drawers   TIP 72

All drawers should have a simple pivoting piece of wood or aluminum bar stock bolted to the back of the drawer to prevent them from sliding all the way out and falling (see top photo).

TPI imports very good German door and drawer catches that have a pop-out unlock feature and are flush when locked. The latch is available from TPI. The push-button (see bottom photo) is available for various wood thicknesses. Another source is Sugatsune America, but this lock uses plastic components.

This simple piece of pivoting wood prevents the drawer from falling out when the boat is heeled. (Tip 72)

This handsome, positive-lock push-button drawer lock from TPI is inexpensive. These catches work well on drawers and are made by several manufacturers. Avoid ones made with plastic components. (Tip 72)

Berth Top Access Lids   TIP 73

Berth top access lids can be easily held closed with pieces of ¼-inch-thick by 1-inch-wide aluminum bar stock about 4 to 5 inches long. A ¼-inch hole for a pivot point is drilled on centerline about 1 inch from one end of the aluminum bar. A ¼-inch stainless steel round-head bolt goes through the hole in the aluminum, and then a plastic washer is placed between the aluminum and the berth top. The bolt passes through a hole drilled in the berth top and is secured underneath with an oversized stainless steel washer (commonly called a *fender washer*) and an aircraft nylon insert locking nut (e.g., Nylok). The berth top hole should be located so the aluminum bar can be pivoted parallel to the opening to give access to the locker lid, then turned 90 de-

A pivoting aluminum bar keeps this berth lid in place, even should the boat capsize. Note the aluminum angle screwed to the bulkhead; the horizontal leg of the angle holds the berth lid in place on the side against the bulkhead. (Tip 73)

grees to hold the lid in place when offshore. Tighten the nut enough so that the pivoting bar stays in place (see photo).

With a spacer to allow for the thickness of a door or drawer face, this same scheme can be used to hold doors and drawers closed. In this case, the hole is drilled into the surrounding frame. Unlike their use on berth tops, however, where the bolt head and turning mechanism are hidden by the cushion, here they are visible and less than aesthetically pleasing. Consequently, I have devised various other systems of rods, barrel bolts, and other devices too numerous to describe. But the idea is the same.

Cabin Sole Floorboards   TIP 74

How one secures the removable boards in a cabin sole is largely dependent on the weight of the boards and the contents stored under the sole. Over the years, I have used about ten different methods of securing cabin soles. No one way works on all boats.

For lightweight boards with no stores underneath, ¼-inch shock cord secured to stainless steel hammock hooks is adequately strong (see photo).

A much stronger method is to install an ABI turning lock lift handle. The locking arm, however, must have its set-screw dimpled into the vertical shaft (see photo, next page) for a more positive attachment. Set-screws without dimples will slide under load.

Shock cord is sufficient to retain lightweight floorboards, but only if there are no stores beneath. (Tip 74)

A third method uses barrel bolts, most of which have a knob that unscrews, allowing the knob to be repositioned on what would normally be the underside of the barrel bolt. A slot routed into the floorboard allows the knob to slide back and forth so that the bolt pin also can move. The pin should engage a piece of aluminum angle at least ⁷⁄₁₆ inch thick, bolted to a sole-bearing timber.

Hinges   TIP 75

Almost all boatbuilders use screws to secure hinges. Frequently, the screws are of small diameter and very short. In almost all cases the screws can be replaced with through-bolts with oversized washers under the nuts. Especially susceptible to failure are piano hinges held with flathead screws—the engagement of the screw head into the hinge is very small. Replace each flathead screw with a round-head bolt, washer, and nut; or if bolts cannot be used, with a round-head screw one or two sizes larger in diameter than the original screw (see photo).

A stronger method of securing floorboards is with this ABI handle. (Tip 74)

With heavy stores behind, hinges secured with screws can give way. Replace with through-bolts, even if you have to countersink the woodwork for the nuts. And, of course, don't forget a strong latch on the other side. (Tip 75)

Holding Down Batteries   **TIP 76**

Securing batteries is always a problem. A battery in motion is a dangerous missile; a restrained battery cannot develop inertia and is therefore much safer in a rollover.

Batteries often are housed in plastic battery boxes. These boxes are great for retaining spilled acid, but have several problems when it comes to rollover security. The polypropylene straps and plastic buckles that come with most battery boxes are seldom strong enough. They may meet the American Boat and Yacht Council's (ABYC) *Standards and Recommended Practices for Small Craft*, E-10.7.4, which most surveyors and insurance companies follow, but the standard only restricts battery movement to 1 inch with a 90-pound pull. Plastic straps and buckles probably will not withstand the effects of a vessel being thrown off a wave and capsized.

Even worse are the plastic fittings supplied with some battery boxes to secure the strap to the boat. I have never found one of these plastic fittings that I could not break with a quick tug. Replacing plastic hold-down hardware with a stainless steel tang through-bolted to a structural member of the boat is an inexpensive improvement.

Also in order is upgrading to a stronger strap. Even a synthetic sail tie would be an improvement over cheap, polypropylene straps.

Most plastic battery boxes have extra space between the top of the battery and the underside of the lid. This space is useful for connecting battery cables, but allows the battery to move and therefore develop inertia. To fill this gap, a piece of wood often can be fitted to the battery box lid. The wood should be located directly under the strap, and can be held in place with a couple of screws through the battery box lid into the wood spacer. Battery acid will eventually attack the wood; a sheathing of fiberglass will prolong the wood's life.

On boats with built-in battery trays, be sure the tray is fiberglassed inside and is structurally supported. The best material to use across the top of a battery is fiberglass bar stock or angle, with wood a second choice (see photo). Under no circumstances should any metal be

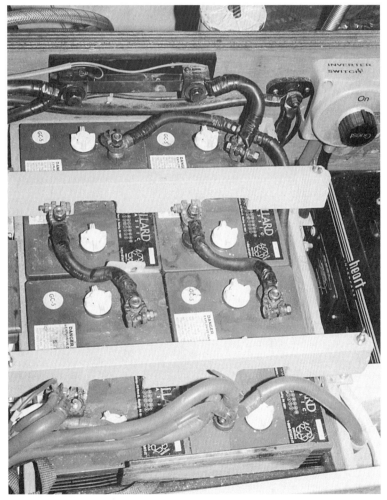

Nonconductive wood and fiberglass are the best materials to restrain batteries.

used, as it is electrically conductive and could short the batteries. Two sources I have used for extruded fiberglass shapes are Ryerson and McMaster Carr. The latter sells ¼-inch-thick 2-by-2-inch fiberglass angle in 10-foot lengths. Angle can be bolted through the sides of a battery box (if they're high enough) to clamp the sides of a battery to the box, giving unrestricted access to filler caps.

As a Marion–Bermuda Race inspector, I have seen very impressive large bars installed across the top of batteries, only to find the brackets holding the bars secured with a few small screws. For smaller batteries of case sizes 24, 27, and 30, Gil Marine makes battery hold-downs designed for offshore powerboat racers.

Because configurations differ, each battery hold-down installation must be engineered *in situ*, keeping in mind high strength and the need to absolutely restrict movement (see drawing).

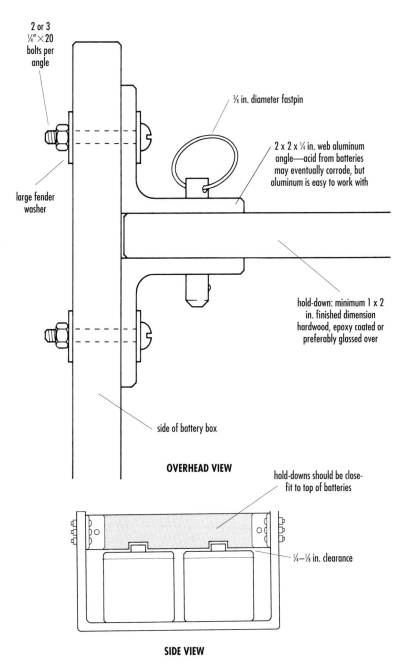

2 or 3 ¼" × 20 bolts per angle

⅜ in. diameter fastpin

2 x 2 x ¼ in. web aluminum angle—acid from batteries may eventually corrode, but aluminum is easy to work with

large fender washer

hold-down: minimum 1 x 2 in. finished dimension hardwood, epoxy coated or preferably glassed over

side of battery box

OVERHEAD VIEW

hold-downs should be close-fit to top of batteries

¼–⅛ in. clearance

SIDE VIEW

Construction details show how the restraining bar over the batteries must be positively fastened to the sides of a battery box or to structural members of the boat, such as a bulkhead tabbed to the hull. (Tip 76)

Construct Fiddles TIP 77

On tables and countertops, numerous tall fiddles make passage-making easier and safer. Having to balance a plate on one's lap because the table lacks fiddles gets very frustrating on long passages. Opening a locker only to have its contents come tumbling out can cause injury to crew and ding up the interior. Watching one's laptop computer slide off the chart table is heartbreaking and usually terminal to the machine.

Here are some boatbuilder's tricks for making removable fiddles. For most applications, #10 2-inch bronze wood screws make very good pegs (see photo 1). To ensure alignment of the fiddles with their mounting holes, and to make them interchangeable, it is very worthwhile to make a jig to space the holes. I use a piece of metal, usually ⅛-inch-thick steel or ¼-inch aluminum. Fiddles up to 18 inches long generally only need two pegs. For longer fiddles, it is simpler to use one jig with the two-hole pattern repeated several times. With a little planning, I have been able to make one jig so that all the fiddle pegs on a boat are spaced the same. This way, a short two-peg fiddle can replace part of a longer multi-peg fiddle.

For #10 2-inch wood screw pegs, use ⁵⁄₃₂-inch holes in the jig. On each fiddle, draw a line down the centerline of the mounting edge, and then use the jig to spot-drill ⁵⁄₃₂-inch holes into the fiddle. Final hole depth is 1⅜ inch. A drill press with a vise is very helpful, as

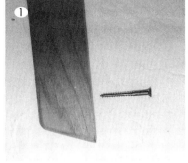

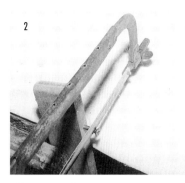

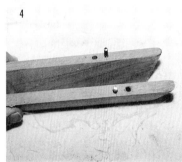

Making removable fiddles. *1. Drill teak fiddle and install screw. **2**. Cut off screw head. **3**. File cut edge smooth. **4**. Extra holes allow fiddles to fit into each other for compact storage. **5**. This cockpit table has two sets of holes, one inboard (shown) and another set farther out at the table edges.*

it is essential that the screws be perpendicular to the underside of the fiddle in both axes.

Drive the screw in until only the nonthreaded portion of the shank is exposed. A hacksaw cuts off the screw head (photo 2, previous page), and a few passes with a file rounds off the remaining peg (photo 3).

I use the same jig to spot holes in the surface on which the fiddle is going to mount and then enlarge the holes to $\frac{3}{16}$ inch. For heavy-duty use, ferrules can be made from $\frac{1}{4}$-inch OD copper tubing, with the top blossomed out with a flaring tool. Mounting holes for ferrules are enlarged to $\frac{1}{4}$ inch, and the tops chamfered with a countersink. A drop or two of epoxy permanently sets the ferrules. To prevent rot, fiddle mounting holes should go all the way through the mounting surface so that liquids can drain.

Most boatbuilder-installed fiddles are not high enough. To have half a chance of retaining a beverage can at sailing angles, 2 inches is the minimum height (photo 5). High fiddles, however, are not comfortable to rest one's arms on, and because they are a snap to make, on some boats I have fabricated a second set of shorter fiddles for use at anchor .

For storing fiddles, after years of having surfaces scratched by the pegs of extra fiddles, it dawned on me that I could drill mounting holes into the fiddles themselves, offset about $\frac{1}{2}$ inch from the pegs, and mate two fiddles to each other (photo 4).

Place Fiddles   TIP 78

Tables. Install a set at the perimeter and another set down the middle to hold condiments and beverages.

Galley. Any athwartships countertops will benefit from fiddles to stop cooking items from sliding. I have even made rows of holes to position fiddles a little farther apart than the width of sliced bread to facilitate making sandwiches when the boat is rolling.

Chart table. In addition to the mandatory fiddle on the inboard side, smaller fiddles work well to make a home for tide tables and other publications that you like to keep handy.

Bureau tops. I have seen many scars in interior varnish that could have been prevented by using fiddles to make small "compartments" on bureau tops so that flashlights, tools, and other items do not roll around.

Inside lockers. Besides the mandatory fiddles on the inboard edges of shelves, additional fiddles separating athwartships spaces will keep locker contents organized and reduce noise from movement.

Shock cord stretched across the inside of a locker keeps its contents in place when the door is opened (see photo).

Even the high fiddles on this Hinckley Sou'wester 51 galley locker needed additional shock cord to retain the contents during a transatlantic passage. (Tip 78)

Avoid the Toilet Seat Toss   TIP 79

Here's a simple modification every toilet seat ought to have. Designed by the owner of *Spirit*, a Hinckley Sou'wester 51 yawl, this chock system of holding the seat in place proved invaluable during our 1999 transatlantic crossing.

When one sits while the boat is heeled, uneven body weight puts pressure on toilet seat hinges, frequently causing dislodgment or breakage. Adding chocks to the underside of the seat stops any wobble and preserves hinges (see photo).

Chock height should allow at least ½ inch engagement inside the lip of the bowl. Chocks can be made from polyethylene, Starboard, or other strong plastic. The outside edge of the chocks should be curved to match the curve of the inside of the bowl. Temporarily hold the chock in place with tape while drilling pilot holes for the screws. For more tips on toilet maintenance, see Plumbing in appendix 1.

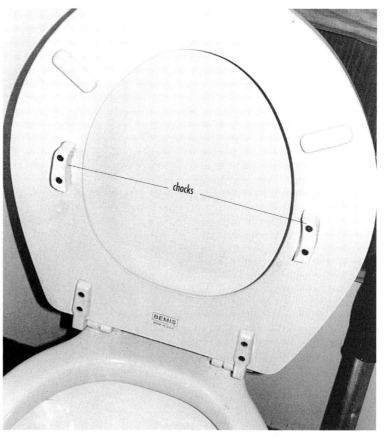

Chocks screwed to the underside of the toilet seat keep it firmly in place when it is occupied at an angle of heel.

SEA BERTHS

For most people, sleeping in the middle of the boat is certainly more comfortable as there is less motion. Back when sailing yachts primarily made offshore passages, the saloon or main cabin was always configured with pilot and transom berths on each side. The forepeak was used for sail storage, with perhaps pipe berths for paid crew. This gave four good underway berths in the middle of the boat.

Modern boats, however, relegate sleeping areas to the bow and stern, with the middle of the boat devoted to dinettes and chairs. In a seaway, sleeping forward of the mast makes a roller coaster seem calm by comparison. I'm one of the few people who do it, because I like to get away from everyone else yet still remain aware of how the boat, rather than the crew, is performing.

As I came on watch during one rather lumpy Gulf Stream passage, one of the crew asked if he could take the leeward side of the V-berth to escape being plastered against a leeboard in the saloon.

I said, "Sure."

Half an hour later, he was on deck feeding the fish. When he recovered, he asked me how I managed to stay in the berth, as he was airborne each time the boat came off a wave. I asked if he remembered how heavy my seabag was, and told him that I put it on top of me to hold me down in the berth.

Here are two good types of sea berths you can make and install yourself.

Removable Sea Berth TIP 80

Faced with making a decent sea berth over two swiveling armchairs in the saloon of an Alden 50, I built what became the most sought-after berth on the vessel (see photo 4). The berth readily adjusts to any angle of heel. The only custom parts are brackets for the outboard sides of the berth (photo 1), and these cost less than $100. Additionally, they are the only perma-

nently installed components; the rest of the berth rolls up to 5 inches diameter and stows on a forepeak shelf (photo 3).

This berth is fabricated from straight, 1-inch OD, heavy-wall (minimum 0.065 in. thickness, with 0.120 in. preferable) polished stainless steel tubing, available from most metal supply houses. Heavy-duty crutch tips cover the forward and aft ends of the tubing to prevent them from gouging the bulkhead. When I have been unable to

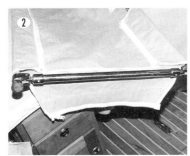

This removable canvas berth proved to be the most popular sea berth aboard an Alden 50.
1. *A bulkhead fitting to receive the pipe end.* ***2***. *The canvas zips tightly around the frame to keep it rectangular.* ***3***. *The berth neatly rolls up out of the way behind the saloon seats.* ***4***. *Suspended by tackle secured to the overhead, this berth is comfortable and lightweight.*

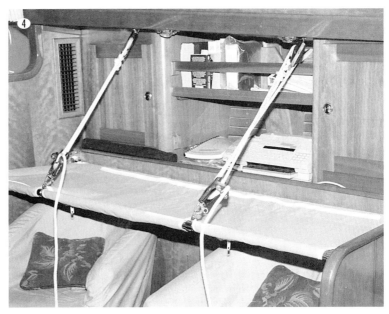

REMOVABLE SEA BERTH PARTS LIST

- two custom stainless steel U-shaped brackets to hold outboard pipe with crutch tip in place. If at all possible, through-bolt in place. If screws must be used, increase number.
- two fastpins to secure outboard pipe in bracket
- four heavy-duty crutch tips
- four 1-inch OD stainless steel washers, if crutch tips do not have metal inside end as required
- four pieces of 1-inch OD polished stainless steel tubing with minimum 0.065-inch wall
- one custom zippered fabric berth bottom
- four socket ends, Sea-Dog #270111, with set-screws

- removed and sockets drilled and through-bolted to athwartship berth tubes
- four #10-24 × 1½-inch round-head machine screws
- four #10-24 stainless steel nuts for above. A little more work, but more streamlined installation is to use barrel nuts so only the nicely rounded head protrudes.
- four slides, Sea-Dog #270171. Replace set-screw with #10-32 round-head machine screws protruding through wall of tubing to lock slides in place.
- two sleeves with eyes, Sea-Dog #270531, for adjustment tackle

- two pad eyes for tops of tackle, Sea-Dog #088721. Other pad eyes can be used. If not possible to through-bolt, mount so screws are not in tension.
- two fiddle blocks with snap-shackles, Garhauer #25-03S
- two fiddle blocks with beckets, cam cleats, and snap-shackles, Garhauer #25-08S
- two lengths ⅜-inch rope, with eyes spliced around beckets
- two stainless steel D shackles; use on sleeves to attach lower ends of adjustment tackle, Sea-Dog #147006 or equal

find crutch tips with an internal metal insert, a 1-inch OD stainless steel washer serves to reinforce the rubber socket.

The connecting hardware consists of heavy-duty cast dodger and bimini components from Sea-Dog. I slightly modified the hardware to through-bolt sockets and replaced some machine screws with fastpins. The drilling goes quickly with cobalt bits and a slow-turning drill.

The secret of the design is the fabric berth bottom, which is a tight fit and holds the berth in a rectangle. Heavy-duty KY plastic zippers secure the fabric around the stainless steel frame (photo 2). The combination of a partially inflated air mattress on the fabric berth bottom and adjustment tackles provides a level platform as comfortable as a water bed at home.

See also appendix 1, page 186.

Root Berth TIP 81

On boats where a full-height bulkhead is available both forward and aft, a root berth is a simple way to make another sea berth.

Charlie Britton, founder of Tartan Marine, built the prototype Tartan 44, *Twain*, with six root berths in the saloon, enabling all the off-watch to sleep to windward. To save weight and improve rigidity, the forward and aft tubes were 1¼-inch IPS (for Iron Pipe Size) schedule 80 aluminum pipe (see drawing).

The downside of a root berth is its lack of adjustment once one is in it. This was hard on *Twain*'s off-watch, as the boat only had notches to raise the inboard berth side — so when the boat tacked, the crew member was automatically rolled out and had to climb to the new high side.

Lee Cloths TIP 82

The best sea berths, as noted, are generally amidships, where motion is the least. Settees work well, but they need lee cloths added to keep the occupant from falling out.

The most comfortable lee cloths are made from a plastic mesh material called Textilene, which allows air to circulate. Canvas or other strong fabric also is suitable, but not as comfortable in the tropics.

Lee cloths should extend a minimum of 22 inches above the berth cushion. Higher is better if overhead space is available. Pad eyes for lee cloth lines must be very secure. I like to pass the line through the pad eye and then tie the end back on itself with a rolling hitch (see illustration on page 8). This allows the line to be slackened (by sliding the knot up) to drop the lee cloth

for ingress, and be tensioned by sliding the knot down when in the berth.

Fuzzy three-strand spun Dacron rope is ideal for lee cloth lines. For fore-and-aft berths, the pad eyes should be positioned well outboard of the berth edge so the occupant is cradled into the berth, not sagging over the edge, as happens if the pad eyes are in line with the inboard edge of the berth (see photo).

Lee cloths should have a hem in the bottom through which a

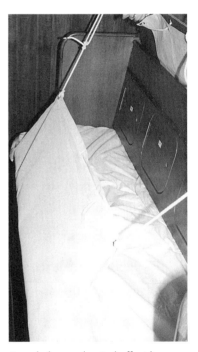

Lee cloths can be tied off with ropes tied to the overhead, or a single bolt rope through the hem to eyes in bulkheads fore and aft. Note how the cloth slants outboard at the top to keep the person from hanging over the side. (Tip 82)

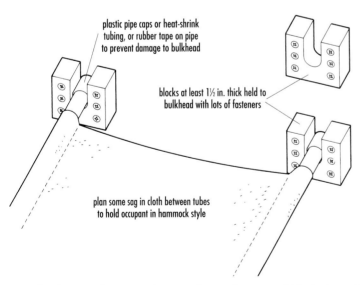

plastic pipe caps or heat-shrink tubing, or rubber tape on pipe to prevent damage to bulkhead

blocks at least 1½ in. thick held to bulkhead with lots of fasteners

plan some sag in cloth between tubes to hold occupant in hammock style

A root berth is simply two sturdy pipes dropped into wood blocks through-bolted to the bulkheads, with canvas stretched between. (Tip 81)

piece of aluminum bar stock (minimum ⅛ in. but recommended ¼ in. thick by 1 in. wide) is run. The lee cloth should be secured to the bottom of the berth with at least eight #10 bolts passing through the top layer of mesh, the aluminum, and the bottom layer of cloth. Oversize flat washers should be used under bolt heads to prevent tearing the mesh. Where the underside of the berth is not accessible, use at least twelve #10 screws with oversize washers (see illustration and photo).

Berth Cushions TIP 83

If you are going to spend more than an occasional night on board, it is worth the extra money to have the cushions made of high-resiliency (often called HR) foam and to vary the density. I find a very comfortable berth cushion is made from 2-inch firm foam on the bottom with 2 inches of medium foam and 1 inch of very soft foam on top.

On my boat, to avoid the cost of replacing the cushions, I started with 1-inch foam as a separate pad on top of the stock 4-inch cushions. As the original cushions aged, the foam became compressed and now I have 3 inches of soft foam topping.

Incidentally, the term "berth cushion" is used because "mattress" gets one into all sorts of federal regulations.

In the tropics, "egg crate" foam mattress pads laid over normal berth cushions give better air circulation.

For more information on berth cushions and cover fabrics, see appendix 1, page 186.

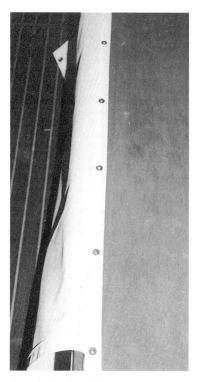

Lee cloths should have aluminum bar stock battens in the lower hem with bolts through the fabric, bar, and berth bottom. Use washers. (Tip 82)

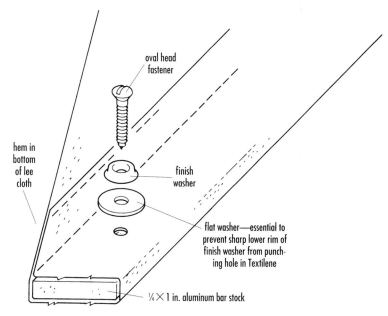

Assembly details show a fabric hem around aluminum bar stock. (Tip 82)

CLIMATE CONTROL

Adequate air flow is important because it reduces mildew, cools the interior, and makes crew generally more comfortable. Most boats, unfortunately, aren't delivered with good ventilation in place. You may need to add fans and vents. And if you decide to go all out for a genset to power air-conditioning, be sure to buy a carbon dioxide monitor-alarm.

Fans TIP 84

While the oscillating feature of fans such as the Guest and other brands is nice, their longevity is short. Hella Turbo and Caframo fans use a very small amount of electrical current for the air they move, and last a lot longer than oscillating types. Even air-conditioned yachts benefit from a large number of fans

to move air around. As a minimum, install fans at the chart table, galley, and over berths.

After two fires with fans, I now install an in-line fuse on each fan, sized just large enough for the individual fan's amperage draw (½ amp for a 12-volt Hella fan). Because fans are frequently ganged on one circuit or connected to cabin lighting circuits, individual protection is necessary so the fuse will blow at the first sign of overheating.

Washboard Vents TIP 85

Aboard the Hinckley Sou'wester 51 *Spirit* there is an extra set of companionway washboards made from stock aluminum floor grating that provide ventilation as well as security.

Carbon Monoxide Detector TIP 86

After a September drive from Boston, the crew and I arrived in Five Islands, Maine, at close to midnight. We boarded the Alden 54 ketch we were to deliver south. The interior of the boat was very cold, so I turned on the generator to bring the refrigeration down, charge the batteries, and run the reverse-cycle air-conditioning for heat.

At five the next morning I was awakened with a report that the couple in one of the aft cabins had gotten up during the night and collapsed due to carbon monoxide poisoning. If the man had not needed to go to the head, he and his wife might never have awakened.

Hella fans have the longest-lasting motors, but anything electrical can burn up, especially if run constantly. (Tip 84)

Washboard vents. (Tip 85)

When removing the generator exhaust system the following winter, I found traces of water leaks in the hose. Because carbon monoxide (CO) molecules are smaller than H_2O molecules, I then understood the source of the deadly gas. I have now installed a CO detector in the boat and strongly recommend this precaution to anyone using combustible fuel aboard, such as for auxiliary engines, gensets, propane stoves, and kerosene or diesel heaters.

WHAT'S WHAT AND WHERE

Labels   TIP 87

Label everything that is not readily evident to all members of the crew. Invite a stranger to your boat, and ask him or her to identify the function of each winch, stopper, switch, and so on. Label what is not immediately identifiable.

Permanent waterproof labels can be made on a Brother label machine. It is battery-powered and makes labels in two sizes, both horizontal and vertical. Various tapes are available: black lettering on a clear background, white on clear, white on black, and assorted colors.

After getting awakened in the middle of the night by a well-meaning person saying, "Your bilge pump has been running a long time," I put a label on the outside of the hull: "Refrigeration outlet: flow of water is OK." The label has lasted for 10,000 miles.

Yacht Inventory Database   TIP 88

While there has been a proliferation of computer software programs for yacht management, a plain old database program works nicely to keep track of what's on board. I establish a field for each possible storage location, generally numerically coded; a field for the items; and various other fields as needed for source, additional information, and other headings. As I enter items, I try to think of as many different names as possible for each item and enter them all. I make a master printout of items listed alphabetically and with the storage venue referenced, and a locker-by-locker inventory of their contents. Where possible, I keep a printout of the locker contents in a plastic envelope taped to the locker door or lid. When anything goes in or out of the locker it is easy to mark up the printout. On a rainy day I update the computer database and print out new locker contents sheets.

CHAPTER 4

ELECTRONIC AND ELECTRICAL EQUIPMENT

In October 1997, I helped the new owner of an Alden 44 take his vessel to Bermuda en route to the Caribbean. Just as I was serving prime rib on the third night, the owner asked if the oven was smoking. I moved aft from the galley and opened the hatch to the engine. Smoke was coming from the aft end of the engine. I poured a little water on the transmission, which immediately vaporized. It turned out that the transmission was not engaged fully in forward, and the clutch was slipping, which caused the overheating. We could not use the engine now.

In the calms between gales we had to hand steer, as the autopilot could not steer at speeds under 3 knots. I ordered a new transmission via SSB radio, which arrived in Bermuda the day after we did. I got the transmission installed and then flew home.

The boat left for St. Maarten, and 340 miles south of Bermuda all pulleys on the front end of the engine began turning independently. The engine raw-water pump, both alternators, and the refrigeration compressor no longer worked. The crew went into energy conservation mode—hand steering, not using navigation lights, not cooking as the propane gas solenoid draws 1 amp, and not using freshwater as there was no manual freshwater pump.

The cause of the problem was the addition of multiple pulleys bolted on to the front of the original pulley on the engine. The original pulley was held to the crankshaft with one small key, which broke from the additional pressure of the two high-output alternators, refrigeration compressor, and pump. The engine had to be removed from the boat to remachine a keyway, and a second one was added in the crankshaft—a very

expensive job that could have been avoided by calculating the load strength of additional peripheral equipment versus strength of the key in the original pulley.

I had outfitted the boat with pipe fittings to bypass the propane solenoid but had not made this clear to the owner. The crew could have cooked the freezer contents as they thawed rather than discarding.

The vessel has subsequently been equipped with a manual freshwater pump at the galley. Incidentally, there must be a shut-off valve on the piping to a manual pump because the pressure water

system will suck air through a manual pump.

Fortunately, this boat has solar panels. Every yacht should have more than one method of charging batteries at sea.

This story illustrates how much a part of passagemaking electrical and electronic devices have become. We must make our peace with the ghosts in the machines, and have redundancy in systems, and retain enough manual backup systems so as not to find ourselves helpless at sea in the event of electronic/electrical systems failure.

ELECTRONICS

This chapter doesn't advise which brands of equipment to buy. Electronic technology changes so rapidly I know that if I don't get a speeding ticket coming home from the store, the computer I purchased is outdated and I paid too much.

Electronic equipment also is becoming increasingly disposable. More instruments are manufactured completely sealed, which means they cannot be opened for repair. If they fail, you throw them away and buy new ones.

As a technology matures, such as the GPS (global positioning system), differences in models and brands decrease. Today, most GPS units have twelve-channel receivers with essentially the same level of accuracy. About all that differs is

the software—the task sequences programmed by the software designers. Some units are more intuitive than others, but this is often a matter of personal preference.

Electronic circuitry undergoes what technicians call a "burn-in" period of up to 50 hours. This means that if the instrument is going to fail, it will probably do so during this settling-in period in which the circuitry is energized and heated. Therefore, it is a good idea to operate all new electronics for a reasonable period of time before heading offshore with them.

Most brands of electronic equipment are made overseas, much of it in Asia. Mainland China has taken over much of the manufacturing from Taiwan and Japan. Of-

ten the same company will make equipment for competing U.S. and European firms. Therefore, for this and other reasons cited above, it has become increasingly difficult to predict reliability. About the best advice one can give is to choose from the long-standing name companies. If a piece of equipment is critical—such as GPS—you should buy and carry a backup.

Interfacing Electronics
TIP 89

A conversation between a couple overheard at an electronics vendor's booth at a boat show:

Man: *"Now, Edith, I know you think we have too many toys on the boat, but wouldn't it be neat if the autopilot was interfaced to the GPS?"*

Woman: *"Sure, George, go ahead and do it . . . then you can send the damn boat out all by itself!"*

For a variety of reasons, I never interface autopilots to position-determining electronics:

- When interfaced to an electronic device—loran or GPS—the boat must create crosstrack error before the autopilot is prompted to correct course. On calm days I have watched boats making lazy S-shaped courses, and I know they are using an autopilot to steer to an electronic waypoint rather than steering to the autopilot's fluxgate compass.

- Electronics have failed me on many occasions, and for unpredictable reasons. An accidental jibe is bad enough when caused by a human helmsman, let alone by turning on an electric can opener in the galley.

- Some GPS receivers only output a great circle course, and while it will be the shortest, it is not necessarily the best if currents are encountered.

- Interfacing leads to a complacent crew, which is a crew unprepared for trouble.

Once I was returning a boat from the Marion–Bermuda Race with an inexperienced crew. Canadian meteorologist Herb Hilgenberg of Southbound II VAX 498 (see pages 140–42) had a special early-morning weather broadcast for the returning boats, and after breakfast I talked to him on the SSB (single-sideband radio).

Then, since I'd been up since 4 A.M. and we were powering with nothing happening on deck, I took a nap. When I woke up about noon I sat down at the chart table and noted that the crew had been very diligent in filling out the log every hour. It struck me that the recorded latitude was getting smaller. I went on deck, and sure enough, the boat was heading south, not north. What had happened was that the SSB had caused the autopilot to deviate from course, and the crew on deck had not noticed the change. I gave the crew a little education on what latitude and longitude numbers mean, and made lunch. Just before dinner we got back to where we were at breakfast.

Electronic and Other Devices That Belong on Every Boat
TIP 90

One can debate the necessity of just about any piece of gear. Practitioners of ancient Polynesian navigation methods have crossed oceans without so much as a compass to guide them. But for the rest of us, the following list of equipment itemizes the essential tools and instruments:

- Barometer. Old-fashioned aneroid barometers rarely fail but can be difficult to read. Electronic barometers that record pressure over several hours are handy, but I prefer hourly log entries. Whatever type, take yours to a small airport to calibrate it to their altimeter. See chapter 6, page 141, for barometric pressure conversions.

  One can confuse the normal diurnal variation of a barometer with a real change as a low-pressure area moves in. The effect of diurnal variation is greatest at the equator where 5 millibars is not abnormal and subsides to nothing at the poles.

  The normal pattern in local time is
     0400–1000 = rising
     1000–1600 = falling
     1600–2200 = rising
     2200–0400 = falling

- VHF radio, 25 watt, connected to masthead antenna with low loss coaxial cable like RG-213.

- GPS, handheld or fixed-mount. If handheld, it should be connected to ship's power due to short battery life.

- Paper charts of the area, parallel rules or other method to lay out courses, pencils, dividers.

- Handheld VHF radio with waterproof enclosure and lots of spare batteries packed in an abandon-ship bag; also a back-up handheld GPS with lots of extra batteries. It is very helpful if both the handheld VHF and handheld GPS take the same size batteries, preferably AA (see tip 92).

• Depth-sounder.

When going offshore, add

• SSB (single-sideband) radio, properly installed and tested.

• 406 MHz EPIRB.

• Autopilot of adequate size for the vessel; when in doubt, use a larger drive unit. Determining size involves calculating rudder torque, and most manufacturers have a form with instructions to assist in this. If there is a question, go to the larger size or strength. When it comes to autopilot drives, overkill is desirable.

• Wind vane steering. Yes, this seems like caveman technology, but steering vanes are very powerful and considerably reduce electrical power requirements. Plus, a very inexpensive autopilot made for steering a small boat with a tiller can be fitted to some vanes to steer the boat in light winds with minimal power consumption. If these are not reasons enough to buy a wind vane, it's important to have backup self-steering, especially a system that doesn't depend on microchips. For more information, see the Steering section in appendix 1.

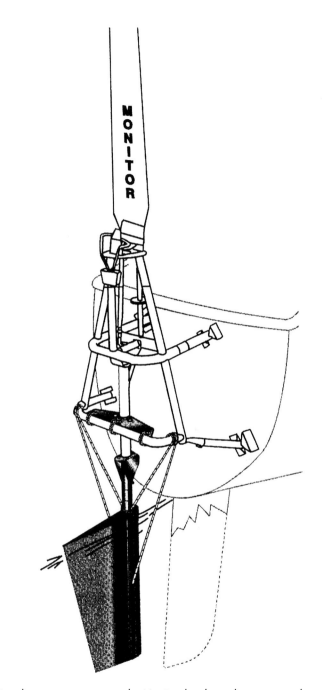

During the past twenty years the Monitor has been the most popular vane steerer in the U.S. It is shown here with the optional EMRUD emergency rudder fitted. (Courtesy Scanmar International)

Servopendulum-type wind vane steerers are very powerful and can handle most cruising boats up to about 50 feet or so in varying wind conditions. (Courtesy Scanmar International) (Tip 90)

- If going to non-English-speaking countries, carry a Navtex receiver (see tip 93).

Note that I have not included a computer and fancy electronic charts. While these are nifty, gee-whiz gadgets, people tend to become mesmerized watching the boat move along an electronic chart and forget to maintain a watch for other vessels, or even to look on deck to visually confirm their position. Computerized navigation is handy in fog, but under no circumstances should it be a vessel's sole means of determining position.

EPIRBs   TIP 91

A high-ranking U.S. Coast Guard SAR (Search and Rescue) officer admitted to me that his service does not pay much attention to signals from 121.5 MHz EPIRBs anymore. Indeed, in 2000 the International COSPAS-SARSAT Program announced it planned to cease processing distress signals from 121.5 and 243 MHz EPIRBs; no timetable was given.

I can personally attest that the coast guard pays a lot of attention to signals from 406 MHz EPIRBs. In the 1993 Marion–Bermuda Race, I was making a midday check around the deck on the third day out and noticed that the switch on our EPIRB was in the off position. I locked the switch in the automatic position, which would turn the unit on if it were released from its hydrostatic mount. As dusk approached, the crew on deck asked why the strobe on the EPIRB was

- Radar with at least 24-mile range, with antenna mounted no more than about 22 feet high so that close-in targets are not missed. This height gives a range of 5.5 nautical miles, range=$1.17 \times \sqrt{h}$ in which range is distance in nautical miles and h is the height of the object above water level in feet. Detection of targets farther off depends on the height of the transmitter and target above water. In this example, the target is on the horizon and only the antenna is elevated. In the real world, you must solve for the height of both radar and target.

- Sextant. High-quality plastic is OK, with tables and instructions on use. You also need an accurate timepiece (chronometer), which can be a digital wristwatch (don't wear it), kept as vibration-free as possible. Celestial bodies have been around a lot longer than GPS signal transmitting satellites, and cannot be turned off. Practicing celestial navigation is a good diversion from the boredom of passage-making and builds confidence in your abilities.

- Wind direction and wind speed instrumentation with readouts at the navigation station and on deck. Units that automatically provide true wind direction and speed are very handy (to do so, the instrument must process boat speed and course as well as apparent wind direction and speed).

flashing. We immediately turned the unit off and called the coast guard on the SSB radio. The first response from the coast guard was from a C-130 aircraft coming to rescue us. The coast guard had called the owner's wife and informed her that our EPIRB had been activated, and she had called the other crew members' wives.

We realized the EPIRB had become slightly dislodged from its mounting and had activated. During daylight the strobe was not visible, and we were unaware of its operation. This experience has caused me to be extremely careful around EPIRBs!

Handheld VHF and Handheld GPS   TIP 92

When purchasing both of these essential pieces of equipment, be sure to buy models that have the option of using replaceable alkaline batteries; some operate only on rechargeable nicad batteries. If your vessel suffers catastrophic electrical failure, knowing where you are and being able to communicate with passing ships can be a lifesaver.

I keep both units in the abandon-ship bag along with a supply of fresh batteries. (See Abandon-Ship Bag in appendix 4 for other items to include.) When I stock up on batteries, the new ones go in the abandon-ship bag, with the previous inventory used for shipboard flashlights, etc. According to *Practical Sailor* tests, Duracell makes the longest-lasting batteries in the popular AA and D sizes.

Navtex   TIP 93

Although not especially popular in the United States, a dedicated Navtex receiver is useful when cruising abroad. Navtex gives you everything from notices to shipping to the local weather, in English text, displayed or printed.

The Navtex service is a low-frequency (518 kHz), short-range (several hundred miles) transmission, so the receiver is not useful on the high seas. Almost all Navtex receivers can be programmed to receive only the data you want. A unit that stores 200 lines of data costs about $300. Navtex data also can be input to a computer through a modem connected to a SSB radio. Be careful when doing this to use the correct sideband.

The synthesized voice of weather broadcasts by the coast guard is actually announcing Navtex weather, which is easier to understand by reading in text form than listening to it.

Emergency Radio Antennas   TIP 94

VHF. The emergency VHF antenna with a little springy metal coil that affixes directly to a VHF radio is basically useless. It is much better to have a duplicate of the masthead antenna with enough coaxial cable to reach from the radio through the companionway and up at least 20 feet (or to the height of the lower spreaders, as masts tend to fail there). Because VHF range is basically line of sight, the higher an emergency antenna can be rigged, the greater its range. (Actually, range is slightly more than line of sight, due to bending of the waves, and hence also more than radar.) The formula is range = $1.17 \times \sqrt{h}$, where range is distance in nautical miles and h is height above the water in feet.

Remember to get an adapter to connect the antenna on your handheld VHF to the PL-259 fitting on the spare antenna cable. RadioShack (see appendix 7) is a good place to start the search for this adapter.

A brief note on coaxial cable for VHF radios: The best cable is RG-213, which is available in a tinned marine version from Ancor and Berkshire. Signal loss of RG-213 is significantly less than that of the little RG-58 cable that comes with most VHF antennas, and the cable is worth the premium price.

SSB. After a dismasting, a very good high-frequency radio antenna can be rigged from any piece of standing rigging (preferably 32 feet or longer, but anything over about 10 feet will work with a good tuner). It should be supported on deck as vertically as possible. Use nonconductive material (dry rope or equal) to insulate the ends of the antenna from the supports. Affix the lead-in wire from the tuner to the makeshift antenna anywhere along its length; a small hose clamp works well for this. If the lead-in wire from the tuner also is broken, any piece of #10 or larger electrical wire will work. Keep people away from the emergency antenna and lead-in wire while transmitting.

Also, it's a good idea to stay away from any metal, as RF (radio frequency) may resonate and make non-attached metal "hot." I have an Icom M-700 SSB in my office that is connected to a tuner mounted on a tree with 20 feet of old standing-rigging wire held up by a rope slung over a branch. I get good reception with this rig, and so far have been able to resist the temptation to key the mike when squirrels are playing on the wire.

A small aside on SSB radios: it is buried in manuals, but the normal marine SSB upper sideband mode is often labeled A3J. AM operation (for WWV, BBC, VOA, etc.) is A3H mode. Lower sideband is required for some weather fax reception.

I like to have a pair of good headphones with built-in volume control and the right adapters to plug into the SSB's auxiliary speaker jack. This generally cuts off the radio's speaker to avoid waking the off-watch when I listen to the 6 A.M. weather.

Intelligible Boat Name   TIP 95

In choosing a name for your vessel, always imagine trying to make someone understand the name on a radio filled with static.

Of course, I don't heed my own advice, and all my boats have been named *Synergism* because to me a boat is more than the sum of its parts. There have been lots of times when I felt like a good boat name would be *Christ Child*, because

with boats it seems you are always bearing them gifts.

Emergency Use of Ham Nets (Amateur Radio Networks)   TIP 96

Although ham radio frequencies are generally not supposed to be used by SSB, it's permissible in an emergency. The current ones can be downloaded from the World Wide Web (see page 222 and www.mmsn.org/others.htm). Keep the list handy to the radio, perhaps taped to the underside of the nav table. Be sure your SSB radio is capable of operating on ham bands; some brands must be modified or reprogrammed. (See also Weather on the Web, tip 191.)

Other Useful Radio Services and Frequencies   TIP 97

Times and SSB frequencies of various broadcasts are of great interest and use to offshore sailors. For example, cruisers have long depended on the BBC (British Broadcasting Corporation) and VOA (Voice of America) for international news, although as of July 2001 the BBC discontinued shortwave broadcast targeting to North America and the Pacific (it does provide FM rebroadcasts to those regions). Station WLO Radio will transmit messages to ships on the high seas, though the advent of satellites and e-mail are quickly overtaking this service. This information changes periodically, so be sure you have updates

before setting sail, and check for updated information as needed if you're on a long cruise. Appendix 8 contains tables with current data from a number of sources.

If you are new to SSB radio operation, I suggest you read one of several good books on the subject.

BBC World News, www.bbc.co. uk/worldservice/schedules/ frequencies/index.shtml

VOA (Voice of America), www. voa.gov/allsked.html

WLO Radio, www.wloradio.com

Coast Guard High Seas Frequencies,www.navcen.uscg.gov/ marcom/ms/cgco/mms/ call.htm

Common SSB Frequencies, www.bitwrangler.com/wt/ ss-ssb-freq.html

Worldwide Marine Radiofacsimile Broadcast Schedules, http://205.156.54.206/om/ marine/rfax.pdf

High Frequency Marine Radiotelephone Channels, www.navcen.uscg.gov/ marcomms/cgcomms/ rtchan.htm

Electronic Timer and Clock   TIP 98

A very handy item to have on board is an electronic timer. The ones sold for kitchen use are fine if at least 12 hours can be programmed. I set the timer for the next weather broadcast or radio check to make sure I don't miss it. Crew who do not record in the log on time are admonished to set the timer as a reminder. My favorite timer is a West Bend (see photo) that can keep track of three events simultaneously.

An inexpensive stick-on, battery-powered digital clock is handy at the nav station, set to Universal Coordinated Time or UTC (formerly known as Greenwich Mean Time). Even if the clock is not particularly accurate, you won't have to mentally calculate UTC each time you need it.

RadioShack has several models of small battery-powered talking clocks that can be set to announce each hour with a human voice. One on deck and one below are good reminders to fill in the log every hour.

Serial Numbers   TIP 99

Record the serial numbers of all equipment in the ship's log. Also note fuse type and size. I keep a copy of this information off the vessel in my laptop, for insurance claims, corresponding with manufacturers about problems, and settling disputes with customs officials.

A kitchen timer has numerous useful applications aboard, not the least of which is reminding you when to tune in radio weather forecasts. (Tip 98)

Uninterruptible Power Source   TIP 100

Some electronics are highly susceptible to erratic behavior caused by momentary low voltage. If you have to start the engine in an emergency, you do not want to lose navigational data or the radar picture. It is easy to power electronics from their own 12-volt battery, preferably a small gel-cell, which is kept charged by the ship's batteries through a diode. I generally run this circuit through an extra 30-amp breaker installed on the electrical panel (see drawing next page).

The downside is that a diode causes about 0.5 voltage drop. If the battery is a gel-cell, it's not a problem, however, because gel-cells should be charged at just 14.1 volts, compared to 14.4 volts for wet-cells. In this case, the alternator or battery charger output does not have to be adjusted downward to avoid damaging the gel-cell.

One must be sure to turn off all electronics powered by a dedicated battery when shutting down the boat. Turning off the breaker feeding the battery will only stop flow of power into the dedicated battery.

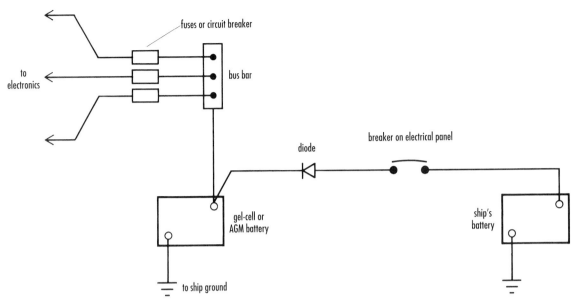

Because most electronic devices use minimal electrical power, it is fairly easy to wire them to a backup battery, thereby ensuring uninterrupted power. (Tip 100)

BATTERIES

Types   TIP 101

The electrical needs of a cruising sailboat are ever increasing. The advent of electric-drive terrestrial vehicles is leading to improved battery technology. While AGM (absorbed glass mat) and gel-cell batteries are not the same, for this discussion we'll lump them together because they do share some common and desirable attributes: zero maintenance, low self-discharge rate, and spill-proof design. Neither type is permanently harmed by being stored in a less than fully charged condition.

On the down side, the number of times AGM and gel-cell batteries can be cycled (discharged and then recharged) is measured in the hundreds, while a properly maintained flooded lead acid battery is capable of thousands of cycles. Also, the cost of gel-cell and AGM batteries is substantially greater, and replacement in foreign ports can be a problem. An additional drawback of gel-cells is that they cannot be recharged at as high a voltage as conventional batteries. Lowering the finishing voltage can be a big problem, unless a "smart" voltage regulator or an adjustable battery charger is used.

Deep-Cycle versus Starting   TIP 102

The electrical requirements of a sailboat underway fall into two categories. First, a relatively small current draw (less than 20 amps) over a long period of time is needed for operating the autopilot, electronics, and lighting; we'll refer to this as the "house" load. The second requirement is a high amperage for just long enough to start the engine. A diesel engine needs 2 CCA (cold cranking amps) for each cubic inch (or 16 cc) of displacement.

Think of batteries forming electricity by the reaction of chemicals to a metal plate. To make a lot of power, you need a large surface area of metal plate. Engine starting batteries generally have more and thinner plates to provide the requisite area. Unfortunately, thin plates do not last as long as thick ones. For house loads, a lot of plate area is not required. More important is the number of times the battery can be cycled—discharged and recharged. For this job, thicker plates last longer. These batteries are called *deep-cycle*.

While marine deep-cycle batteries are readily available in the U.S., they are very difficult to acquire elsewhere.

My preference for boat batteries is 6-volt golf cart batteries wired in series/parallel (see drawing; see also Batteries in appendix 1) to produce ship voltage (usually 12 volts on smaller boats). Golf cart batteries are easier to handle, as they are only half as heavy as a 12-volt battery of comparable amp-hours. Golf cart batteries are made to be deeply discharged and charged back up again often. Golf cart batteries also are capable of handling physical abuse, as a duffer follows his ball into the rough. A disadvantage is that golf cart batteries are often somewhat taller than conventional batteries.

Battery Bank Configurations   TIP 103

Most typical is option 1, where the boat comes with two batteries of equal size, the idea being that you use one until it is fully discharged, then switch to the other, start the engine, and charge both batteries. There is a lot wrong with this process. Without a dual-output alternator or a charge divider, the master battery switch must be placed in the "All" or "Both" position to charge both batteries. If charging is stopped before the batteries are full, you'll be left with both banks partially charged. The more fully charged battery will discharge into the lower-charged battery. Also, it is easy to forget to turn the switch from "All," permitting all the boat's batteries to discharge at once and leaving you without a backup bank for emergency engine starting or radio transmission.

Battery switch E is normally left in position 1 to feed engine from engine start battery. **Battery switch H** is normally in position 2 to feed power distribution panel from house battery bank. Should either alternator fail, putting either switch E or H into the Both position will allow the remaining alternator to charge both battery sources. **Battery switch HS** divides the house battery bank, and is optional. It is normally left in Both, and only placed in 1 or 2 if one house bank fails. West Marine Battery Combiner charges both house battery banks, and is deleted if there is only one house battery bank.

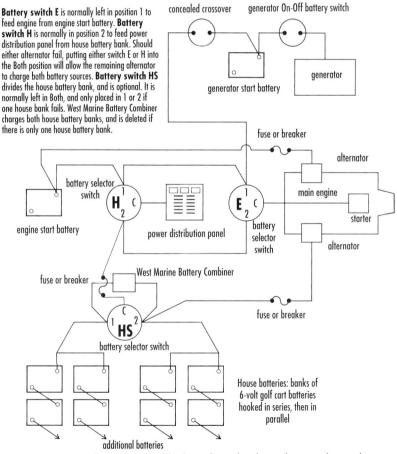

Batteries wired in series double the voltage but keep the amp-hours the same. Batteries wired in parallel double amp-hours but keep voltage the same. This schematic shows how both are used in wiring a typical battery bank. Note that all negatives are common. (Tip 103)

Option 2 is a large house bank to run the boat and a separate engine-starting battery. Again, without separation, a voltage regulator will read the average voltage of the two and neither bank will be optimally charged.

Option 3 is two equal, large house battery banks, and no separate engine-starting battery. A bank of an adequate number of golf cart batteries has sufficient plate area to start an engine. A dual-output alternator, or preferably two single-output alternators, charge each bank separately. And, of course, there are yet more choices, such as two large house banks and a dedicated engine start battery. Which one you choose depends on the size and sophistication of your electrical needs.

For an interesting case history of what can go wrong charging batteries, see Battery Charging, tip 111.

A word of caution on battery isolators, often called charge dividers: they contain diodes that suck up 0.5 volt or more from the charging voltage, so the batteries never get fully charged unless the reference voltage for the alternator is picked up after the isolator.

West Marine sells a device called a Battery Combiner that senses high voltage and closes contacts to connect batteries together for charging, then disconnects when charging stops. Budget allowing, preferable to of any of these devices, a dual-output, high-amperage alternator, such as those made by Lestek and sold by Balmar.

To avoid long engine run times, alternator output should be at least 30 percent of the battery bank's amp-hour capacity.

Also, I'd install a "smart," multistage regulator to maintain charge rate until the batteries are nearly full. Standard automotive-type regulators taper the charge too quickly.

Wire size from alternator output to batteries should be increased to handle the additional amperage, and to comply with ABYC standards. Overcurrent protection (large fuses, such as those available from Blue Sea) should be installed within 72 inches of the alternator.

Charging Profiles   TIP 104

Battery capacity is usually measured in amp-hours. While it is convenient to think that a 200 amp-hour battery will provide 20 amps for ten hours, this is not the case. Amp-hour capacity is measured to the dead battery point, which one wants to avoid. For greatest life, batteries should never be discharged below 50 percent of their capacity. I recharge when battery voltage falls below 12 volts.

Additionally, batteries have an acceptance rate curve. When discharged, they will accept a lot of charging amps. As they near the fully charged state, however, resistance in the battery increases and decreases the rate of charge. Therefore, it is only efficient to recharge batteries to about 90 to 95 percent

of capacity. The net result is that only 30 to 40 percent of the amp-hour capacity of a battery bank is usable.

It has been my experience that over a 24-hour period many modern cruising boats average 15 to 20 amp-hours every hour while underway. That's 360 to 480 amp-hours per day that must be replaced. If you want to recharge just once each day, you need quite a sizable battery bank. Because a maximum of 40 percent of the capacity is usable, divide 480 by 0.4 and determine that a 1,200 amp-hour battery bank will be required. And that's a minimum.

Common GC-2 size golf cart batteries provide about 200 amp-hours at 6 volts. Because they are wired in series to make 12 volts, the amp-hour capacity stays the same per pair of golf cart batteries. To make up one 600 amp-hour bank, you'll need three pairs of 6-volt batteries, with the pairs wired in parallel.

LIGHTS

Flashlights ␣␣␣ TIP 105

Carry a supply of disposable flash-lights on board and issue one to each crew member to keep in his or her pocket when on deck after dark. Also encourage the use of low-power flashlights below decks at night to avoid disturbing the off-watch.

If you do not have rotating crew, Pelican brand flashlights are worth their high cost—they're waterproof and last a long time.

When your standard flashlights stop working (note I say *when*, not *if*), clean the contacts with a pen-cil eraser, not sandpaper.

Spotlight ␣␣␣ TIP 106

Twelve-volt, 1-million or more can-dlepower spotlights are inexpensive and are invaluable for finding un-lit buoys at night, crew overboard, and illuminating sails to make them visible to other maritime traffic. RadioShack has 10-foot, 10-amp ex-tension cords with cigarette lighter ends that are very useful for taking the spotlight forward to get the glare out of the cockpit.

Before going to RadioShack, take a look at your compass light-bulbs. I have found LEDs at Ra-dioShack that are a perfect re-placement for the $15 compass bulbs sold by compass makers, and their cost is less than $1.

Running Lights ␣␣␣ TIP 107

When on soundings and likely to encounter small craft, I use the deck-level navigation lights. Off-shore I use the masthead tricolor, which is more visible to commer-cial traffic and conserves power. Re-member that it is illegal to use the masthead tricolor when under power, as the steaming light must be above the level of the red-green-white running lights.

ORC regulations require emer-gency running lights with a power source independent from the ship's batteries. Unfortunately, running lights of equal intensity to the COL-REGS (name commonly given to the International Regulations for Preventing Collisions at Sea, 1972, adopted and amended by the In-ternational Maritime Organization) are not available with built-in dry-cell batteries. The Marion–Bermuda Race allows a masthead tricolor light, provided it has adequate in-tensity for the vessel, to fulfill the requirement for emergency navi-gation lights . . . if a separate battery is installed to be used only for the tricolor.

The best type of battery for this purpose is a gel-cell, as gel-cell bat-teries do not self-discharge as much as conventional lead-acid batteries. A well-charged motorcycle starting battery is an inexpensive alternative to a gel-cell. Remember that the battery for the tricolor light must be well secured in place.

Most tricolor lights use four or five wires. Be sure to label which wires activate the single bulb that illuminates the red and green side-lights and the white stern light.

While COLREGS limits the size vessel on which a masthead tri-color light is legal (and then only when it is under sail), ship captains tell me that a masthead tricolor is always more visible than deck-level lights.

Anchor Light ␣␣␣ TIP 108

Most of us rely on a 360-degree masthead anchor light. While this is convenient, a masthead light is not easily visible to small vessels, and is likely to be obscured by fog. Much preferable is an anchor light hanging in the foretriangle. A legal and very handy combination is to attach an all-around white light to the bottom of an anchor ball, cov-ering both day and night signals with one hoist.

Because it is prudent to leave power on to a windlass at all times while anchored, one can take power from the windlass supply, run through a low-amperage breaker or fuse and then to a watertight deck fitting. While it is not approved un-der COLREGS, Davis Instruments' Mini Amp Mega Light only draws 0.074 amp and has a built-in photo cell. Unless night is substantially longer than day, this light should draw less than 1 amp-hour in 24 hours.

Laser Pointer   TIP 109

I have a small, but very powerful laser pointer I use during my slide show on preparing for offshore passages. When I am walking at night, I carry it in my pocket, figuring I can hold it well away from my body and aim it at any undesirable characters I come across. I have also used it to point out to a launch driver which boat I want to go to. The most fun I have with it, however, is to get kids or animals to chase the beam around the floor!

GHOST IN THE MACHINE: SOLVING WEIRD ELECTRICAL PROBLEMS

Watertight Junction Box   TIP 110

The following two case histories illustrate the potential danger in trying to waterproof the electrical system.

An Alden 50 had an elaborate electronics installation, originally installed by a prominent East Coast electronics firm. To install a new holding tank I had to move the junction box for radar wires at the base of the mast. Subsequently, the radar stopped working. I checked the dislocated connections carefully, and they looked fine.

Then I hired the same company that had done the installation. At first, they diagnosed the problem as a bad microswitch in the scanner, necessitating many trips up the mast. Then we disassembled the plugs on deck and after that we followed all of the radar wires, taking out copious joinerwork. Finally, buried behind a remote part of the nav station we found a watertight junction box for the radar cable. Wire from the mast entered the box at the top and wires to the deck plug and navigation sta-

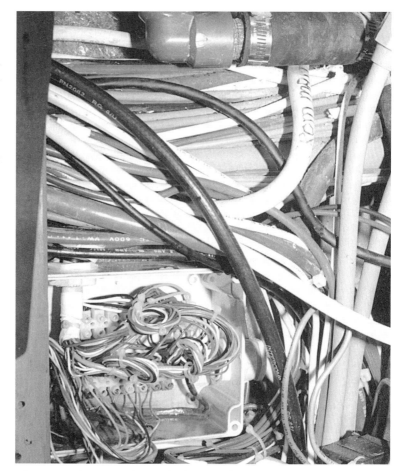

The watertight junction box at the bottom of the picture was filled with water from an improperly sealed top wire entry and from a cracked PVC elbow immediately above.

tion exited at the bottom. The outside of the box looked perfect, but opening it let out a deluge of water and revealed a mass of corroded connections.

Eighteen inches above the box was a deck scupper with a cracked PVC elbow that had dripped water on the wire entering the top of the box, which must not have been properly sealed (see photo). A $1,200 electronics company bill and a lot of time on my part disassembling woodwork taught me that watertight junction boxes are not always the best idea, and a diagram of all junction points is very worthwhile. A box with drain holes probably wouldn't have retained water and caused corrosion.

On another occasion, I was bringing the Alden 46 *Gannet* back to Newport from the Marion–Bermuda Race and the weather was a little lumpy. On the third day the loran showed an antenna fault. Because we did not have a GPS on board, and I had not taken a celestial sight in years, I traced the loran antenna wire from unit to deck, and everything looked good. The problem persisted, and I finally cut into the heat-shrink-covered junction of antenna wire just inside the deck feed-through. The connectors were full of seawater, and after drying them out we had loran again. This experience has made me very careful to install a drip loop in all wires entering a vessel (see photo), and *not* to use heat-shrink tubes over electrical connections. Allowing any collected water to drain is a better strategy.

Troubleshooting system problems requires a general understanding of DC and AC systems, plus a few tools such as a good multimeter. I won't try to explain it all here, as there are other good books on the subject, such as Nigel Calder's *Boatowner's Mechanical and Electrical Manual* (International Marine), but I do want to emphasize the importance of being able to troubleshoot your own boat's systems.

Battery Charging   TIP 111

The owner of a big cruising boat stopped me in the yard one day to ask a question.

"It takes forever to charge my batteries from the engine alternator," he said. "I've installed an alternator output controller, and even pulling 50 amps from the alternator does not bring the batteries up unless I motor all day. What is wrong?"

After looking at the boat, the answer was obvious. There was an expensive 12-volt, ½-horsepower holding plate refrigeration system installed with an oil pressure switch that allowed the system to run only when the engine was on. Almost all alternator capacity was operating the refrigeration with little left over for battery charging. The solution was a very high-output alternator.

The same thing can happen with an inadequately sized battery charger, as people tend to forget that any DC current being used by

Drip loops in wire runs prevent moisture from entering terminals and/or equipment. (Tip 110)

the ship must be deducted from that available for battery charging.

The bottom line is this: When you want to fully charge the batteries, turn off other loads until the job is done. This is especially necessary when equalizing batteries with a modern multistep alternator controller.

One must be careful when charging batteries that only one source is used at a time. A lot of boats have an inverter with a built-in battery charger and a separate multiple-bank battery charger. Battery chargers work by sensing battery voltage and adjusting output accordingly. Until the batteries are full, a charger outputs voltage higher than the battery voltage. Using two charging sources simultaneously causes them to read each other's higher output voltage and reduce output. Yes, some chargers can be ganged and wired to eliminate this problem, but we won't go into that here.

Before the Alden 50 *Elena* went across the Atlantic in 1996, I installed a battery charger that operates from both 50 and 60 Hz current, along with a step-down and isolation transformer. The charger worked fine at the dock, and it did not dawn on me to try it with the auxiliary generator (genset). The crew got underway and called several days out to report that the charger was not working. A lot of expensive calls resulted. The solution was to disconnect the small alternator built into the generator that was artificially increasing voltage, causing the charger not to output.

A last thought: ferroresonant battery chargers (they hum) do not charge batteries nearly as fast as modern solid-state chargers because of their lower output voltage.

For more on battery chargers and isolation transformers, see appendix 1, pages 179–80.

Shore Power Problems　　TIP 112

After a transatlantic passage from Rhode Island to Horta in the Azores, we rafted to another boat whose owner offered to let us plug into his boat, saying he had a step-down transformer for the 220-volt dock current. The owner of our boat thought that running our generator might be offending the neighbor, and that this was his tactful way of asking us to stop the noise. Although I reminded the owner that our battery charger wouldn't work on 50 Hz, he went ahead and plugged us in, anyway. Later, we unplugged, and the next time we started the generator, it output only 6 volts instead of 120.

Seven thousand dollars later, after flying in a new electrical part of the generator to Portugal and importing someone to install it, we surmised that our neighbor must have had a step-down transformer without windings to isolate the ground. Because European AC current is not grounded like U.S. power, we had fried the generator due to its being installed to the U.S. standard of bonding the neutral and ground to the vessel's underwater components.

See appendix 3, Foreign Adaptation, for more information.

Spontaneous Ignition　　TIP 113

It was a beautiful warm night. *Tandem* was running with spinnaker and blooper up the Florida coast, far enough offshore to be well in the Gulf Stream. Speed over the bottom was 13 knots and higher when surfing. I hated to go to bed when my watch ended at midnight. I came back on watch at 0400 and made coffee.

Temperatures were 40 degrees cooler than during the last watch. A norther had blown in, and *Tandem* was beating under #4 genoa and reefed main. As the wind was now blowing in the opposite direction of the Gulf Stream current, seas were very lumpy, and a fast run to finish the St. Pete–Ft. Lauderdale Race was now a long, hard beat.

I was just pouring the first of the coffee mugs when the diesel auxiliary started. I slid back the hatch and asked why the deck crew had started the engine.

The reply was: "We didn't start the engine. Why did you start it?"

"I can't start the engine from down here," I replied.

The crew tried turning off the key, but the engine kept running. I opened the engine hatch and could smell a hot starter motor. I turned off the master switch, which killed power to the whole boat, and the engine stopped.

"Hey! We need lights and instruments!" the deck crew hollered down.

I turned the master back on, and the engine restarted. Cutting the wires running to the back of the ignition switch killed the engine. Taking the switch apart later, I found that the boat's vibration had caused an internal short in the switch, connecting the B and S terminals, thus engaging the starter. Since the engine stop was an electric solenoid, killing power didn't turn off fuel or stop the engine.

Engine Wiring   TIP 114

Many engines come with the engine and instrument panel pre-wired and a plug-in harness to connect the two. While this is handy for the boatbuilder, corrosion eventually works into the harness plugs and things either stop working or get sluggish. I have improved performance and reliability on a lot of engines by removing the harness and installing new wiring from the engine senders and solenoids directly to the corresponding items on the instrument panel. If the distance from the engine to the instrument panel is long, I increase the wire size on the starter solenoid supply and actuation runs to give less than a 3 percent voltage drop.

PLAYING IT SAFE

Avoiding electrical burns at sea, far away from medical facilities, is a no-brainer. See also Electrical Systems in appendix 1 for more information on electrical safety.

Making the Connection   TIP 115

I was advising the owner of a Hallberg-Rassy on preparing his boat for ocean passagemaking, and he was doing most of the work. One afternoon I noticed a large burn on one of his wrists, and asked him what had happened. He said he had been wiring the SSB radio.

"Oh, an RF burn?" I questioned.

"Nope, got it in the electrical panel."

"You didn't disconnect shore power before opening the panel?" I queried.

"Shore power was already off," Alan answered.

"Then how did you get that big burn from 12 volts?"

"When your metal watch band goes across the main DC positive and negative buses, it sure gets hot in a hurry," Alan replied, pulling a disfigured band from his pocket.

Lightning   TIP 116

Lightning and its byproduct thunder can be terrifying, not to mention damaging to yachts. Thunderstorms show up well on most radar equipment with their intensity discernible. Even the best-grounded boats can have problems.

ABYC recommended practices call for a minimum of #8 stranded conductor for lightning ground. I have never thought this adequate. Instead, I use #4 solid copper from the mast step to the keel primary ground.

One Tartan 30 was returned to the factory after a direct strike. All the wood screws in the boat were backed out and required a screwdriver to re-install. There were small pinholes through the hull at the waterline. Even the copper wire was vaporized for over a foot, and electrical parts on the engine had melted.

Cloud-to-ground lightning occurs when negative charges in the base of a cloud are attracted to earth's positive charge. A surge is created carrying a typical current of 1 billion volts at 10,000 to 20,000 amps. The flash is the return stroke of superheated air in the realm of 15,000 to 50,000°F, and appears wide from the glowing air. By comparison, the surface of the sun is about 11,000°F.

One Tartan 41 was hit and a crewman immediately aft of the mast had permanent, irreversible damage—his electronic wristwatch stopped. I have experienced St. Elmo's fire, with lightning jumping off spreader ends—literally a hair-raising experience.

Lightning hits the earth 100 times per second. If you are unfortunate enough to be in one of the 8 million strikes per day, immediately check all electrical devices on board. Metal items, especially tanks, deserve scrutiny. Also inspect the hull for watertight integrity, including tacking to check the windward side. When conditions permit, make a trip up the mast. If you have a nonmetallic mast, there is a strong possibility that the intense heat of a strike may melt resin, resulting in a spar that may look OK, but has diminished structural integrity. Tap it with a plastic hammer all over. A dull thud may indicate delamination.

A properly grounded sailboat has a "cone of protection" starting at the masthead. Stay as far away as possible from any metal, and if possible, get below.

The best tactic is avoidance. However, a thunderstorm 10 miles away can generate ground strikes from high-altitude anvil clouds. Remember that the sound of thunder does not travel far, generally not more than 10 miles, but high-altitude cloud-to-cloud lightning is visible from quite a distance.

MISCELLANEA

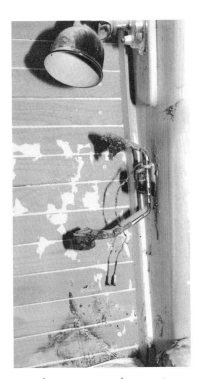

Very low amperage draw equipment should have a properly sized fuse close by. This fan caught fire well before the breaker in the fan circuit tripped. **TIP 117**

Junctions in wiring should be made with terminal blocks. Wiring should be supported to take the strain off terminals. I make clear Plexiglas covers for all terminal blocks to prevent accidental contact and to allow inspection for corrosion. **TIP 118**

Type ANN fuses are compact and available in high-amperage ratings.

TIP 119

These Buss #4512 fuse holders are much preferable to in-line types commonly used for AGC fuses.

TIP 120

Compare this new zinc with the remnants of an eroded zinc. Rapid zinc deterioration should be investigated promptly. See also Copper Alloys, tip 158.

TIP 121

This corroded connection was heavily wrapped with tape and took hours to track down. These spade connectors are more likely to cause problems than the preferred terminal blocks.

TIP 122

Terminals must be crimped with a proper tool that won't release until the terminal is fully crimped. A good ratchet model can do the trick; its only downside is that it requires more space to operate, which can be a problem when making a crimp in place. Combination stripper-crimpers don't do an adequate job.　**TIP 124**

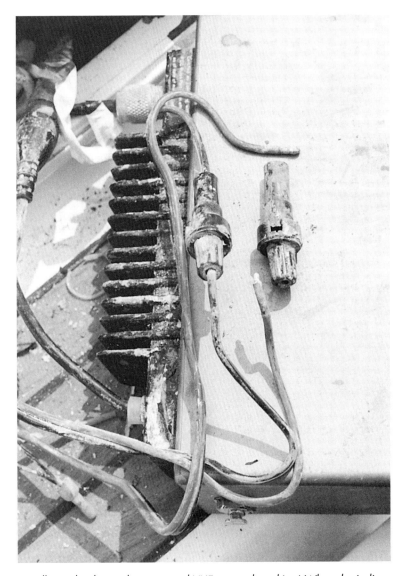

Small wonder this cockpit-mounted VHF stopped working! When the in-line fuse holders rotted out, I replaced them with a fuse block mounted in a dry location inside the vessel.　**TIP 123**

CHAPTER 5

ENGINE, MECHANICAL, AND PLUMBING SYSTEMS

Upon leaving his boat at the yard for the winter, one owner commented that there must be a bad connection in his fuel system because the engine would not run with fuel from the port fuel tank. To prevent condensation, we filled the fuel tanks as part of the fall decommissioning practice. Over the winter, the mechanics disassembled and reassembled the plumbing from the engine to the tank. In the spring the engine ran fine from the port tank, and we considered the matter closed.

In the middle of the summer, however, the customer called to say we must not have done a good job, as the port tank was again not working. We took all connections apart and redid them again, but the engine still would not take fuel from the port tank. In desperation, we took the inspection cover off the tank top and shined a flashlight at the pickup tube, which we saw was welded to the top of the tank. There was some pitting visible on the outside of the tube, but nothing major seemed wrong.

On second look, however, I noticed a little light. It turned out there was a pit all the way through the pickup tube halfway down on the side away from the inspection port. With a welded-in pickup tube, we were in a quandary as to how to repair the tube because the tank could not be removed from the boat for welding.

The ingenious answer was to cut the withdrawal tube 3 inches from the tank bottom and then slip a piece of hose over the exterior of the tube, clamping it on the tube near the top of the tank. A mechanic with long, skinny arms accomplished this through the inspection port, and the tank has been fine for the past ten years.

At times like this, it seems that no amount of preventive maintenance can guarantee problem-free operation of your boat (though it certainly helps). When confronted with a mysterious failure, your only consolation is knowing that there is a cause for everything and that eventually good detective skills will uncover it.

This chapter covers a variety of products, tricks, and do-it-yourself upgrades that can minimize the potential for failures in the mechanical systems aboard your boat—principally, the engine and fuel supply, plumbing, and water systems.

ENGINE AND FUEL

Engine Education

Charlie Britton, cofounder of Tartan Marine, was a superb sailor, having sailed around the world, largely with a dysfunctional engine. I once watched Charlie sail his boat into a very congested harbor with a Twelve-Meter-size spinnaker up, drop it, and coast the 30-ton boat into her dock slip without turning on the engine. Oh yes; he was alone!

Sails were Charlie's thing.

One rainy Saturday, Charlie and I were aboard *Tandem*, his new racing boat. Charlie said, "OK, Seif. I suppose you ought to tell me what I need to know about the engine" (a 4-108 Westerbeke diesel).

"Sure, Charlie," I answered, opening up the engine hatch. "What do you want to know?"

"Let's start with where the spark plugs are," Charlie said. I knew then this was going to be a long day.

Mechanical Oil Pressure Gauge TIP 125

Most boats have all-electric engine instrument panels that are subject to corrosion. The panels also come prewired with plug-in harnesses, in which the plugs are great incubators of grunge.

One can tell the temperature of an engine by feel and its speed by sound, but nothing will alert you that the engine's internal oil pressure has fallen if the idiot lights and buzzers on the ignition-instrument panel fail.

For about $40 at auto parts stores you can buy a high-quality, old-fashioned oil pressure gauge, which works directly from oil. If a tee off the present electric sender does not mount the gauge in an easy-to-view place on the engine, for about $5 more you can pick up a remote kit with about 5 feet of

The F. W. Murphy Mfg. oil pressure gauge, Model A20P-100, part #05-70-4255, has adjustable cut-in and cut-out pressure so you can set an alarm to your own limits.

tough tubing that allows the gauge to be mounted somewhere easily visible.

F. W. Murphy Mfg. (see appendix 7) makes a neat combination oil pressure gauge, mostly from high-strength plastic, which in addition to a dial for oil pressure has both normally open and normally closed electrical contacts with adjustable cut-in/cut-out pressure. These can be used to replace a malfunctioning low-amperage oil pressure switch or to activate an alarm. Model A20P-100, part #05-70-4255, is the 0–100 psi gauge I use most frequently (see photo).

Changing Oil the Easy Way   TIP 126

To expedite oil changing, I borrowed one of those 5-gallon buckets with a power pump mounted on top. I pushed the rubber hose into the dipstick tube and flipped the toggle switch on the pump. I kept pumping until I heard air sucking. Then I shut off the pump and pushed the pump tube farther down the dipstick pipe to be sure I had gotten all the old oil out. I hit the toggle switch again, and to my amazement the rubber hose shot from the dipstick and whirled around like a snake, covering me and most of the cabin with used engine oil.

I had not realized the pump switch was reversible!

I had to replace some of the berth cushions because the dirty engine oil spots did not come out, even after several dry cleanings. Now I pump oil with a one-way hand pump. It takes a little longer, but it's certainly safer.

Oil Analysis   TIP 127

While laboratory analysis of engine oil is a common practice on large motor yachts and for industrial engines, it is not a common practice for sailboat auxiliaries. Sailboat engines often are used in a very abusive manner—infrequently and either for short periods (motoring out of a harbor) or extended running (when the wind dies). Cruisers without generators often run engines with a low load to charge batteries and/or to run refrigeration compressors; both practices are harmful to the engine, as it may not come up to operating temperature and so develop carbon deposits.

Whenever I change oil on yachts under my management, a sample of the used oil is collected in a container provided by Southworth-Milton Wear Analysis Laboratory and then mailed to them. (Their engine oil analysis kit includes ten prepaid bottles, a pump with which to withdraw the oil, and a carrying case.) Inside of a week I get back a full analysis of the oil, including wear trends on bearings and things to look for. If there is a big problem with the engine, they will, at my direction, even call. A sample analysis is shown here. In addition to metal readings indicating internal bearing wear, the percentages of fuel, antifreeze, water, and soot give me advance indication of problems with gaskets, rings, and the cooling system. Other companies provide similar service.

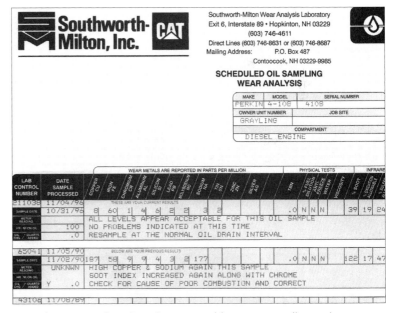

Periodic engine oil analyses by a reputable company will provide you with information you need to keep abreast of problems developing with the engine. (Tip 127)

Engine Water Flow Alarm   TIP 128

While making an offshore passage on an Alden 50, the Aqualarm engine low water flow alarm suddenly sounded. I checked the strainer, which was relatively clean, and with the top off the strainer I momentarily opened the through-hull to confirm that we had water flow. I then pulled the cover off the raw-water cooling pump, and the impeller looked OK.

Next I had the crew jog the engine so I could confirm that the impeller was turning, which it was. I then blew out all the raw-water cooling water hoses and pulled the ends off the heat exchanger to confirm the tubes were not blocked. When everything was put back together, we still had an alarm for low cooling-water flow. I let the alarm ring for a short time and noted that the engine was indeed getting hotter than normal.

I took everything apart again, but this time put in a new impeller. The engine ran fine. I left the removed impeller out on a countertop. A few days later, still perplexed, I held the center brass portion of the impeller with a pair of pliers, and to my surprise the fins turned. The bond between the rubber impeller and the brass center bushing had broken. Turning the engine over without the water pump cover in place put no load on the unit, and the rubber fins rotated. Now, I routinely change impellers whether they look OK or not.

Waiting for an engine overheat alarm to come on can result in damage to the engine. It's better to install a device that monitors the flow of water through the engine and gives advance warning of clogged sea strainers, worn impellers, internal engine blockage, or a clogged heat exchanger. Such a device is the Aqualarm #210 Cooling Water Flow sensor mentioned above. It is installed in the hose from the engine to the water injection elbow of the exhaust. When the flow of cooling water out of the engine is reduced from normal, the sensor closes contacts to activate an alarm. Properly adjusted, the alarm comes on one to two minutes prior to an engine overheat alarm, allowing one to fix the problem or prepare for an engine shutdown.

Alarm Annunciator   TIP 129

The buzzers that come with engine instrument panels generally are not made for marine use and do not last very long. I have had very good luck replacing these devices with a Preco model ELT-248 truck backup alarm made to mount on the undercarriage of a truck. The beeping is loud and attention-getting. Buy them at auto parts stores.

Electric Fuel Pump   TIP 130

If your diesel engine is not self-priming, it is easy to add an electric fuel pump. This makes bleeding air from the fuel system much easier.

I use an Airtex model #E8012S electric fuel pump installed be-

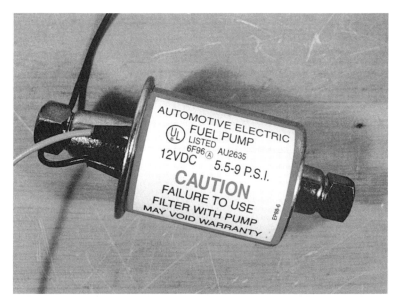

An electric fuel pump, such as the Airtex #E8012S, makes bleeding air from a diesel fuel system much easier, especially in a seaway. (Tip 130)

tween the primary filter and the engine (see photo). This pump allows fuel to flow freely through it when off, which is essential because otherwise the engine wouldn't get fuel when supplied only by the standard pump.

I install an electrical circuit breaker for the pump close to the engine so I can flip it on while bleeding the engine. After changing the primary filter cartridges (Racor or other brand) or the secondary filters on the engine, it sure is easy to flip on the pump and open a bleed screw until fuel without air comes out. The alternative, of course, is manual operation of the small hand pump provided on some engines, or having a helper turn the engine over with the starter. Final bleeding at the injectors must be done with the engine on, or at least while cranking over, but I have found that bleeding most engines to the injector pump will get them running, albeit roughly.

As a bonus, if the engine's mechanical fuel pump fails, the electric pump will supply the engine with fuel.

Most boats these days have water lift exhausts. Cranking the engine for a long time without the engine firing may fill the water lift muffler pot with water to a level where it backs up into the engine. This ruins your whole day. Anytime the engine doesn't start right away, either open the drain screw on the muffler or close the cooling water through-hull at the seacock. Once the engine starts, of course, close the drain and/or open the seacock.

Adding Tees to Tanks   TIP 131

All pickup tubes in tanks end short of the bottom of the tank to prevent settled sediment from being sucked up. But when a vessel is bounced around offshore, the sediment goes into suspension and is picked up. This is most serious in fuel tanks where water and gunk can quickly foul filters and shut down the engine (see Diesel Engine SAD Syndrome, tip 132).

On a passage from Rhode Island to the Azores, the crew of an Alden 50 had to clean the potable water filter twelve times. The filters kept getting clogged with a white powdery substance created by the reaction of chlorine in city water with the aluminum tank. (Never add bleach to an aluminum tank, as it accelerates the creation of these white deposits.)

Fortunately, I had installed tees in the fuel tanks (see photo) and had withdrawn all sediment from the tank bottom before the passage, so the engine ran fine.

On diesel fuel tanks, I install the tee in place of the elbow in the fuel

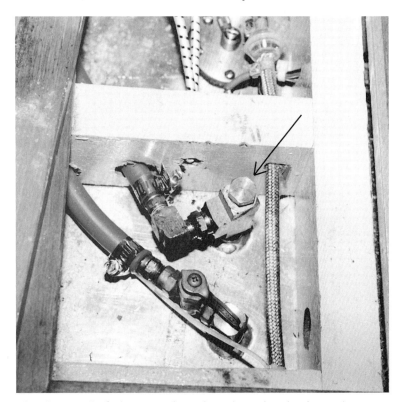

The elbow on the fuel return to the tank can be replaced with a tee having a pipe plug on the top. This makes it easy to access pump crud from the bottom of the fuel tank. Insert the hose from a manual pump through the tee. (Tip 131)

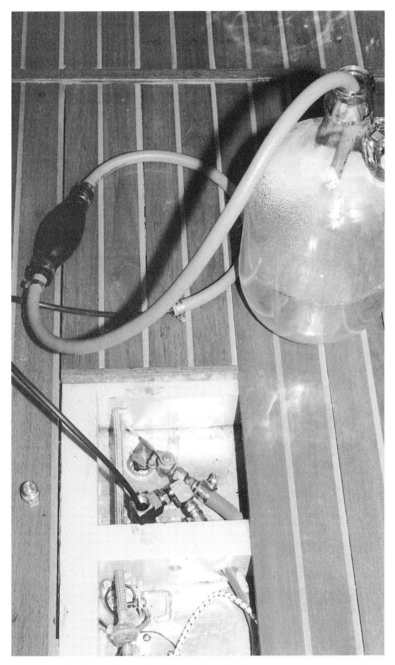

A semirigid plastic tube pushed through the fuel return access connected to an outboard-engine hand fuel pump discharges into a clear bottle so you can watch the crud get sucked from the bottom of the tank. (Tip 131)

return; the return line is plumbed to a branch of the tee, and a pipe plug is screwed into the other branch. By removing the pipe plug I can run a tube down to the bottom of the tank and pump the contents into a clear plastic jug until I get clean fuel (see photo). On water tanks, I use the vent fitting.

On aluminum tanks, never use brass or bronze fittings in direct contact with the aluminum tank. To attach the tee, install a stainless steel nipple into the tank. For a pipe sealant, I like RectorSeal better than Teflon tape.

Diesel Engine SAD Syndrome TIP 132

Unless you are meticulous about pumping water from the bottom of fuel tanks on a regular basis, especially in climates with warm days and cold nights, you will probably experience diesel engine SAD (surge and die) syndrome. During cold nights, condensation forms in diesel fuel tanks, which ends up in the bottom of the tank. Algae only lives in the interface between water and fuel. When the boat is taken offshore, tank contents are shaken up and the algae is picked up in the fuel withdrawal system. Algae plugs the fuel filters, and the engine's governor opens to admit more fuel, which causes a surge in rpm. However, more fuel cannot get through plugged filters, and eventually the engine becomes starved and stops.

It is *imperative* that several people on board know how to change fuel filters and bleed the engine.

The SAD syndrome generally happens in rough weather. Working near the smell of diesel fuel can be very nauseating in harbor, let alone when head down, butt up in a rolling boat underway. The crew may have to work in shifts to get the engine restarted.

When you think you are proficient at bleeding the engine after a routine filter change, try turning off the valve on the fuel tank supply with the engine running. This duplicates totally plugged filters. Open the valve after the engine stops, then bleed the engine. You will probably find you have to bleed more extensively, perhaps even to the tops of the injectors, to get the engine running again.

It is helpful to dab a little contrasting-color paint on all the bleeding points of the engine so you don't have to look through a manual to find all of them.

V-Belts   TIP 133

Always buy the highest horsepower rated V-belts you can find. Frequently, auto parts stores have to order the extra-strength V-belts, but in terms of longevity and lower stretch they are worth the wait and cost.

Unfortunately, pulleys for V-belts come with different angles to their sides. Many cases of premature belt wear eventually can be traced to dissimilar pulleys and a belt that only fits one of them properly.

Aerosol belt dressing is helpful to prevent slippage and consequent belt wear, but is not a substitute for matched pulleys.

As a rough rule of thumb, all but very short V-belts should be tensioned so it is only possible to twist the belt 90 degrees when grabbing it in the middle. An overly tight belt causes wear on bearings. One that is too loose will slip, resulting in heat that may eventually cook the alternator.

NAPA auto parts stores sell an inexpensive belt tension gauge that gives a more precise measurement. It's called the Krikit, part #KR1.

Engine Space Ventilation   TIP 134

Diesel engines need a lot of air to operate properly. The rule of thumb for square inches of ventilation is engine horsepower divided by 3.3. For example, a 40-horsepower engine needs about 12 square inches of ventilation; that's a duct 4 inches in diameter.

Most engine installations rely on air scavenged from the bilge and cabin, which works unless the boat is all buttoned up for storm conditions.

Alternators are especially heat sensitive, and their output declines with increased temperatures. I like to position blower ducts up high in the engine compartment, close to the alternators to induce airflow past them.

While safety standards do not require exhaust blowers for diesel engines, I always run a power blower any time an engine is on, and generally for at least half an hour after shutdown to rid the engine space of residual heat.

Fueling   TIP 135

At the fuel dock I always smell the nozzle before pumping to be sure it is diesel, not gas. What made me cautious was an experience in the early 1970s aboard a Tartan 41. The owner's son was delivering the boat back from a long race. He stopped at a fuel dock and told the attendant to "fill it up." He then left to find a store. On returning he paid for the fuel and started the engine. A few minutes later, the engine briefly ran fast and then stopped with a loud crack. The owner complimented Tartan on the strength of the fiberglass engine box, which stopped a connecting rod after it punched through the block when the gasoline reached the engine.

Although diesel fuel is not that explosive, I always take the precaution of grounding the nozzle against a shroud after pulling the hose on board. This prevents static electrical charges from accidentally igniting the fuel.

Miles per Gallon   TIP 136

Powerboaters worry about fuel consumption more than sailors, and rightly so, as they cannot wait for a favorable wind. A lot of sailors baby their diesel engines by running them at low rpm. In most cases, this is not doing the engine any good. Most experts assert that diesel engines are happiest when operated at about 80 percent of maximum rpm.

Most engine manufacturers publish fuel consumption curves showing the amount of fuel burned at various rpm. Unfortunately, the data is often in strange units like pounds per horsepower per hour. The unit does not really matter. After being sure your tachometer is calibrated properly (see tip 137), on a calm day record boat speed at 200 rpm increments. Give the boat time to settle in on each speed, generally at least three minutes. Make a graph of the boat speed versus rpm, using the same axis for rpm as the fuel consumption curve. Transpose the fuel data onto the same graph, and it will be easy to select the rpm at which you get the best mileage for the fuel consumed.

As a very rough rule of thumb, a diesel engine consumes about 1 gallon per hour for every 18 horsepower. Look again at the manufacturer's data to locate the horsepower produced by various rpm. Another rough calculation can be made on the assumption that a diesel engine will burn 0.4 pound of fuel per hour per horsepower.

If you want to be more precise, and it pays to be, put the engine fuel pickup and return hoses in a measuring cup full of fuel. Run the engine for a period of time, say 10 minutes, and accurately measure how much fuel has been consumed. Note, of course, the rpm. Repeat at different rpm and enter this data on the curve rather than the manufacturer's predicted figures.

We did this test on a 110-horsepower turbocharged diesel on a long passage when we were running low on fuel. At 1,600 rpm the engine burned 0.88 GPH (gallons per hour); at 1,800 rpm, 1.13; and at the normal cruising rpm of 2,100, 1.88 GPH. Running at 1,600 rpm cut the boat speed about three-quarters of a knot, but meant that we could stop struggling to sail at 3 knots and could power for the rest of the passage.

Calibrating Tachometers   TIP 137

Most sailboat engine tachometers operate from a terminal ("tap") on the alternator. This type must be calibrated with a hand tach, and is subject to inaccuracy as the alternator belt wears, or heavy charging loads cause slipping. After a lengthy time motoring, the batteries may not be able to accept any more charge and the voltage regulator will stop charging, leading to erratic tachometer readings.

One time an owner woke me up to tell me that the tachometer had stopped working. On inspection, it was only coming on at intervals, when the voltage regulator let the alternator output check voltage. I turned on half a dozen cabin lights, which put enough load on the alternator to cause it to maintain output, and then went back to sleep. The owner was amazed that I could "fix" the tachometer without going near it or the engine.

A simple way to check a tach is to use a fluorescent lamp, operated from a line frequency ballast and powered from shore power. All you need to do is place a piece of contrasting-color tape on the front of the engine crankshaft pulley. Illuminate the pulley with the fluorescent light. With 60 Hz shore power and the engine operating at 1,800 rpm you will see four pieces of tape. Adjust the throttle to make the tape stand still and then adjust the tach to read 1,800 rpm. You can also check at 3,600 rpm, where you will see two pieces of tape. The speeds for 50 Hz power are 1,500 and 3,000 rpm. This check is precise, although limited to only the speeds indicated.

Runaway Diesel Engine   TIP 138

Fortunately, it is very rare, but a diesel engine can experience governor failure, or even worse, start to burn its own crankcase oil through leaky piston rings or seals. In such instances one cannot shut off the fuel supply, so one must instead cut off the air going to the engine. The temptation is very strong to put your hand over the air intake, but you will be badly injured. Grab anything solid like a piece of plywood or metal and slide it quickly over the air intake. A large carbon dioxide or Halon fire extinguisher will also eliminate the oxygen needed for combustion, but the extinguisher must have sufficient capacity to keep discharging until the engine stops.

Fire Extinguishers   TIP 139

Common practice is to mount dry chemical fire extinguishers vertically. Unfortunately, this causes their powder contents to settle to the bottom. If there is no convenient way to mount dry powder fire extinguishers horizontally, shake them at least once a month to keep the powder from caking up.

Charging Refrigeration   TIP 140

Here's a novel use for a fire extinguisher I bet few have thought of. On the longest Newport–Bermuda Race in history (1976), we were becalmed 150 miles north of Bermuda for 36 hours. There were ten crew, and we had ten cans of beer left. Unfortunately, the refrigeration was not working in the tepid water south of the Gulf Stream.

After some brainstorming, the crew boiled a pot of water and put a can of Freon in it. Then a CO_2 fire extinguisher was discharged onto the refrigeration compressor. The cold compressor accepted warm Freon, and the ice box started to get cold. After all that, however, we could not wait and drank the beer as soon as it started to chill, pretending we were in England.

Engine Beds   TIP 141

In preparing for offshore passage-making, check how the engine mounts are held in place. Some boat manufacturers use lag bolts into wooden stringers that are covered by fiberglass. If the boat rolls over, it is doubtful that any lag bolts can hold the engine.

Additionally, check that engine mounting stringers are heavily glassed to the hull. Even after a severe knockdown, it is prudent to check shaft alignment to be sure the engine has not shifted on its beds.

Engine bed design could consume an entire chapter. Suffice to say that beds must be strongly fixed to the hull with engine mounts bolted to them.

PROP AND SHAFT

Propeller Type   TIP 142

Props for sailboats fall into three basic categories—fixed, folding, and feathering. Which one you choose depends a lot on where you plan to sail.

An interesting study was done in the mid-1970s that compared the drag of folding and fixed props. Going upwind, drag of a fixed propeller was equal to 5 feet of IOR handicap on a boat rating 25. Dead downwind, the drag was negligible. Other tests have shown that on a given boat on a given point of sail, a fixed prop can slow a boat almost a full knot.

Years ago, I made an interesting test with Tartan 33 hull #1. I got six different propellers of various combinations of diameter and pitch. I borrowed a hanging scale from Tartan's glass shop and connected one end to a piling. The other end had two mooring lines with loops to go over the boat's stern cleats. I rented a Travelift for half a day and tested the speed and pull of each propeller. None gave the best combination of pull and speed, but I was able to interpolate the data and specify a two-blade 16-inch-diameter-by-12-inch pitch propeller for production models that gave 7 knots at wide-open throttle and could stop the boat from this speed in less than 50 feet, all with a 24-horsepower engine.

Today, I manage two Alden 50s of about equal displacement and sail plan. One boat has a 22-inch-diameter three-blade fixed prop and an 8-inch-diameter bow thruster tunnel forward. On the average passage, this boat is about half a knot slower than the other boat with a feathering prop and no thruster.

Unless you are going around the world in the trade winds (in which case you will be spending a lot of time downwind, where prop drag is negligible), I recommend a three-blade feathering propeller. Most of the boats I manage have the Max-Prop, which has very good reverse thrust owing to its flat blade design.

Stopping Shaft Rotation   TIP 143

To be sure a Max-Prop feathers, I always get the boat going fast under power, then stop shaft rotation so that forward momentum folds the blades. Most manual transmissions stop shaft rotation when the gear is put in reverse. But if the engine is going to be used to generate power while under sail, the transmission must be put in neutral, which allows the shaft to rotate. If this is the case, you must manually grip the shaft.

While it is preferable to have a fancy shaft lock, a pair of Vise-Grip pliers, *loosely* clamped to the shaft, stops rotation, yet will open if the engine must be used in an emergency.

On *Spirit*, a Hinckley Sou'-wester 51 on which I sailed from Miami to Belize in 1999, a safety interlock, which prevents the engine from starting unless the transmission is in neutral, forced us to heave-to whenever we needed to start the engine. Here's why: Under sail, the shaft would rotate unless the transmission gear was in reverse. But the transmission would not shift from reverse to neutral (so we could start the engine) with pressure on the shaft from water passing over the fixed blades. Normally, I would jog the engine with the starter and shift quickly to neutral. But *Spirit*'s safety interlock switch would not allow the Yanmar engine to be started. To avoid this Catch-22 position, a bypass switch was later installed on the safety interlock.

Correct Pitch   TIP 144

A good prop shop will have a computer program that fairly accurately determines the correct diameter and pitch of a given prop for your boat. The pitch of a propeller is the theoretical amount the propeller would move forward during one revolution in the absence of any slippage; picture a screw turning in wood. Diameter affects the power a prop can transmit. A tugboat with a 1,000-horsepower engine might have a 10-foot-diameter prop, geared to turn slowly. A lightweight hydroplane of equal horsepower will have a small-diameter prop turning at high rpm.

In the absence of expert advice, you can do some experimenting yourself and come pretty close. Ideally, your boat should achieve cruising speed (perhaps a bit less than theoretical hull speed, that is, a comfortable speed) at about 80 percent of the engine's maximum rpm. Therefore, if it takes more than 80 percent of maximum rpm to reach cruising boat speed, consider increasing propeller pitch. Conversely, if cruising boat speed cannot be achieved at about 80 percent of maximum rpm, decrease propeller pitch.

The other variable, of course, is diameter. One inch of diameter is equal to about 2 inches of pitch. Generally, it's better to add diameter than pitch, but that's not always possible, especially if the prop is in an aperture. Also, there should be at least 10 percent prop length clearance between the prop and hull or appendage.

Propellers are a difficult subject and I will not go into all the intricacies here, but suffice to say that sailboat props should not be "over square," that is, having more pitch than diameter. For those who want to really study this subject, I recommend Dave Gerr's *Propeller Handbook* (International Marine, 2001).

Removing the Prop Shaft from the Engine Coupling   TIP 145

One day I was backing out of my slip, and all of a sudden engine speed increased and the boat stopped moving backward. Worse, the rudder could not be turned and the power bilge pump came on. Luckily, we were able to lasso a piling and get the boat into her slip.

Tartan's service manager was on board, and the promised evening cocktail cruise turned into a lot of work for him. He found the prop shaft had not been dimpled for the set-screws, and reverse gear had pulled the shaft out of the coupling and almost all the way out of the boat. It was only held in place by being jammed against the rudder.

He ground a point on the set-screws and dimpled the shaft to receive the point. He also placed a hose clamp on the shaft just forward of the stuffing box as a prophylactic measure.

In general, couplings for the prop shaft to the transmission are made from steel that eventually rusts, making even stainless steel

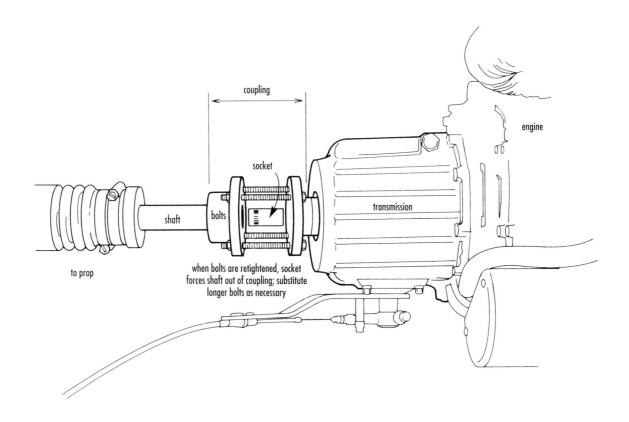

coupling

engine

socket

transmission

shaft

bolts

to prop

when bolts are retightened, socket
forces shaft out of coupling; substitute
longer bolts as necessary

*Often it is difficult to remove a prop shaft from its coupling. Insert a socket
between the shaft and transmission half of the coupling, and then reassemble the joining bolts, turning them alternately and evenly until the shaft is
pushed out of the coupling.*

shafts difficult to remove. Heating the coupling with a torch sometimes expands it enough so that the shaft can be pulled out, but I learned an easier way:

Separate the halves of the coupling by removing the bolts that hold them together. Find a nut or a wrench socket that is slightly smaller than the diameter of the prop shaft. Use tape to hold it over the end of the prop shaft in the coupling. Reassemble the coupling and tighten the bolts evenly. The socket will force the shaft out of the coupling (see drawing). It may take several disassemblies and assemblies to add sockets or other spacers, and you might also have to use longer bolts.

PLUMBING

We have all seen the plaque on how to use a head that ends with the admonition, "There are no plumbers at sea."

Actually, there are plumbers at sea—you!

Plumbing problems are fairly prevalent. Vessel movement often causes leaks in hose joints, and insufficient protection where hoses pass through bulkheads or over corners eventually causes the hose to chafe through.

One time, a friend who owned a Shannon called and asked me to come look at a leak in a metal freshwater tank. He had filled the tank and then gone out for a sail on a blustery day. The end of the tank with the hose fittings was positioned tight against a bulkhead in which holes had been drilled for the fittings. After a lot of investigation I found that the tank had shifted, placing the tank's weight on a plastic hose barb, which, naturally, cracked. I enlarged the hole in the bulkhead for the barb, and the problem was solved. But we had treated the symptoms, not the disease.

It turned out that the tanks were not adequately secured in place. There were pieces of foam rubber under them, which is good for the tanks, but not for securing them.

Hose   TIP 146

I frequently see the wrong type of hose used for a given application, which can cause problems.

All intake hose—whether for the engine, toilet, or sink—should be wire-reinforced to prevent collapse. All hose below the waterline should be a minimum of two-ply rubber or vinyl, not clear or clear with nylon mesh. Avoid any hose not having a smooth interior wall, as corrugations slow the flow of liquids and, in the case of sewage, may collect waste and lead to premature failure of the hose.

For sanitation, all hoses eventually fail, allowing odors to permeate the wall and enter living spaces. But laboratory tests have shown that SeaLand Technology's OdorSafe 1½-inch white PVC hose lasts more than ten times longer than other hoses. (See the Sanitation Hose section in appendix 1.)

Rigid PVC does not allow odors to permeate. It's cumbersome to route through a boat, but rigid PVC can solve smelly head problems, especially if used where there are unavoidable low spots in the sewage lines. You will, of course, need to revert to hose for connections to seacocks and pumps. The only possible drawback to rigid PVC is potential cracking of joints caused by excessive boat vibration or flexing.

Cleaning Hoses   TIP 147

We left Mentor, Ohio, on a Tartan 37 bound across Lake Ontario for Toronto. At noon I drank a glass of water that tasted terrible. The owner assured me he had cleaned the water tanks. I pulled off a ⅝-inch inside diameter hose running to the faucet under the galley sink and found that the foul water was caused by deposits in the hose.

I was able to take off short pieces of hose and push a rag through to clean them. The long runs, however, had me baffled until I looked in the ship's medicine cabinet. I found the perfect cleaning implements for water lines: they were cylindrical, expandable with moisture, and they even had strings attached to affix a messenger line.

I removed one upper lifeline to use as a snake, and pulled the cleaning implements through the hoses. Water taste problem solved! When we stopped at a harbor, I found a drug store to replace the feminine hygiene items we'd used.

Fouled Freshwater Tanks   TIP 148

I was making the trip from Bermuda to St. Maarten on *Agape*, a center-cockpit Alden 50, in rough conditions, when the boat's freshwater turned bad. I switched tanks, but within a day the water again tasted salty. After investigation, I found that gear stored in the sail locker had shifted and partially opened the three-way valve that selects between sea- and freshwater for the deck washdown. I was glad the boat had a watermaker, as we had to dump the contents of both freshwater tanks, which had become fouled.

Another unusual experience occurred on an aluminum ketch. On a passage, freshwater from one of the tanks tasted bad. The boat has five freshwater tanks and a watermaker, so this was not a great hardship. At the next port, we flushed the tank and refilled it. Again the water was bad.

Not until the vessel was hauled was the mystery solved. Two days after hauling, the exterior hull was still wet in the area of the tank. Removing the bottom paint and barrier coating revealed pitting through the hull into the integral tank. Actually, the pitting appeared to be from inside the tank to the outside, probably caused by chlorine in the city water.

Be Alert to Variations in Muriatic Acid Concentration   TIP 149

Saltlike deposits (actually calcium carbonate) build up in hoses, and I have seen inside diameter reduced from 1½ inches to the diameter of a pencil.

Ian Hughes brought his Alden 46 to Nanny Cay, Tortola, to get my advice on several matters. He asked me to show him how to do the muriatic acid toilet effluent hose interior cleaning trick on his aft head, which was not working well. Ian had found

muriatic acid at a local store, and I did the usual procedure of filling the toilet bowl half full of freshwater and then adding acid. I pumped the toilet while Ian slowly closed the discharge seacock to fill the hose with the acid-water mix. Temperature in the aft head compartment was about 95°F, and we had to close the door to access the seacock. Soon, acid fumes drove me on deck, and Ian joined me.

We began talking about another subject when we heard a loud *whoosh*, followed by the sound of running water. Opening the aft head door revealed liquid dripping from a large storage compartment. I opened the compartment to find towels and what must have been a year's worth of feminine products floating in a sea very far in color and smell from the Caribbean. Knowing that the acid would quickly affect the wood, we removed the locker contents and bailed it out.

Inside I found that a hose had been blown off the head's Y-valve.

Through the head window, I spotted Ian's female companion coming down the dock. I rushed on deck and told her to go to a bar for at least the next hour and drinks would be on me. Ian and I spent an absolutely miserable hour cleaning everything. I surmised that muriatic acid from outside the United States may be sold in greater concentration than I was used to, or the high cabin temperature resulted in a greater reaction. I have now altered my recommended mix to one third acid and two thirds water for starters: it takes less time to repeat the process than to clean up after.

Seacocks   TIP 150

To facilitate removal of clogs in seacocks, install a plumbing tee on each intake seacock (see photo). Plumb the intake hose from the

Seacocks occasionally clog. Installation of a tee at the hose fitting, with a plug in the unused end, allows you to jam a round implement down the seacock and through-hull to dislodge the obstruction. (Tip 150)

horizontal branch of the tee, and put a pipe plug in the upper end of the fitting (in line with the end screwed into the top of the sea-cock). If the seacock clogs, remove the pipe plug and thrust a round implement into the seacock and through-hull to push the obstruction straight through the bottom of the boat. Have a towel handy, and be sure the seacock can be closed to stop water flow while the pipe plug is being reinstalled.

I was once cleaning a blocked engine intake with wire. I un-spooled 10 feet of wire through the seacock and out the bottom of the boat, and still no water came in. I figured a plastic bag could have not been that big, so next I used a round bilge pump handle to dislodge what I am convinced now was a jellyfish sealing itself around the wire!

The tee fitting also is handy for winterizing. Close the seacock and use a funnel to feed antifreeze through the top of the tee while running the device that the in-take supplies—engine, washdown pump, etc.

Softwood Plugs   TIP 151

ORC regulations require softwood plugs for each through-hull fitting. This is a good idea, though it is un-likely that all fittings are going to let go at once . . . unless the boat suffers a very unusual lightning hit.

The regulations also ask that the plugs be affixed near each through-hull fitting. I am against this prac-tice. The idea of softwood is that it swells when wet, providing a watertight seal. If the plug is stored in a location where it is likely to get wet, it will swell *before* being driven in place.

I like to keep a supply of plugs in a plastic bag in a dry locker, each marked with the name and location of the through-hull fittings they fit.

Even better than plugs for stop-ping leaks are "bowl waxes" sold by plumbing stores for seating toilets. These cost but a few dollars each and can be molded by hand to form irregular shapes. Buy about six.

For large-diameter hoses or plumbing, stop at a commercial plumbing supply company for ex-pandable test plugs. On these, screwing down a wing nut expands a bellows that will seal against the inside diameter of the hose or fit-ting. Lash the test plug in place.

Bilge Pump Strainers   TIP 152

Most bilge pumps have a strainer at the bottom of the pickup hose that is easily clogged by debris in the bilge. Unless the pump is run-ning, the crud falls off as the strainer is withdrawn from the bilge for cleaning. I prefer to eliminate this foot strainer (also called rose or strum box) from the bottom of the pickup hose and instead mount an engine intake–type strainer such as a Groco ARG series or Perko #493 up high in the bilge where it is read-ily accessible (see photo).

I connect as large a pickup hose as possible to the strainer intake, and cut a V-shaped notch in the bottom end of the hose so it cannot suck itself flush to the inside of the

Replacing small strainers with larger ones improves efficiency and extends intervals between cleaning. The bilge pump on this boat has oversize hose on the pickup with no foot strainer, just a notch cut in the end of the hose so it will not suck itself tight to the bottom of the bilge. (Tip 152)

Seawater draining back into the pump body from the discharge hose totally destroyed this Edson aluminum bilge pump. At right, note the condition of the corroded flapper valve seat versus a new valve seat. (Tip 153)

bilge. If possible, I try to avoid elbows in the pickup hose connection to the strainer, as debris gets caught in them.

All bilge pumps that discharge underwater (remember to think of the boat heeled and at speed, which may put the stern area underwater) must have a vented loop in the discharge hose. Many cases of boats mysteriously taking on water when under sail have been traced to backflow through a bilge pump. Do not rely on a check valve, as it may be held open by debris.

Aluminum Bilge Pumps   TIP 153

All of the Edson aluminum bilge pumps on the yachts we manage have failed (see photos). Some boats also have Whale aluminum bilge pumps that also have stopped working due to corrosion from seawater. If your boat has an aluminum bilge pump, take it completely apart . . . if the fasteners have not already corroded so much that disassembly is impossible. If the pump comes apart and is not yet so badly corroded that it must be replaced, reassemble with lots of antiseize compound on the stainless steel threads going into aluminum. Test the pump only with freshwater, and leave a sign on it that the pump must have a lot of freshwater pumped through it immediately after each pumping of seawater.

A large manual bilge pump nestled away is supposed to provide peace of mind that you will be able to cope with a leak. Edson readily admits that if serviced regularly, and always left with only freshwater inside, the service life of their aluminum bilge pump is only seven to ten years. Their bronze pumps are about 40 percent more expensive than aluminum, but have an unlimited useful expectancy.

In *Practical Sailor* tests, the top-rated, large, plastic, manual bilge pump was the Henderson Mk V.

Emergency Bilge Pump   TIP 154

A three-way valve mounted on top of the engine intake seacock (see top photo next page) allows the engine to withdraw water from the bilge as an emergency pump. Be sure to monitor continuously so debris doesn't clog the intake hose. And label each part of the valve so you know which hose the valve is set for.

I once drove from Rhode Island to Milwaukee for the spring commissioning of an Alden 50. Working in the bilge shortly after launching, I noticed that the water level was rising. I tasted the water, which was not salty, and continued reconnecting the water heater, figuring there was a leak in the pressure water system. When the water reached my elbows, it finally dawned on me that Lake Michigan was freshwater, and perhaps I ought to find out where the water was coming from.

I finally found that I had bumped the three-way valve that allows emergency use of the engine intake as a bilge pump, and it was letting water in. By then I had the opportunity to test the boat's high-capacity bilge pump.

Conserving Freshwater — TIP 155

Aboard a small boat, tankage is usually limited. Despite the growing popularity of watermakers (12-volt and engine-driven), freshwater should not be wasted.

In showers. Personal cleanliness goes a long way toward crew happiness. If your crew likes hot showers, install a tee in the hot water line at the shower mixer. Put a ball valve on the branch of the tee. Plumb the outlet from the valve to a tee fitting in the water tank vent line (see photo). Opening the valve allows water to run back to the tank, so no freshwater is wasted waiting for it to run hot.

Typically, there is more pressure in the hot water line than the cold water line until the pump kicks in, increasing the cold water flow. When the pump shuts off, hot again has more pressure, causing the shower temperature to once more fluctuate. Pressure-compensating shower mixers solve the problem. On land, they are required by most building codes for commercial installations, and some cities require them for new home construction. I buy them at the local Home Depot for about $75, and

A three-way valve mounted on top of the engine intake works as an emergency bilge pump. (Tip 154)

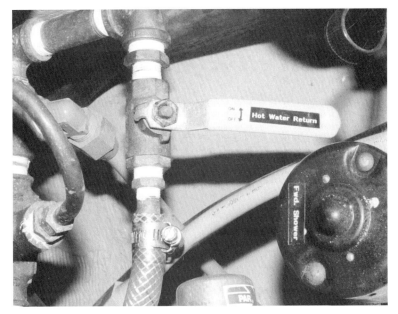

A tee installed in the shower mixer with a hose led back to another tee at the tank vent fitting saves water while you wait for it to get hot. (Tip 155)

most boatowners agree that they are a good investment.

An experienced cruiser replaced the normal shower hose and handheld wand with a kitchen sprayer hose and nozzle. Because this type of sprayer must be held open and stops when released, water consumption is held to a minimum. When I take a shower on board, I get wet, turn off the water, soap up with a washcloth, then rinse quickly. This uses only a few gallons of water and makes me so refreshed that I always wonder why I didn't do it yesterday.

In the galley. A supply of seawater to the galley saves more freshwater than any other conservation method. Offshore, I use seawater for all dish washing (lemon Joy works well) and rinsing, and then give plates and cups a quick freshwater rinse (see Washing Dishes, tip 212). The handiest outlet for seawater is a standard kitchen sink-type sprayer on a hose. If your boat has a seawater anchor washdown, tee into it to supply the galley sprayer. If seawater is provided via a foot pump, connect it to the sprayer.

Insecticide-Sprayer Shower TIP 156

A pressurized plastic insecticide sprayer with hand pump, filled with freshwater, provides a fine mist spray that washes off salt after swimming or showering in seawater. If you cannot find a dark-colored sprayer, make a dark cloth cover to absorb solar heat. Because the mist is pressurized, a sprayer gives a more satisfactory rinse than a gravity-operated solar or sun shower. Buy them at garden supply or hardware stores.

Pipe TIP 157

There is much confusion regarding pipe. Pipe is measured in nominal sizes that have nothing to do with any dimensions of the pipe, except in very large sizes.

The abbreviation IPS (for Iron Pipe Size) is often used to denote nominal pipe size.

The most common pipe is schedule 40, which is considered to be the "standard." Schedule 80 has a thicker wall and is sometimes referred to as "extra strong" or "XS." Schedule 10 has a very thin wall, often used for crop irrigation where there is little pressure.

Pipe is available in a variety of materials. The most common on yachts is black iron, which is used for engine exhaust. Bronze/brass pipe is sometimes used for through-hulls. And, of course, there is PVC (polyvinyl chloride). Any PVC used below the waterline should be schedule 80, which is generally dark gray.

Other common abbreviations are MPT (male pipe tapered) and FPT (female pipe tapered).

A lot of spinnaker poles are made from schedule 10 aluminum pipe, a fact that once came in handy to a Tartan 41 owner. He was racing in the St. Francis Yacht Club big boat series, and the crew managed to break the pole. At the time, I was employed at Tartan, and I got a panic call asking me to air-freight overnight a new spinnaker pole. I told the owner that the cost would be exorbitant, and recommended that he send the crew out to forage the irrigated fields. He called back the following day to say that a San Fernando farmer had one less length of pipe, but a full case of beer. The spinnaker pole worked fine, but smelled of fertilizer.

In addition to IPS sizes, plastic PVC pipe is available in nominal inch sizes with a thin wall, called DWV (drain, waste, vent). This pipe should not be used for any pressure applications, and is usually terminated with solvent-weld fittings. PVC pipe-to-hose adapters are readily available, but they are made to fit the ID (inside diameter) of plastic pipe, *not* the ID of hose. Only one size works well: a ½-inch IPS barb adapter fits ⅝-inch ID hose. Do not use any other sizes, as forcing hose on may collapse the fitting internally or rupture the hose. Shields and Forespar make reinforced plastic pipe thread-to-hose adapters that are sized to the ID of marine hose. A note on Forespar fittings: there is an unthreaded portion at the end of the threads that must be ground off to allow the fitting to screw into anything.

Most pipe threads are tapered (think of a wood screw). NPS (National Pipe Straight) threads are used on some through-hull/seacock combinations to allow the through-hull to screw into the seacock body by varying amounts, depending on hull thickness.

At the top of the seacock, however, where the tailpiece screws in, NPT (National Pipe Tapered) threads may be used. NPT threads are designed so that when two NPT fittings are screwed together the threads will jam after a few turns and make a watertight seal. The accompanying table shows the necessary thread engagement length to achieve a tight joint with tapered pipe threads. There is justice in the world: 14 and 16 IPS pipe (not given in the accompanying table)

actually measure the same outside diameters in inches!

In short, don't mix NPS and NPT threads.

For pipe joint compound, I like RectorSeal #5. Unlike Teflon tape, fittings can be backed off a little and still not leak.

Copper Alloys   TIP 158

Bronze is an alloy of copper and tin, and brass is an alloy of copper and zinc. The color of the alloy cannot be used to determine what is suitable for use under water, nor can

one say unequivocally "do not use brass under water."

Most through-hull fittings and seacocks are made from alloys having about 85 percent copper, 5 percent tin, 5 percent zinc, and 5 percent lead. This SAE #40 alloy is commonly called "bronze" by marine hardware manufacturers but "red brass" by machinists. Propeller shaft struts and powerboat rudders are commonly cast from manganese bronze because it is over twice as strong as red brass. Manganese bronze contains 55 to 60 percent copper, 38 to 42 percent zinc, and small amounts of manganese, tin, lead, iron, and aluminum. Cutless-bearing shells are usually naval brass, which is 59 to 62 percent copper, plus very small amounts of tin, lead, iron, and the rest zinc.

Copper alloys immersed in seawater are susceptible to a process called dealloying, with alloys having a lot of zinc becoming weak and porous. Galvanic and electrolytic corrosion is a very complex subject, and is not the only type of corrosion that happens in marine environments. Recommended reading for anybody installing underwater hardware is *The Boatowner's Guide to Corrosion* by Everett Collier (International Marine, 2001).

I always try to use through-hull fittings and seacocks from the same manufacturer, and stick to the large, well-established names. A cheap off-brand through-hull fitting is not a bargain when your boat sinks or, in the best case, the fitting has to be replaced.

PIPE SIZES (TIP 157)

Nominal Size (IPS), in.	Outside Diameter, in.	Approx. Fraction Equivalent, in.	Minimum Thread Engagement, in.	Comments
⅛	0.405	⅜	¼	used on oil pressure senders and lamps
¼	0.540	½	⅜	engine zincs are frequently ¼ in. IPS
⅜	0.675	⅝	⅜	nipple is good fit in ⅝ in. ID hose
½	0.840	¾	½	nipple is tight fit in ¾ in. ID hose
¾	1.05	1	⁹⁄₁₆	nipple is slightly tight fit in 1 in. ID hose
1	1.315	1⅜	¹¹⁄₁₆	
1¼	1.66	1⅝	¹¹⁄₁₆	used on head discharge plumbing with 1⅝ in. hose
1½	1.9	1⅞	¹¹⁄₁₆	used on engine exhaust
2	2.375	2⅜	¾	larger engine exhaust
2½	2.875	2⅞	¹⁵⁄₁₆	larger engine exhaust
3	3.5	3½	1	aluminum light wall used on spinnaker poles
4	4.5	4½	1⅛	same
5	5.563	5⅝	1¼	
6	6.625	6⅝	1⁵⁄₁₆	

TOOLS AND MAINTENANCE

Large Tools   TIP 159

Most passagemaking boats do not carry an adequate inventory of large tools. Underway, exerting a lot of pressure can be difficult, and large tools help. For a suggested inventory, see the accompanying list.

A requirement of the Pacific Cup race from California to Hawaii is a steel strap banding machine, which is very helpful for splinting broken booms and spinnaker poles. The recommended tool is made by the Band-It Company; part #C001 bands from ¼ to ¾ inch wide. Supplies include

- ⅝-inch stainless banding, 100-foot roll, part #C205
- ⅝-inch buckles, part #C255
- ⅝-inch screw lock buckles, part #C725 (enables one to make custom hose clamps)

OFFSHORE TOOL LIST

This may seem like a lot of tools, but I have needed every single one offshore for repair and routine maintenance. Not listed are tools for extensive modification projects or cosmetic maintenance.

Screwdrivers

1 very small flat blade; for adjusting electronics
1 ea. ⅛-, ³⁄₁₆-, ¼-, ⁵⁄₁₆-, ⅜-, ⁷⁄₁₆-inch-wide flat blade
1 right-angle flat blade
1 stubby flat blade
1 wedge tip for #8 screws (QuickWedge and Vaco #k34 are popular brands); look in electrical supply houses; invaluable for working on electrical panels
1 very small Phillips
1 ea. #0, #1, #2, #3 Phillips
1 right-angle Phillips
1 stubby Phillips
1 ea. ⁵⁄₁₆-, ⅜-inch flat blade by ⅜-inch drive socket
1 ea. #2, #3 Phillips by ⅜-inch drive socket; add #4 if boat has large Phillips screws
1 set impact driver with bits
if your boat uses square-drive or other esoteric screws, bring a screwdriver to fit them

Pliers

1 ea. 6-, 8-inch common slip-joint pliers
1 ea. 10-, 16-inch (or preferably 18-inch) arc-joint pliers (Channellock is a popular brand)
1 ea. 10-inch locking pliers, straight and curved jaw (Vise-Grip is a popular brand)
1 ea. 4-, 6-inch needlenose pliers
1 ea. 8-inch diagonal cutting pliers

Wrenches

1 ea. 6-, 12-, 18-inch adjustable (Crescent is a popular brand)
1 set very small combination wrenches (commonly called ignition wrenches)
1 set combination open-end and box wrenches, ⅜ to 1 inch
1 set combination open-end and box wrenches, 6 to 28 mm
1 set socket wrenches, standard depth, ¼ to 1 inch, ⅜-inch drive, six point.
1 set same, deep sockets (or buy a set which has both standard and deep)
1 set socket wrenches, standard depth, 6 to 28 mm
1 ratchet for above (if not included with set)

1 ea. extensions for ⅜-inch drive sockets, 3, 6, and 12 inch
1 universal joint for ⅜-inch drive socket
1 breaker bar for ⅜-inch drive
1 chain wrench; these have a bicycle-type chain that wraps around irregular shaped objects; can be used on propeller-shaft packing boxes
1 oil filter wrench to fit your filters
1 fuel filter wrench (if your engine fuel filters are screw-on type)
1 hex key set (or sets), ¹⁄₁₆ to ⅜ inch (these are commonly called Allen wrenches)
1 hex key set (or sets), 2 to 12 mm

Chisels and Punches

1 ea. ¼-, ¾-inch-wide wood chisels
1 ea. ¼-, ½-inch-wide cold chisels
1 centerpunch
1 ea. ⅛-, ³⁄₁₆-, ¼-inch small-diameter drift punches (useful for removing roll pins)
1 drift punch, ⅜-inch small-end, 12 inches long; add a wrist lanyard; this is essential for knocking out clevis pins after your rig goes over the side

(continued next page)

Taps

3 ea. #6-32, #8-32, #10-32, #10-24, #¼"-20 (see table page 118)
2 ea. ⁵⁄₁₆-18; ³⁄₈-16
1 ea. tap handle to fit above (the kind with a sliding handle for working in tight spaces)

Hammers

1 4- to 5-pound short-handled sledgehammer; add a wrist lanyard; use with large drift punch to drive out clevis pins after a dis-masting
1 20-ounce claw hammer

Drills and Bits (see table page 117)

1 hand drill, ³⁄₈-inch chuck capacity
1 battery-powered drill, ³⁄₈-inch chuck capacity; I like the Makita right-angle drills, which are useful for working in tight spaces
1 charger for above that works off ship's voltage (usually 12-volt)
1 extra battery for above
1 cobalt drill set, ¹⁄₁₆ to ³⁄₈ inch; stainless steel cuts nicely with a slow-turning cobalt drill, but you must be able to see the flutes on the drill bit as it turns; use lots of pressure
1 drill bit, ½-inch with ³⁄₈-inch shank
2 ea. #36, #29, #25 drills for tapping holes; a proper-size tap drill helps to make properly tapped holes
1 ea. #7, #F drills for tapping holes
1 countersink
1 set EZ-Out screw removers; for removing broken-off screws and bolts

Clamps

2 4-inch C-clamps
2 10-inch C-clamps
2 plastic spring clamps; useful for keeping charts from blowing away and as heavy-duty clothespins

Files

1 10-inch mill file
1 10-inch round file
1 6-inch round file
1 6-inch triangular file

Cutting Tools

1 heavy-duty frame hacksaw
6 min *carbide* blades for above; carbide cuts stainless steel nicely
6 bi-metal blades for above, with both fine and coarse teeth; lubricate blade with beeswax when cutting aluminum, and teeth will not load up
1 small cabinetmaker's wood-cutting saw
1 rotary rasp to fit drill
1 small block plane
1 10-inch combination fine and coarse wood rasp

Electrical

1 auto-ranging Volt Ohm Milliampmeter (VOM), plus spare batteries
4 test leads, about 2 feet long with alligator clips each end
1 50-watt lightbulb of same voltage as ship's DC, and a socket with wire leads; for circuit testing (frequently a bad circuit will show voltage on a meter, but fail to illuminate the light)
1 ratchet electrical crimper that will not release until crimp is properly made (the crimpers that come with sets of terminals are terrible, only useful as wire stripper)
1 wire stripper, #22 to #10 wire capacity
Misc. electrical terminals—buy only marine-grade, quality terminals (frequently the ones included in sets are plated steel, not plated copper); check sizes used on your boat and buy lots, as you can go through a dozen easily on one minor electrical project
1 butane-powered soldering iron, low-melting-point electrical solder, rosin flux

Miscellanea

1 propane torch; since disposable gas cylinders do not last long in a marine environment, go to a plumbing supply and buy a torch with hose that will fit the ship's cooking propane tanks; also get a soldering iron tip
1 high-quality rubber plunger (commonly called a plumber's helper)
5-minute epoxy
high-strength epoxy
Krazy Glue
underwater epoxy putty
1 putty knife, ¾- or 1-inch-wide blade, stiff type; useful for prying up hardware
1 crowbar, 24-inch minimum
1 claw-type remote-pickup tool; invaluable for retrieving things dropped in a deep bilge
1 tape measure, inch and metric
1 6-inch dial-type caliper, 0.001 resolution is fine, stainless steel or plastic
1 pump for changing oil and transmission fluid

DRILL BIT SIZES

Drill bits come in numbered, letter, and fractional sizes. Here is a listing through ⅝ inch, in ascending decimal size order.

Drill Size	Drill Diameter, in.
60	0.0400
59	0.041
58	0.042
57	0.043
56	0.0465
³/₆₄	0.0469
55	0.052
54	0.055
53	0.0595
¹/₁₆	0.0625
52	0.0635
51	0.067
50	0.070
49	0.073
48	0.076
⁵/₆₄	0.0781
47	0.0785
46	0.081

Size	Diameter, in.
45	0.082
44	0.086
43	0.089
42	0.0935
³/₃₂	0.0938
41	0.096
40	0.098
39	0.0995
38	0.1015
37	0.104
36	0.1065
⁷/₆₄	0.1094
35	0.110
34	0.111
33	0.113
32	0.116
31	0.120
⅛	0.125
30	0.1285
29	0.136
28	0.1405
⁹/₆₄	0.1406
27	0.144
26	0.147
25	0.1495
24	0.152
23	0.154
⁵/₃₂	0.1562

Size	Diameter, in.
22	0.157
21	0.159
20	0.161
19	0.166
18	0.1695
¹¹/₆₄	0.1719
17	0.173
16	0.177
15	0.180
14	0.182
13	0.185
³/₁₆	0.1875
12	0.189
11	0.191
10	0.1935
9	0.196
8	0.199
7	0.201
¹³/₆₄	0.2031
6	0.204
5	0.2055
4	0.209
3	0.213
⁷/₃₂	0.2188
2	0.221
1	0.228
A	0.234
¹⁵/₆₄	0.2344

Size	Diameter, in.
B	0.238
C	0.242
D	0.246
E & ¼	0.250
F	0.257
G	0.261
¹⁷/₆₄	0.2656
H	0.266
I	0.272
J	0.277
K	0.281
⁹/₃₂	0.2812
L	0.290
M	0.295
¹⁹/₆₄	0.2969
N	0.302
⁵/₁₆	0.3125
O	0.316
P	0.323
²¹/₆₄	0.3281
Q	0.332
R	0.339
¹¹/₃₂	0.3438
S	0.348
T	0.358
²³/₆₄	0.3594
U	0.368
⅜	0.375

Size	Diameter, in.
V	0.377
W	0.386
²⁵/₆₄	0.3906
X	0.397
Y	0.404
¹³/₃₂	0.4062
Z	0.413
²⁷/₆₄	0.4219
⁷/₁₆	0.4375
²⁹/₆₄	0.4531
¹⁵/₃₂	0.4688
³¹/₆₄	0.4844
½	0.500
³³/₆₄	0.5156
¹⁷/₃₂	0.5312
³⁵/₆₄	0.5781
⁹/₁₆	0.5625
³⁷/₆₄	0.5781
¹⁹/₃₂	0.5938
³⁹/₆₄	0.6094
⅝	0.625

PROPER TAP DRILL BIT SIZES

Repairs or working with metal, such as the mast, sometimes require a tap or threaded hole into which a machine screw can be fastened. The pilot hole for the tap must be the right size. This table shows the correct pairings of drill bits and taps.

Size of Machine Screw		Number of Threads per Inch	Tap Drills	
No. or Diameter	Decimal Equivalent		Drill Size	Decimal Equivalent
6	0.138	32	36	0.1065
		40	33	0.1130
8	0.164	32	29	0.1360
		36	29	0.1360
10	0.190	24	25	0.1495
		32	21	0.1590
12	0.216	24	16	0.1770
		28	14	0.1820
¼	0.250	20	7	0.2010
		28	3	0.2130
⁵⁄₁₆	0.3125	18	F	0.2570
		24	I	0.2720
⅜	0.375	16	⁵⁄₁₆	0.3125
		24	Q	0.3320
⁷⁄₁₆	0.4375	14	U	0.3680
		20	²⁵⁄₆₄	0.3906
½	0.500	13	²⁷⁄₆₄	0.4219
		20	²⁹⁄₆₄	0.4531

Maintenance Log

TIP 160

While it is satisfying to cross a job off a "to do" list, take time to maintain a maintenance log. No only will the log answer the question "Was it one or two years ago that I had to disassemble the port cockpit winch?", but it also helps schedule preventive maintenance, predicated on experience. When the time comes to sell your boat, a well-kept, up-to-date maintenance log is a valuable selling feature.

Miscellanea

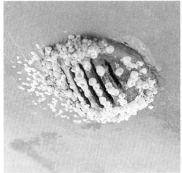

Exterior scoop strainers for engine cooling or other intake should be readily removable, as barnacles also grow inside the strainer and through-hull. **TIP 162**

At least the forward third of the hull, keel, and all of the rudder should be free of growth. The cleaner the hull, the better, of course. While the cruising sailor does not have to be as fanatical as the racer who wet-sands his bottom, severe growth can slow a vessel in double-digit percentages of normal speed. It is especially important to keep the propeller perfectly free of barnacles. Manufacturers go to great expense to get perfectly fair curves on propeller blades, so one barnacle can cause cavitation and very inefficient operation.

On one passage I stopped to have the prop cleaned by a diver. The boat was a 54-foot ketch with a 70-horsepower engine. The result was an increase of 2.3 knots at the same engine rpm.

For more on making the best time on passages, see tip 187.

TIP 161

CHAPTER 6

AT SEA

Early one April I was helping an Alden 54 owner bring his boat back from the Bahamas to Annapolis, Maryland. We rode the Gulf Stream as far north as possible, but south of Cape Hatteras we headed northwest for Norfolk, Virginia. As the water was cold out of the stream, we put up the side curtains on the bimini and were enjoying a dry ride in the enclosed, greenhouse-like cockpit.

This photograph was my 1996 Christmas card, which read, "Season's Greetings from the Gulf Stream."

When we left the Abacos, I had offered to take a berth in the forward cabin, but the owner said he wanted to be in "his" cabin. Fifty miles east of Cape Hatteras the waves built, and the owner told me he would take me up on my previous offer and take my aft cabin, especially because it was on the leeward side. I snuggled in for my afternoon nap up forward, with my sea bag on top of me to hold me from becoming airborne. I was just falling asleep when I felt a wave smack the boat's side, immediately followed by a string of expletives from the owner. Coming aft to see what had happened, I saw the owner standing dripping wet in the cockpit. He had left open both aft cabin portlights to the cockpit. I watched his pillow float back and forth on his berth. The bimini frame was bent, and most of the windward-side curtains were split open.

I had to bite the inside of my mouth to stop from laughing, and very generously offered the owner a dry pillow from my bunk. I was glad the one rogue in 300,000 waves happened on the owner's watch.

(Incidentally, the scientific journal *Sea Frontiers* reported in 1973 that one wave in 23 will be twice the height of the average wave; one in 1,175 will be three times bigger, and one in 300,000 will be a minimum of four times higher than the average.)

At sea, comfort and safety are enhanced by learning to make the unexpected expected.

SAFETY FIRST

Safety Video   TIP 163

One of the yachts I manage has a professionally filmed and edited video in which her owner explains various safety procedures and features of the vessel. While most owners will not go to the expense of professional filmmaking, a friend with a video camera can record the following information, which will be helpful to all crew:

- How to launch the life raft; abandon-ship procedures (see pages 132 and 205).

- How to wear the inflatable harnesses, where to clip them on.

- Rigging and hoisting the storm trysail (see page 44).

- Rigging and deploying the storm drogue (see pages 123–24).

- Deploying Lifesling or other MOB retrieval devices, and use of the spinnaker halyard and winch for lifting the person on board (see page 131).

- Location and operation of seacocks; procedures in event of flooding (see pages 131–32).

- Operation of valves to use the engine intake as an emergency bilge pump (see pages 111–12).

- Location and operation of below- and above-decks manual bilge pumps.

- Location of emergency gear, tools, and medical supplies (see pages 204–5).

- How to broadcast Mayday message on all radios.

In addition to the video, checklists for much of the above are in the front of the deck log. Crew must flip past these pages to fill in the hourly log, and I am adamant that position and conditions be recorded hourly.

Large-scale drawings showing locations of all gear and through-hulls are always on top in the chart table.

Maintaining Night Vision   TIP 164

A very handy and inexpensive addition to a boat is a piece of dark-colored cloth snapped to the after side of the companionway and hanging down to cover the companionway opening (see photo, next page). With the cloth dropped, lights below will not interfere with the vision of those in the cockpit. The cloth is easy to move aside for egress.

The bottom of the cloth should have a hem filled with lead shot or sand to weight it so it will not blow open. On one boat I used a length of ⅜-inch stainless steel threaded rod as a bottom weight. Ten thousand miles after having the cloth made, an alternator pivot bolt broke on the boat. We were 800 miles from our destination. To hold the alternator on the engine block, I ripped out the hem and used the threaded rod in place of the bolt.

Heaving-To   **TIP 165**

Unfortunately, the practice of backwinding the jib, sheeting the main in tight, and lashing the helm is becoming extinct.

Very lightweight boats with fin keels simply will not heave-to. Most nonradical cruising boats, however, will heave-to satisfactorily, reaching

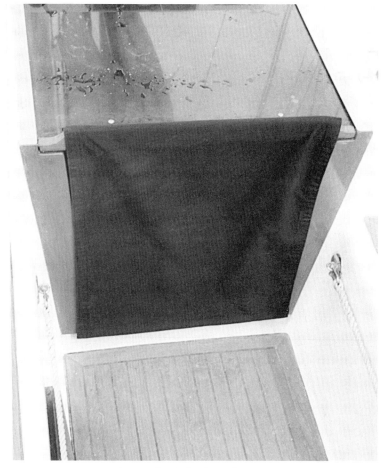

Here's an easy way to keep cabin lights from destroying the night vision of crew on deck: Sew a dark-colored cloth slightly larger in size than the companionway. Snaps across the top affix it to the hatch. Lead shot or sand can be used in the hem at bottom to keep it from blowing open. (Tip 164)

a little off the wind at about a knot. It is helpful to have a jib of no more than 95 percent of the foretriangle to avoid chafe on the shrouds, or to roll in a furling genoa to this size.

Here's how to heave-to: With the reefed mainsail sheeted in hard (or the storm trysail if conditions warrant), tack the boat but do not release the windward jib/genoa sheet. As soon as the sail is aback, reverse the helm to keep the boat headed up. Wind pressure on the backed headsail holds the bow off while wind pressure on the mainsail keeps the vessel from falling off. You'll probably have to hand steer awhile to find the rudder angle at which the boat is happy, making a scalloping course and little headway. Lash the wheel in this position, using slipknots that can be easily undone if an emergency arises. A pedestal brake is not adequately strong to hold the helm when hove-to; a lashing must be used. If the boat does not have pad eyes outboard of the wheel for this purpose or port and starboard cockpit jacklines (see photo page 5), try lashing to a spoke around the pedestal.

Because the pressure of wind is exponential, the sail combination that works for heaving-to in 20 knots may not be effective in 30 or 40 knots. Practice heaving-to in various wind strengths, and record the combinations that result in a good ride. Once mastered, the practice of heaving-to may become addictive for such mundane reasons as eating meals comfortably, or even using the head.

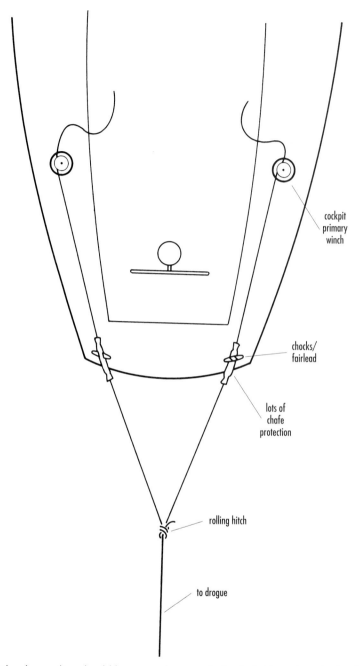

cockpit
primary
winch

chocks/
fairlead

lots of
chafe
protection

rolling hitch

to drogue

The drogue line should be secured to a cockpit winch. To reduce the load on the line, tie a second line to the first and lead it to the opposite winch, forming a bridle. (Tip 166)

Drogues and Sea Anchors   TIP 166

Sea anchors are deployed off the bow and keep the boat more or less headed into the wind and waves. Drogues are smaller and are trailed from the stern with the boat running downwind. Do not deploy a drogue from the bow, as it doesn't sufficiently slow the boat; papers presented at a Society of Naval Architects and Marine Engineers (SNAME) symposium stated that a drogue from the bow allows a vessel to slide stern-first down waves, often resulting in rudder damage.

The best drogue is a series of small cones on a long line (such as the Jordan Series Drogue—see appendix 7), as some of the cones will always be in solid water, not in breaking wave crests. Very popular and less expensive is the Galerider from Hathaway, Reiser & Raymond sailmakers.

A drogue should be set up with the line led fairly to the primary cockpit winches. A second line should be tied to the main line with a rolling hitch (see illustration page 8) and led to the primary winch on the other side of this cockpit to form a bridle (see drawing, here); this halves the load on each winch.

As with all safety gear, try using a drogue before you really need one. Slowing boat speed so the vessel does not surf down a wave and then plow under the next wave makes for a safer ride. You might also deploy a drogue in rough weather if your boat is short-handed, to give the crew a rest. Current thinking is that lying *a-hull*, parallel to the waves, is a bad idea and is likely to result in a rollover.

Centerboards   TIP 167

While most offshore boats do not have centerboards, there are exceptions, especially among larger boats in which a centerboard is a viable means of reducing draft (when up) yet still providing additional lift (when down) for upwind sailing. Most Aldens and a number of Tartans as well as some other brands have centerboards.

To windward. Use the board to balance the helm. Pulling the board up slightly moves the center of lateral resistance aft, relieving weather helm. I have been able to sail for days with the autopilot off by occasionally adjusting the board to neutralize the helm just enough so that the boat sails itself to windward quite happily.

Close reaching in heavy air. Use some board to alleviate weather helm.

Broad reaching/running in waves. Lowering about one-third of the board increases lateral plane aft, which helps directional stability and decreases the tendency of the bow to wander.

Maneuvering under power. While it seems incongruous, try making tight turns at slow speeds with the board all the way down. If the centerboard is a narrow, daggerboard type, most hulls tend to pivot around the board and turn better.

Freeing Lines Under Load   TIP 168

One of the most common mistakes newcomers make is having no idea of the pressure on a line when it is removed from whatever is holding it. I have watched people uncleat a dockline and almost get pulled off the boat by the pressure on the line. If they had just kept a turn on the cleat and gradually released the load, they would have been fine.

A common injury is caused by freeing a sheet, either from a cleat or self-tailing mechanism, and having your hand holding the line get sucked into the winch. When releasing the load on the sheet, always hold one hand against the turns on the winch drum to act as a brake, especially if the force on the tail is too great.

In short, never release a line until you have an idea of the amount of pressure on it and how you are going to deal with it!

I learned my lesson on the maiden sail of a big boat I crewed on for many years. There was virtually no wind. We hoisted the ½-ounce spinnaker. I was hand-holding the sheet and tweaking it to get the sail to fill. When the sail filled, I was pulled 15 feet across the deck until I came to a winch, on which I was able to take a turn of the sheet. After that, I learned never to hold any line that is not wrapped around a stationary object.

Spinnaker Takedown   TIP 169

On Tandem, the big boat I used to race on in the mid-1970s, the spinnaker afterguy led to a coffee grinder winch just aft of the mainmast. This position gave the winch grinders and tailers a good view of the chute. Kevlar rope had not yet been invented. The afterguys were 7×19 wire, the only material with low enough stretch for close reaching. Our spinnakers were 71 feet luff and 40 feet wide.

On a St. Pete–Ft. Lauderdale race we were close reaching with a 2.2-ounce star-cut spinnaker to Rebecca Shoals one afternoon when a line squall closed with us. Our general battle plan for line squalls was to ride them for a few minutes to determine their duration before shortening canvas. (We did not have radar to check the intensity of squalls.) This one turned out to be especially vicious, and Tandem took a major knockdown that put the upper spreaders in the water. With the spinnaker sheet winch underwater, we could not ease the sheet, and the strong spinnaker full of water was holding the boat down. I was close to the afterguy coffee grinder and happened to look at the mast—not up, but horizontally.

The middle of the mast had what appeared to be a 4-foot bow. I waved to the crew in the cockpit to keep down, and unwound the afterguy from the grinder. The 108-foot-long afterguy zinged through its blocks and spinnaker pole end. Tandem came upright rapidly. The flailing wire afterguy cut the chute into three pieces like a sword.

After we took down the remains, Charlie Britton, Tandem's owner, questioned my actions. A sanitized version is "Seif, why did you run the afterguy?"

My reply was, "Charlie, I was looking at the mast and thought it was about to bust. We have five spinnakers, but only one mast." Charlie huffed and told the crew to put any dry portions of the spin-naker in his bunk, as he wanted the world's most expensive bed-sheet.

Evacuation by Helicopter TIP 170

If a helicopter lowers a basket to evacuate an injured person, let the line dangling from the basket drag in the water before grabbing it. The line is meant to dissipate static elec-tricity, which will injure anybody touching it before the charge is bled off. No matter how much you are tempted, do not secure the static line of the basket to your vessel. The lift line on a helicopter has an easy-to-use cutter, which will be used if the mobility of the aircraft is com-promised.

Downdraft from a hovering he-licopter may reach 100 knots. Be sure all loose items on deck are se-cured, canvas is removed, and all crew are tethered.

DESIGN AND LOADING CONSIDERATIONS

Sailing and Center of Effort TIP 171

A little naval architecture is nec-essary to understand the dynamics of sail trim. All hulls have a cen-ter of lateral resistance (CLR), which can be thought of as the fore-and-aft pivot point of the vessel. The sails have a geometric center of ef-fort (CE), which may be thought of as the fore-and-aft middle of the combined forces of the sails.

Going to windward. Most sail-boats are designed so that full sail puts the CE somewhat aft of the CLR. The difference is called *lead*. Lead produces some weather helm to help the vessel sail to windward. This is also a built-in safety feature; when the helm is released, the boat naturally heads up into the wind and the sails luff.

Most often, a naval architect will design the CE to be a little aft of the mainmast. Unfortunately,

reefing the main and roller reefing the genoa moves the CE forward, which causes lee helm—if the boat is not heeled. I will not go into pris-matic coefficients and other fancy terms, but suffice to say that most hulls have more buoyancy aft than forward, and when a boat heels it causes the bow to go to windward— the same effect as weather helm. Perhaps you remember dinghy sail-ing where hiking hard in puffs kept the boat under control.

To restore the relationship of CE to CLR (move the CE aft to balance the boat), the furled genoa should be completely struck or furled and a staysail set on an inner forestay.

Off the wind. Boats, like people and chains, are happiest being pulled, rather than pushed. Broad reaching in heavy wind, a boat will behave much better with a jib or genoa and no main than with a mainsail alone. Even in less than gale conditions, reefing the main so it is not blanketing the genoa results in easier steering and faster speeds. Genoa area is usually more than mainsail area on modern boats, and using the larger sail to pull rather than a smaller area to push is prefer-able. One must be *very* careful that concentrating loading at the mast-head from reducing or eliminating mainsail does not result in the mast developing compression bends. An inner forestay and running back-stays will help stabilize the stick. Be sure to sight up the mast in heavy weather to observe pumping. All mast materials are subject to fatigue from repeated bending.

I once owned a boat in which the designer placed the CE too far aft of the CLR. The vessel was very close winded, but on a reach I would often have to reduce main-sail area to avoid broaching. After the windward mark it sure seemed funny to be putting in a reef while other boats shook theirs out.

Fore-and-Aft Weight Distribution   **TIP 172**

All racing boats, and some cruising vessels, make a great effort to concentrate weight amidships. Yes, locating everything heavy (engine, tankage, etc.) in the middle of a vessel does improve performance so the bow and stern have less inertia to overcome going through waves. With decreased inertia comes quick movement. Spending time on the foredeck of a modern racing boat beating into a moderate chop is somewhat akin to being on a trampoline.

There are safety questions about decreasing the ability of a bow or stern to quickly ride up on waves, but weight in the ends of a yacht will make for a smoother, albeit wetter, ride. One must remember that inertia is the product of an item's weight multiplied by the distance from the center of gravity *squared*.

Unfortunately, most naval architects are more performance than cruising oriented, and do not allow for the weight of a windlass and a lot of chain in the bow. Compounding the problem is that most modern designs have less wetted surface (read buoyancy) forward than aft. The formula for determining longitudinal center of buoyancy (LCB) is very long, and some naval architects simply cut out a piece of cardboard equaling the areas of the immersed hull and balance it on a knife blade to determine LCB. In *Principles of Yacht Design* (International Marine), Lars Larsson and

Rolf Eliasson state that this method is as accurate as a mathematical model. In any event, one has only to look at the underbody of a yacht to estimate the relative forward and aft volume of the hull, both upright and heeled. Because the aft portions almost always have more volume, more weight will be required aft to sink the hull to a level condition. Crew weight in an aft cockpit helps, and a lot of smaller cruising boats are designed to float a little bow-down to accommodate people in the cockpit. Unfortunately, in most boats, one person in the cockpit does not equal a 45-pound anchor on a stemhead roller.

Rather than going through all sorts of mathematics, the yacht owner can use empirical data to determine the effect of heavy objects forward and aft on the vessel. A dinghy, a tape measure, and a piece of wood are all that you need to do this on a calm day. Let's say you are thinking about adding 200 feet of ⅜-inch BBB chain as a primary anchor rode (BBB is a type of chain frequently used with windlasses because it has short links). The catalog will tell you that ⅜-inch BBB chain weighs 1.7 pounds per foot. Therefore 200 feet will equal 340 pounds.

Fill water and fuel tanks to the level you normally carry. Loosen docklines. Get in the dinghy and measure the distance from a point on the stemhead to the piece of wood floating in the water. Also, take the measurement at the vessel's stern. Find a couple of people who together weigh about 340 pounds, and ask them to stand on deck over

the chain locker. Retake the measurements from the same points. You will now know the sinkage forward and slight increase in freeboard aft from the increased weight. As an example, let's use the following hypothetical measurements:

	Forward	Aft
Original measurements	40.0 in.	35.0 in.
With weight of chain	38.5 in.	35.5 in.

Look at the percentage difference:

Forward
1.5 inches ÷ 40 inches
= 3.75 percent

Aft
0.5 inch ÷ 35 inches
= 1.43 percent

Now you have a relative idea of the buoyancy forward and aft of the vessel.

If you want to return the vessel to the original waterline plane (less sinkage, which I'll cover in a moment), throw a party for the harbor. Have the original 340-pound people forward over the chain locker, and then add people aft over storage lockers or places where additional tankage or ballast could be added. Start with at least 680 pounds positioned an equal distance aft of the middle of the waterline as the "chain gang" is forward. All right, the LCB is not right in the middle of the waterline, but you have to start somewhere.

Overall Effect of Adding Weight to a Vessel   **TIP 173**

The term *sinkage* has nothing to do with the galley or the vessel going totally underwater. Sinkage is the term used to describe the effect of additional weight to a vessel. A very rough approximation can be made with the formula:

$$\text{tons per inch immersion} = (\text{length of waterline}) \times (\text{maximum beam at waterline}) \div 500$$

Length of Waterline, ft.	Waterline Beam, ft.	Pounds per Inch Immersion
25	8	750
30	9	1,050
35	10	1,350
40	12	1,800

A closer idea of sinkage can easily be found using the monograph in *Skene's Elements of Yacht Design*. I've picked off a few examples:

The best way to get an idea of sinkage, aside from asking the naval architect, is to obtain an IMS certificate from U.S. Sailing (see appendix 7) for a sister ship to your boat. The IMS certificate has a lot of good data, including speeds the vessel should achieve in various wind conditions.

A word on additional weight on a vessel: adding weight—whether it is gear, stores, or crew to a vessel—increases stability. With increased stability comes more force exerted on the rig and its supports. For years customers have said to me, "I'm going offshore and want to increase the size of my standing rigging."

My answer is, "Proper boats are designed like the proverbial one-horse chaise, and increasing the standing rigging size will just mean that something else will break first."

While naval architects do build in a safety factor to allow for added gear, loading a vessel with a double-digit percentage of her designed displacement is asking for trouble. The stability of the vessel will increase, and things will break, rather than the vessel heeling to spill wind.

PERSONAL COMFORT

What clothing you bring and what accessories you carry in your kit can make all the difference between pain and comfort. Here are some ideas born of experience.

Apparel   **TIP 174**

A frequent source of discomfort among offshore racers has been described as "rail tail" or "fiberglass ass." This itching and burning can be easily prevented. Starting after my last shower before departing on an ocean passage, I apply Desitin diaper rash ointment to the intended areas. On a Bermuda Race that took seven days, the bid among the crew on the sixth day was $5 for a 1-inch squeeze from the tube!

When a shower is not possible, premoistened Baby Wipes are great for a quick wipe-down, and being medicated, they also help with rash problems.

Cotton underwear tends to absorb salt water; I am much more comfortable in synthetic blends.

Although dark clothes don't show dirt, they're considerably hotter to wear in the sun. Also, someone overboard in a dark shirt is very difficult to spot, especially at night.

About a week before a passage, I get a short haircut. The time before departure allows my scalp to get some sun so sunburn is not a problem. Just before departure I cut all body hair about ⅜ inch long, which helps a lot in the comfort department.

For cold weather, I love Patagonia underwear. My favorite top has a turtleneck to stop water from running down, and I love my poly-propylene pile balaclava. The old expression, "If your feet are cold, put on a hat," certainly is true; my whole body warms up when I put on the balaclava.

For steering in cold weather I have a pair of bright orange lined rubber gloves that are frequently passed among the crew. Calf-high sea boots with poly pile socks keep me comfortable down to 25°F; foul-weather pants are tightly cinched around the outside. I put my initials in red on the left boot and green on the right, which helps to identify them in a locker and gets them on the correct foot when coming on watch at 3 A.M. Boots must not fit so tightly that they cannot be removed underwater.

For hot weather, I wear a cotton T-shirt, shorts, and loose-fitting synthetic underwear. A visor keeps glare and sweat out of the eyes. Be careful of suntan oils, which can make fiberglass very slippery. Many people like Hawaiian Tropic gel, which doesn't seem to run into your eyes as much as some other brands.

Sunglasses that wrap around or have side shields are effective in eliminating glare. Polarized sunglasses are recommended. I finally had to get bifocals so I could read a chart without taking off my sunglasses and frying my eyes.

Every boat should have a skindiver's mask on board. Not only is it useful for underwater inspections, but it is great protection from wind-driven spray and hail in storm conditions. Unless all your sailing is going to be in the tropics, also carry a skindiver's wet suit. Hypothermia can occur in water as warm as 70°F, and people work best in the water when not shivering. Make every effort to stay dry. Water sucks body heat twenty-six times faster than air. If fully immersed in 80°F water, a body loses heat at the same rate as in 42°F air.

Sea Bag Checklist for Five- to Seven-Day Passage   TIP 175

Note: For warm climates, add more shorts and shirts.

calf-high sea boots

foul-weather-gear top

chest-high foul-weather-gear pants

vinyl visor to wear under foul-weather-gear hood

cloth visor with terrycloth lining to keep sweat out of eyes

heavy wool or poly pile socks, to be worn inside sea boots

inflatable safety harness with tether plus re-arming pack

balaclava made of polypropylene pile

heavy rubber gloves

leather sailing gloves

two knives, one in foul-weather-gear pocket

small towel to go around neck under foul-weather gear

polypropylene long underwear pants

polypropylene long underwear top

two disposable flashlights with wrist tethers

three pairs nylon undershorts/panties

two to three pairs shorts

one pair synthetic long pants

one bathing suit

three pairs of socks

polypropylene pile jacket

one long-sleeved shirt

three or more short-sleeved polo shirts, light colors

two pairs of deck shoes

two pairs of sunglasses

dress clothes

dull paperback books

toiletries and medications: toothbrush, toothpaste, lip sunblock-moisturizer, SPF 30 sunblock, soap, moisturizer, shampoo and conditioner, Desitin, antihistamines, prescription drugs, comb or brush, nail clippers, tweezers

especially for men: razor, extra blades, shaving cream

especially for women: tampons and/or sanitary pads, medication for menstrual cramps; two sport bras

towel or absorbent chamois for drying off after showers

Sea Bags   **TIP 176**

My sea bags have a removable waterproof inner liner. I start a passage with clean clothes rolled and rubber-banded inside the inner liner. Dirty clothes are placed between the inner liner and the outside shell of the bag. The inner liner has handles on it, and on return trips I frequently remove it to make two sea bags when things are no longer neatly packed and I need more room. The bags also have voluminous pockets at each end and reinforced handles that the airlines have yet to rip off, despite a packed weight that has reached 93 pounds. The bags are custom made by All Hands Canvas in Newport, Rhode Island.

If you don't have a waterproof inner liner, pack clothes in zippered plastic bags. Save the resealable bags for dirty and wet clothes. A marker is handy to identify the bags with dirty clothes, and avoids opening the bag for a sniff.

Sleeping   **TIP 177**

When wet, resist the temptation to sleep in your foul-weather gear. Without air circulation, you will wake up bathed in sweat in all but the coldest conditions, and will leave your clothes wetter than when you started. Getting into dry clothes will make you much more comfortable. The best blankets are made from polypropylene pile. I have slept in the cockpit under a pile blanket and had it soaking wet

from dew in the morning. Wring it out and toss it over the boom; it'll be dry before the coffee is perked. S & S Fabric Products of Portsmouth, Rhode Island, makes polypropylene pile blankets, which they call Snug Sacks.

Foul-Weather Gear   **TIP 178**

All foul-weather gear should have retroreflective tape (*retroreflective* means it returns light in the same direction from which it came) all the way around each arm, on the shoulders, and on top of the hood. Two-inch-wide retroreflective tape with a strong adhesive is readily available and should be added to gear that does not come with it. After dark, I like to put a piece of retroreflective tape on the top of the toe of each sea boot to give better visibility to foot positions.

White foul-weather gear makes spotting a person overboard in breaking waves difficult. My gear is red, which is very visible in daylight, but not that good at night. Perhaps a better color would be hot pink, but then I would not wear it ashore. Best is international orange.

Seasickness   **TIP 179**

There are probably as many remedies for seasickness as there are sailors, but here are a few that my crews have used. I cannot attest to them, as I have not been bothered in the last 100,000 miles.

The pH cocktail. Pour a glass half full of 7-Up or similar soft drink. Add a teaspoon of sugar, which will make it fizz, and then a generous dollop of angostura bitters.

Liqueur. A pharmacist who regularly sails offshore with me has found that the digestive Jägermeister calms stomachs better than anything stocked in his stores. I've tried it and it has worked for me. The first sip tastes awful, but the flavor grows on you.

Ginger. A lot of people find ginger helps a queasy stomach. Keep a supply of gingersnap cookies on board, or use my recipe for Joe Froggers in chapter 7 (see page 158).

Scopolamine. If you plan on wearing Transderm Scop patches on the voyage, be sure to experiment with wearing one at home before the trip. Although undoubtedly the most effective seasickness medicine available, the patches have varying side effects on people, including hallucinations. Carry catheters on board, as the patches can cause difficulty in urination.

On the return passage from Bermuda after the 1991 Marion–Bermuda Race, the crew was from the Midwest and all wore patches. On the second night out, when I came up for the 4 A.M. watch, the crew going off told me about the dancing girls on the foredeck. After talking to them for a few minutes, I determined that they were not kidding, and ripped their patches off.

Stugeron. In Bermuda and elsewhere outside the United States, the best items to buy and take home are seasickness medications not available in the states. Most off- shore passagemakers swear by Stugeron. The active ingredient is cinnarizine, which my pharmacist tells me is not available in the United States even in generic form. If one does not take Stugeron in time, phenegrine suppositories are also available without prescription outside the United States.

STANDING WATCH ORDERS

Cruising offshore, with four equally competent crew, I like two-hour watches at night and three- or four-hour stints during the day, with one person on at a time. This gives everybody plenty of rest. If more hands are needed, the person coming on next is called. The danger with one-person watches is falling overboard. Hooking on with a harness (see Safety Harnesses, tip 2) is essential.

For racing, when the autopilot cannot be used, two people are necessary on watch.

I insist that the latitude and longitude be recorded in the log every hour, and sea temperature every 15 minutes when in the vicinity of the Gulf Stream or other currents with water temperature differentials. Wind direction and strength are helpful to establish trends.

I record the course made good (CMG) from the electronics rather than the course reportedly steered, and advance the DR (dead reckoning) from the electronics (GPS, loran, etc.) or distance log rather than estimates of speed. All helmspersons are optimistic about their speed. Electronics have failed me on passages, and having a position not more than an hour old from which to start an accurate DR is invaluable. If log space permits, I also like to record each hour the range and bearing to the waypoint (destination) from the electronics.

Except on the rare perfectly clear night, I keep the radar on standby; every 10 minutes I turn it on to transmit at least five swings. The range of any radar is essentially just a little more than the visual horizon, and it does a good job of showing up unlit objects. An ungimbaled radar, however, may miss targets, especially to leeward when the vessel is heeled. Radar and guard zones should be used only as an adjunct to visual observations, never a substitute for keeping watch.

I personally like the 4 A.M. to 6 A.M. watch, as my kidneys get me up at about that time anyway. To give me something to do while it is still dark, I precompute the azimuth of the rising sun, and then check it against the binnacle compass at sunrise. On many occasions I have found a flashlight with steel innards or other magnetic interference near the compass that has appeared during the night.

When relieved of my watch, I take a walk around the deck, looking up at the rig and noting any chafe on the running rigging. I also throw the flying fish overboard before they bake in the sun and smell. If they are decent size, I add hooks and use them as bait on the trolling line.

The standing order for the watch on deck just before sunset is to go around the deck, tidy up any sheet tails or halyards, be sure all spare halyards are straight, and generally prepare the boat for squalls that always seem to happen in the middle of the night. Another standing order for the watch coming on is to check the bilges for water. If powering, check the engine gauges at least every 15 minutes.

On every boat, emergency procedures should be planned in advance. Some skippers delegate certain responsibilities to specific people. I do not like to do this, because, for example, the person responsible for the abandon-ship bag might not be available, and the vital bag may be forgotten. I prefer that everybody know what needs to be accomplished. Following are some of the standing watch orders put together for *Agape*, a 1989 Alden 50. The standing watch orders are kept in a notebook at the navigation station, and each new crew is issued his or her own copy, along with diagrams of the vessel indicating locations of through-hull fittings (seacocks), emergency safety gear and tools, and spare parts. You will want to develop your own watch orders predicated on your vessel. Use these from *Agape* as a guide, and customize.

Crew Overboard **TIP 180**

1. Hit COB or MOB button on GPS in cockpit. Holler "Crew overboard!" as loudly as possible to arouse off-watch.

2. Throw cockpit cushions overboard.

3. Throw horseshoe life ring overboard with light and flag on pole. [On *Agape*, a center-cockpit boat, this is unfortunately mounted away from the cockpit.]

4. If at all possible, one person does nothing else except watch and point constantly at the person overboard.

5. Execute Quick Stop maneuver. (See ORC booklet on offshore equipment requirements; see source information for U.S. Sailing in appendix 7.) Remember, the vessel is likely to be moving at 14 feet per second.

6. Only after checking carefully for lines trailing overboard, start engine. Furl sails if required.

7. Return to COB position, approaching from downwind if possible.

8. Deploy Lifesling from stern.

9. Make concentric circles around person in water until person has taken hold of Lifesling. Then *stop* vessel. Shut off engine to avoid accidentally putting in gear and mutilating person with propeller.

10. Take in as much extra line on Lifesling yellow rope as possible. Make fast to any available cleat.

11. Rig spinnaker halyard with snatch block to cockpit winch. Attach shackle on spinnaker halyard around the yellow Lifesling line. (See also Spinnaker Halyard, tip 32.)

12. Hoist spinnaker halyard with cockpit winch, which will bring person on board amidships where there is the least chance of being hit on the head from the hull coming down off a wave.

Flooding Below Decks **TIP 181**

1. Get vessel as level as possible. Head downwind or heave-to if sailing.

2. Taste water. If fresh, there is no danger of vessel sinking (but

see Emergency Bilge Pump, tip 154!). If seawater, proceed with steps below.

3. Unless source of water is immediately evident, close all seacocks. See boat's diagram for locations. When closing seacocks, try to feel around each for a large flow of water entering vessel.

4. If engine is operating, open diverter valve to use engine as emergency bilge pump. Have someone constantly monitor the strainer on the engine bilge intake for clogging (see also Bilge Pump Strainers, tip 152).

5. The highest-capacity manual bilge pump [aboard *Agape*] is the Edson pump, located under galley sole (see also Aluminum Bilge Pumps, tip 153). Insert handle and pump with steady strokes.

6. If there is adequate crew, get buckets from lazarette and bail with buckets. Unless you are sure a cockpit scupper hose has not ruptured, dump buckets overboard rather than into cockpit.

7. The manual bilge pump in the cockpit discharges into a cockpit scupper hose. Buckets will remove water faster than this pump.

8. If water level does not recede, launch life raft, being sure tether is secured to vessel. See Abandoning Ship procedure, tip 182.

9. If water level is reduced to cabin sole level or lower, or extra crew are available, try to locate source of water ingress. Check for upward flow of water from bilge sump area where centerboard mechanism is located.

10. If flow of water is from a crack in the hull, use cockpit cushions wedged in place with cabin sole floorboards or any other members available to reduce flow of water. If needed, plywood from openings in berth tops can be used with a blanket under them.

11. If source of water is determined to be from a leaking hose, cut off hose at leak and drive a wood plug into hose end. See boat's diagram for location of wood plugs.

Abandoning Ship
TIP 182

1. The decision to abandon ship should not be made lightly. A vessel that is floating with the decks awash is a safer platform than a life raft. There is an old adage: "Never get into a life raft unless you have to step *up*."

2. The life raft on *Agape* has a hydrostatic release that will automatically deploy the raft when it is 15 feet underwater. The tether securing the life raft to the vessel is tied to the hydrostatic release, so the raft will come to the surface and rapidly be swept downwind. If the ves-

sel suddenly sinks, swim downwind as fast as possible to rendezvous with the raft when it comes up.

3. To launch the life raft manually, first secure the tether to a strong point on the vessel. Unless there is jagged debris to leeward (most likely from a broken mast), toss the raft overboard to leeward. Keep pulling on the painter until the raft inflates. It may be helpful to put the painter around a winch to take in the slack as the painter is pulled to keep the raft close to the boat. The painter is 30 feet long.

4. After the raft inflates, there *will be the sound of escaping gas. Do not worry* about the raft having a leak. All rafts have an excess capacity of gas to inflate them and a safety valve to release the excess gas.

5. If the raft inflates upside down, there are straps on the underside with which it can be righted. Use the wind to help with this operation.

6. Take abandon-ship bag to the raft. [See appendix 4, page 205, for list of contents.]

7. After all crew are on board the raft, appoint one person to stand by the tether connecting the raft to the vessel. There is a pocket with a knife in it close to the tether attachment to the raft. The knife should only be used to cut the tether when the raft is being pulled un-

derwater by the main vessel.

8. Activate the EPIRB stowed in the abandon-ship bag. The antenna will transmit through the canopy of the raft so there is no need to hold it outside. Hold the EPIRB upright and above body level inside the raft.

9. If a ship or aircraft is observed or heard, turn on the handheld VHF radio and attempt to establish communication on channel 16.

10. The coverage of the 406 MHz EPIRB is worldwide, but it may take days to divert a rescue vessel. Deploy drogue on life raft to stay as close to original position as possible.

11. Keep calm. Maintain one person on watch at all times. Only fire flares when a ship or aircraft is sighted. Be sure to hold handheld flares well away from the life raft, as they may drip burning material.

12. Ration food and water. The abandon-ship bag has a watermaker in it that can make enough freshwater to sustain the entire crew indefinitely. Only use the canned water in the raft if the device fails.

Deck Log Entries
TIP 183

A deck log is used to record information on passages and is distinct from a permanent ship's log. See opposite.

Time	Latitude	Longitude	COG	BRG	Range	Range Delta	Log	Log Delta	True Dir.	Wind Vel.	Bar.		Watch	Comments
									Date 9/25/01					
				Waypoint CCN										
0600	42° 07′	70° 19′	215	216	21.1		40.3		182	12	1019		WS	Powering
0700	42° 01′	70° 21′	213	215	16.5	4.6	46.5	6.2	171	14	1019		WS	Powering Adverse Current
0800	41° 57′	70° 23′	213	214	11.8	4.7	53.4	6.9	160	13	1020		JG	Powering Adverse Current
0900	41° 52′	70° 26′	211	212	4.7	7.1	60.2	6.8	152	15	1021		JG	Sailing—Out of Current

Sample cruising log.

Time. Fill in hourly. If you are not right on the hour, that's OK. Be honest and fill in the actual time the readings are recorded.

Also fill in any course deviation of more than 5 degrees, and record the time of the course change.

Latitude. Record only degrees and whole minutes, unless navigating on soundings in fog. Round decimal parts of a minute up or down to yield a whole number.

Longitude. Same as Latitude.

COG. Record course over ground from GPS. Watch instrument for several minutes and take average of readings.

Waypoint. Enter first few letters of the destination waypoint.

BRG. Record the GPS bearing to the waypoint.

Range. Record the GPS range (distance) to the waypoint in whole number of miles, rounding up or down as appropriate.

Range Delta. Subtract the current entry on "Range" from the previous entry. The difference is the distance made good toward the waypoint. If log entries are made hourly, this number will also be the average speed toward the waypoint.

Log. Record the distance from the trip log in whole number of miles.

Log Delta. Subtract the current "Log" entry from the previous entry. The difference is the distance through the water. If log entries are made hourly, this number will also be the average speed through the water.

True Wind

  Dir. Record true wind direction from nav station or cockpit electronics. Watch display for several minutes and average the readings.

  Vel. Velocity or speed is the same source as Dir.

  Bar. Record barometric pressure from electronic barometer.

(Blank) Use the blank column for various information, possibly:
- Water temperature when in the vicinity of the Gulf Stream or eddies.
- Engine temperature or oil pressure if either are acting abnormally.

Watch. Initials of the person recording log data.

Comments. General information such as weather conditions like thunderstorms or developing clouds.

NAVIGATION AND WEATHER

One of my customers was discussing a planned passage, and said, "I want to avoid heavy weather, so I've picked August, because the pilot charts indicate only a 10 percent likelihood of gales."

My reply was: "The trip is 2,000 miles. Your boat makes about 150 miles a day, so you are looking at about 14 days in transit. Therefore, you should have 1.4 days of gales."

"I never thought of it that way," the customer replied.

I felt vindicated when the trip log indicated 32 hours of Force 8+ winds.

Compasses   TIP 184

Today, accurate headings are available from GPS and most autopilots have fluxgate compasses, making an accurately calibrated binnacle compass less important.

Rod Stephens used to hate built-in compensators, as he alleged

they caused heeling error. I once mounted a compass on a board and inclined the board. At 45 degrees the compass heading changed by 2 degrees. At that angle of heel, I do not know any helmsmen who could steer that accurately.

I have built-in compensators on my binnacle compass only because I took them out and hid them when Rod was on board; otherwise, he would have thrown them overboard. After he left, I replaced them.

The very thorough owner of *Spirit*, a Hinckley Sou'wester 51 yawl, hired a professional compass adjuster to check the binnacle compass before our transatlantic passage in 1999. Once we were out running courses, the adjuster placed a large screwdriver by the compass to cause change and then noted that the compass did not return to its original heading. He told the owner that the compass was shot and needed rebuilding (which he could do) or replacement (which he could provide). I suggested that we remove the built-in compensators. The compass then worked properly . . . and there is a compass adjuster in Miami who is on my black list.

Almost all compass cards have compensating weights for the dip toward the North Pole in the Northern Hemisphere that, when you are well south of the equator, must be moved for accuracy.

Before removing a binnacle compass, be sure you know which screws remove the compass (usually round-head ones), and which seal the unit (generally flat-heads). If the compass develops an air bubble, the fluid can be refilled. A good grade of mineral spirits will work. Remove the compass and find the filler port. Hold the compass with the filler port at the highest point, then fill the compass. A West System epoxy syringe makes a convenient filling tool. It may take several tries to get rid of the last air in the dome.

I once had a compass that developed a hole in its diaphragm and all the fluid leaked out. We were off on a race week, so I sacrificed some old foul-weather gear to make a new diaphragm, and filled the compass with available fluid. At season's end, when I sent the compass back to the manufacturer for proper repair, they sent the repaired compass back with a note asking me to please flush the compass before refilling, as the residual mineral spirits had spoiled the gin I had used to fill it.

Polars on Passages   TIP 185

No, this is not about the Arctic. A polar diagram is a graphic representation of the theoretical speed a sailboat should achieve in different wind speeds and angles to the wind. Polar diagrams use true wind speed, not apparent, and most use true wind angle. Most wind instruments these days output true wind speed and direction, so I will not digress on how to obtain these numbers mathematically. The formulas are found in most texts on navigation.

Polar diagrams obtained from U.S. Sailing (see appendix 7) offer the option of using apparent wind angle. In the following examples, I'll use true wind, which more clearly demonstrates the difference in boat speed.

Quite often the fastest progress toward a destination is not achieved by sailing either the rhumb line or great circle route. Armed with a polar diagram for the vessel, the navigator can determine the fastest course. Here's how.

1. Determine the magnetic heading of true wind.

2. Determine the magnetic bearing to your destination.

3. Subtract wind direction from bearing to obtain the true wind angle, which in the polar you will use as your course to steer. You are looking for a number between 0 and 180 degrees. You may need to add 360 degrees to one of the numbers. If you get confused, draw it on a piece of paper.

4. Locate the true wind angle on the perimeter of the polar diagram. Draw a line from this point to the center of the polar diagram.

5. Determine true wind speed and locate this curve on the polar.

6. Slide a right angle down the line from step 4 until the leg contacts the closest tangent point of the true wind speed curve. Interpolate between wind strength bands if necessary. Mark the point of tangency, that is, where the right angle touches the curve.

7. Draw a line from the center of the polar diagram through the tangent point to the perimeter of polar. Read the number on the polar perimeter.

8. The difference between the number in step 4 and the one determined in step 7 is the number of degrees to alter course, high or low depending on

whether it adds or subtracts boat speed, to make the best speed toward destination *in the present conditions*.

The above explanation probably seems inordinately complicated. Let's do an example (see illustration; see also explanation under You Can't Always Get What You Want in appendix 1):

Inputs:
true wind direction = 280°
bearing to destination = 165°
true wind speed = 10 knots

Therefore, the angle between wind and bearing is 280° − 165° = 115°.

After performing steps 4 through 7 you'll find that the angle from step 7 is 104°. Therefore, deviation from course will be 115° − 104° = 11°. We'll subtract the 11° and head up, making the course to steer 165° − 11° = 154°.

Let's do another example, but with the wind heading us and of a little less velocity.

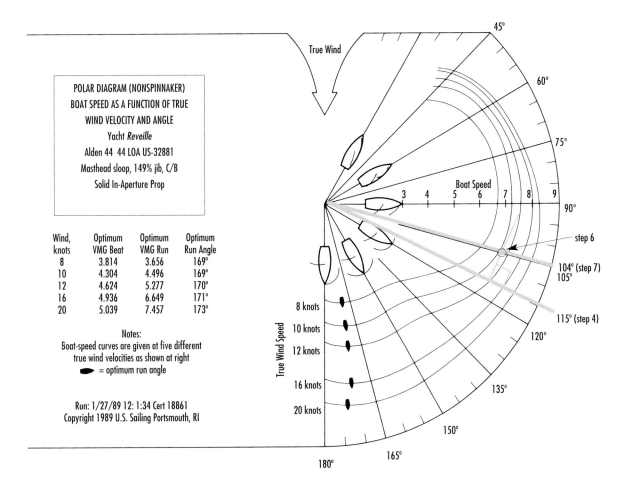

POLAR DIAGRAM (NONSPINNAKER)
BOAT SPEED AS A FUNCTION OF TRUE
WIND VELOCITY AND ANGLE
Yacht *Reveille*
Alden 44 44 LOA US-32881
Masthead sloop, 149% jib, C/B
Solid In-Aperture Prop

Wind, knots	Optimum VMG Beat	Optimum VMG Run	Optimum Run Angle
8	3.814	3.656	169°
10	4.304	4.496	169°
12	4.624	5.277	170°
16	4.936	6.649	171°
20	5.039	7.457	173°

Notes:
Boat-speed curves are given at five different
true wind velocities as shown at right
= optimum run angle

Run: 1/27/89 12: 1:34 Cert 18861
Copyright 1989 U.S. Sailing Portsmouth, RI

Polar diagrams can be used to determine the fastest course between two points.

Inputs:
true wind direction = 210°
bearing is still 165° (we're headed from
Newport to Bermuda)
true wind speed = 8 knots

The angle between bearing and wind is 210°−165°=45°. Great! If we stay hard on the wind we can fetch St. George's! But let's see whether this course will get us to Dark and Stormys the fastest (see diagram).

Using steps 4 through 7, you'll find that the line from step 7 intersects the polar perimeter at 63°. Therefore, the fastest course will be 63°−45°=18° deviation from course. So 165° bearing + 18°=183° course to steer. According to the polars, boat speed should increase a knot by footing off (5.4 knots at 45° versus 6.4 at 63°).

Because most modern GPS units are able to monitor the speed of advance (SOA) toward a waypoint, one can easily check the affect of altering course to the best polar speed. If there are still doubts, make a vector diagram of boat velocity and angles. Draw concentric circles from the destination to intersect the vectors (see drawing, next page).

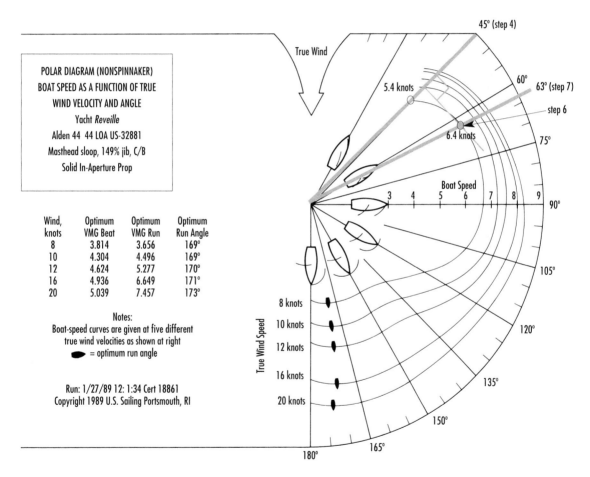

POLAR DIAGRAM (NONSPINNAKER)
BOAT SPEED AS A FUNCTION OF TRUE
WIND VELOCITY AND ANGLE
Yacht *Reveille*
Alden 44 44 LOA US-32881
Masthead sloop, 149% jib, C/B
Solid In-Aperture Prop

Wind, knots	Optimum VMG Beat	Optimum VMG Run	Optimum Run Angle
8	3.814	3.656	169°
10	4.304	4.496	169°
12	4.624	5.277	170°
16	4.936	6.649	171°
20	5.039	7.457	173°

Notes:
Boat-speed curves are given at five different
true wind velocities as shown at right
◆ = optimum run angle

Run: 1/27/89 12: 1:34 Cert 18861
Copyright 1989 U.S. Sailing Portsmouth, RI

In this example, boat speed is increased by 1 knot when footing off 18°.

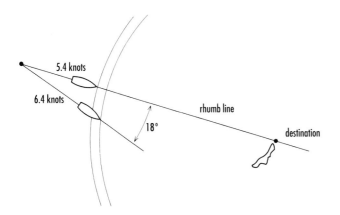

By drawing concentric circles around your destination, you can easily determine which course and speed will get you there fastest. In this illustration, the boat making 6.4 knots and deviating from the rhumb line is closer. (Tip 185)

Note that polar diagrams depict fastest speed *in the present conditions*. Especially when going downwind, small changes in wind velocity will have a large impact on the fastest course. On the sample polar diagrams, look at the 150-degree wind angle. Note that there is almost a knot and a half difference of boat speed between 12 and 16 knots true wind speed. This phenomenon happens with most boats, and is called the *downwind cliff*. After racing boats discovered the cliff, bloopers disappeared and crews began jibing often on downwind legs.

"But if I spend time altering course all over the ocean, I'll never get to the destination," you may think. Remember that 25 miles from rhumb line only requires a 5-degree course change to close over 300 miles. In general, I go for boat speed until about 50 miles from the destination.

Polar diagrams are available from U.S. Sailing as part of a Per-

formance Package. The polars will be customized to your genoa overlap, propeller type, and spinnaker or nonspinnaker.

Altering Course   TIP 186

During a 1996 transatlantic passage, the crew from the Midwest became concerned about crosstrack error displayed on the GPS. Since we were more than a thousand miles from our destination, I was interested in sailing the fastest polar speeds, not in the shortest distance.

"Don't worry, we'll get back on course," I told them.

On my next solitary night watch, I reset the GPS to start from our present position. Bearing to waypoint stayed the same, but crosstrack error disappeared, and the crew was so happy that I made the same adjustment on every solitary watch.

SECANTS (TIP 187)

Angle	Secant	Angle	Secant	Angle	Secant
0°	1.0000	16°	1.0403	31°	1.1666
1°	1.0002	17°	1.0457	32°	1.1792
2°	1.0006	18°	1.0515	33°	1.1924
3°	1.0014	19°	1.0576	34°	1.2062
4°	1.0024	20°	1.0642	35°	1.2208
5°	1.0038	21°	1.0711	36°	1.2361
6°	1.0055	22°	1.0785	37°	1.2521
7°	1.0075	23°	1.0864	38°	1.2690
8°	1.0098	24°	1.0946	39°	1.2868
9°	1.0125	25°	1.1034	40°	1.3054
10°	1.0154	26°	1.1126	41°	1.3250
11°	1.0187	27°	1.1223	42°	1.3456
12°	1.0223	28°	1.1326	43°	1.3673
13°	1.0263	29°	1.1434	44°	1.3902
14°	1.0306	30°	1.1547	45°	1.4142
15°	1.0353				

Making the Best Time on Passages TIP 187

One does not need to use polar data, however, to sail at the maximum speed to a destination if experimentation with various deviations from course and the resultant speed change can be made. Using this method, you can quickly determine the course that will get you to your destination in the least amount of time.

The Secants table shows the percentage of speed increase necessary (under Secant column) to break even at the deviation from rhumb line shown in the Angle column.

The accuracy of the boat's knotmeter is not critical, because only the relative percentage increase is used in the calculations.

Example:

course to destination = 165°
speed on course = 6.0 knots
experimental course deviation = 10°
secant of 10° = 1.0154
speed on experimental course
= 6.1 knots

Question: *Is this speed increase worth the extra distance sailed?*

Answer: *Original speed × secant of angle change: 6.0 × 1.0154 = 6.09 knots*

Therefore, deviation from the first course of 165 degrees is a little more beneficial—albeit just a hundredth of a knot. Stated another way, if falling off 10 degrees, you would need to exceed 6.09 knots to make the course change worthwhile. Because speed on the new course is 6.1 knots, the course deviation will get you to your destination quicker, but just barely.

If you don't have a calculator handy, use the Speed to Exceed at Angles Off the Direct Course chart, below.

Cosines TIP 188

Having the cosines of a few angles can be very helpful. Just in case your high school trigonometry text is not a book you cherish and keep handy, here they are.

5°	0.99619
10°	0.98481
15°	0.96593
20°	0.93969
25°	0.90631
30°	0.86603
35°	0.81915
40°	0.76604
45°	0.70711

Question: *You have run aground. Your boat draws 6 feet when upright. You think you can heel your boat 10 degrees by kedging with an anchor. How much is this going to reduce your draft?*

Answer: *Multiply the nominal draft by the cosine of 10 degrees: 6 × 0.98481 = 5.909. Shucks, only a tenth of a foot!*

SPEED TO EXCEED AT ANGLES OFF THE DIRECT COURSE

Speed Direct (knots)	10°	20°	30°	40°
2	2.03	2.1	2.3	2.6
3	3.04	3.2	3.5	3.9
3.5	3.55	3.7	4.0	4.6
4	4.06	4.3	4.6	5.2
4.5	4.6	4.8	5.2	5.9
5	5.07	5.3	5.8	6.5
5.5	5.6	5.9	6.4	7.2
6	6.09	6.4	6.9	7.8
6.5	6.6	6.9	7.5	8.5
7	7.1	7.5	8.1	9.1
7.5	7.6	8.0	8.7	9.8
8	8.1	8.5	9.2	10.4
8.5	8.6	9.0	9.8	11.1
9	9.1	9.6	10.4	11.7
9.5	9.6	10.1	11.0	12.4

Question: *The toerail is under-water at about 30 degrees angle of heel. What will the draft be then?*

Answer: *6 ×0.86603 = 5.2. Well, that's a little better, but not what we'd hoped for.*

Cosines also work to determine the height of the mast with your boat heeled, just in case you want to sail under any bridges (not recommended!).

Communication with Southbound II VAX 498, Herb Hilgenberg TIP 189

Herb Hilgenberg is the best source of free weather and ship routing for the Atlantic Ocean available on SSB radio.

Following years of cruising, Herb now lives close to Toronto and spends most of his waking hours analyzing weather. He has more than $50,000 worth of operating equipment, all bought with his own funds and contributions. Herb is so busy with weather that he doesn't have time for a full-time job. I always send him a generous donation before departing on an Atlantic passage. To put it in perspective, a commercial weather service may charge $200 or more for a single forecast prior to departure. Talking to Herb every day to get up-to-the-minute weather information is worth much more.

Herb broadcasts on 12359.0 (ITU channel 1253 or 12 Charlie) at 2000 UTC daily.

About 1945 UTC, call "Southbound Two, this is (boat name) at (latitude and longitude—whole degrees only), standing by."

Herb will come up at 2000 UTC and broadcast all the vessel names he has copied, then give a moment for others to call in. If the transmission is your first on a passage, it is essential that Herb have your rough location so he can schedule transmission to you with his directional antennas when propagation is likely to be the best (see SSB Frequency Propagation, page 228).

Depending on propagation, Herb may start talking to boats anywhere in the Atlantic Ocean. His general scheme is to start with boats north of 28 degrees, then cover the eastern Atlantic, moving westward. If there are boats north of Bermuda, Herb may switch to 8294.0 (ITU channel 851 or 8 Alpha) about an hour into the broadcast (approximately 2100 UTC). If you cannot hear Herb on 12359 at 2000 UTC, switch to 8294 and leave the radio on until at least 2130 UTC.

Propagation varies, and if you cannot copy Herb one day, try the next. Herb also maintains contact with commercial vessels, so if you hear a vessel say they are steaming at 20 knots, there's no need to be jealous.

When he calls you, have the following information handy:

- Your location in degrees and whole minutes only.

- Exact barometric pressure in millibars (see conversion table,

opposite). Before departure, take your barometer to the closest airport and calibrate it to the airport's barometer.

- Present wind strength in knots (true, not apparent) and wind direction in compass points, not degrees—e.g., north-northwest.

- Any changes in conditions of significance—e.g., frontal passages.

- Wave height and condition—e.g., 4-foot waves on 10-foot swells.

- Sky conditions.

If I were on the S/V *Agape*, the conversation might go like this:

Herb: *"Let's go to boats headed for the leeward islands, starting with Agape. Do you copy?"*

Bill: *"Roger, Southbound Two, this is Agape. We are at 21 degrees 23 minutes north, 65 degrees, 45 minutes west. Barometer 1021 and steady. Wind east-southeast at 15 knots, gusting to 20. Had squall line pass at 0400 Zulu. Waves 5 feet from the east. 20 percent cumulus cloud cover. Over."*

Herb: *"Good report, Agape. I expect your winds to continue for 6 hours, then gradually shift more easterly and increase to 25 to 30 knots. Tomorrow conditions should moderate with winds becoming 15 to 20 knots and perhaps shifting a little*

Barometric and Temperature Conversions

In.	MB	In.	MB	°C	°F	°C	°F
27	914	30.05	1,017.7	0	32	35	95
27.1	918	30.1	1,019.4	1	33.8	36	96.8
27.2	921	30.15	1,021	2	35.6	37	98.6
27.3	925	30.2	1,022.7	3	37.4	38	100.4
27.4	928	30.25	1,024.4	4	39.2	39	102.2
27.5	931	30.3	1,026.1	5	41	40	104
27.6	935	30.35	1,027.8	6	42.8	41	105.8
27.7	938	30.4	1,029.5	7	44.6	42	107.6
27.8	941	30.45	1,031.2	8	46.4	43	109.4
27.9	945	30.5	1,032.9	9	48.2	44	111.2
28.0	948	30.55	1,034.6	10	50	45	113
28.1	952	30.6	1,036.3	11	51.8	46	114.8
28.2	955	30.65	1,038	12	53.6	47	116.6
28.3	958	30.7	1,039.7	13	55.4	48	118.4
28.4	962	30.75	1,041.4	14	57.2	49	120.2
28.5	965	30.8	1,043.1	15	59	50	122
28.6	969	30.85	1,044.8	16	60.8		
28.7	972	30.9	1,046.4	17	62.6	60	140
28.8	975	30.95	1,048.1	18	64.4		
28.9	979	31.0	1,049.8	19	66.2	70	158
29.0	982			20	68		
29.1	986			21	69.8	80	176
29.2	989			22	71.6		
29.3	992			23	73.4	90	194
29.4	996			24	75.2		
29.5	999			25	77	100	212
29.6	1,002			26	78.8		
29.7	1,006			27	80.6		
29.8	1,008			28	82.4		
29.9	1,013			29	84.2		
30.0	1,016			30	86		
				31	87.8		
				32	89.6		
				33	91.4		
				34	93.2		

south of east. Wednesday a cold front will move off the U.S. East Coast, which could produce squalls and variable winds where you will be by then. Have a good watch."

Bill: *"Thanks, Herb. Copied all. This is Agape, Whiskey Alpha Mike 9er371 clear with Victor Alpha X-ray 49er8."*

Herb may give you a waypoint to go to. If he does, follow his instructions. Chances are he has looked at the long-range situation and has reasons for the suggestion, which he may not have time to explain on the radio.

On the last day of a passage, let Herb know that you will be getting into port before the next transmission time, so he can take you off his list and not waste time preparing

Phonetic Alphabet

The International Phonetic Alphabet was devised by NATO to facilitate radio communications. It's still widely used, particularly at sea.

Alfa	Juliet	Sierra
Bravo	Kilo	Tango
Charlie	Lima	Uniform
Delta	Mike	Victor
Echo	November	Whiskey
Foxtrot	Oscar	X-ray
Golf	Papa	Yankee
Hotel	Quebec	Zulu
India	Romeo	

a forecast you will not need or attempting to contact your vessel.

If you want to send a contribution, the address is Herb Hilgenberg, 5468 Hixon Ave., Burlington, Ontario L7L 3S2, Canada.

Recording the Broadcast   TIP 190

When a synthesized voice announces the weather, it is easy to miss writing down the information. I record the broadcast on a small tape recorder so I can play it back and fast-forward through those portions of the broadcast that are not germane to our position. This way, if I am called away from the radio or attention lapses, I do not have to wait six hours or longer for the next broadcast.

Weather on the Web   TIP 191

In addition to charts that come over the SSB radio, I have found better weather information at the Naval Atlantic Meteorology and Oceanography Center Web site, www.nlmoc.navy.mil.

Nigel Calder has collected a useful list of additional weather sources on the Web.

http://weather.noaa.gov/fax/ marine.shtml and *http:// weather.noaa.gov/fax/nwsfax. shtml:* Synoptic charts, 500-millibar charts, and associated data and analyses for North America and the entire world, from the NOAA and the Na-tional Weather Service (NWS) (the home pages for NOAA and NWS are *www.noaa.gov/* and *www.nws.noaa.gov/*).

www.mpc.ncep.noaa.gov/: NOAA's Marine Prediction Center. Twelve-, twenty-four-, and forty-eight-hour forecasts for the oceans. This is a fabulous free service for the mariner containing an incredible wealth of data and analyses. Go to the Radiofacsimile Charts User's Guide for an explanation of the various products supplied. It is well worth spending some time at this site and familiarizing yourself with many of the products.

www.nhc.noaa.gov: NOAA's Tropical Prediction Center/ National Hurricane Center home page.

www.srh.noaa.gov/tlh/wxhwy.html: Weather information super-highway; links to weather in-formation around the globe.

www.weather.unisys.com: A thor-ough source of graphical weather information (from the NWS) for the United States, including satellite pictures and analysis, and a ten-day 500-millibar forecast.

http://fermi.jhuapl.edu/: Satellite images of sea-surface tempera-tures, especially the Gulf Stream.

www.ndbc.noaa.gov/Maps/rmd. shtml and *http://seabord.ndbc.*

noaa.gov: Near real-time weather data from offshore buoys, primarily around the coast of the United States.

http://weather.msfc.nasa.gov: Weather satellite imagery for the world.

http://manati.wwb.noaa.gov/doc/ ssmiwinds.html: Ocean sur-face wind speeds (but not di-rection).

www.fnoc.navy.mil/: Ocean weather features, including wind speed and direction, for the world.

www.navcen.uscg.gov/: The USCG Navigation Center home page.

www.met-office.gov.uk: The home page of the British meteoro-logical office, with detailed forecasts for the United King-dom and its surrounding wa-ters, and a page of useful links to other meteorological offices around the world.

www.bbc.co.uk/weather/: The British Broadcasting Corpora-tion (BBC) weather services home page. Click on Ship-ping Forecast or Inshore Wa-ters for the United Kingdom–region marine forecasts.

www.marineweather.com: A com-mercial weather site with a great collection of free synop-tic charts, satellite images, wind and current analyses, and more, collected from nu-merous official sources.

www.navcenter.com: A commercial site that has an expanding amount of useful (free) data on wind speeds and directions, and other weather-related information for sailors, with worldwide coverage categorized by region.

Reprinted from *Nigel Calder's Cruising Handbook: A Compendium for Coastal and Offshore Sailors,* courtesy International Marine.

Chart Copies   TIP 192

Charts of frequently traveled routes inevitably get so covered with position records and other hen scratches that it becomes difficult to determine whether the last recorded position was a few hours ago or years ago.

One solution is to carry colored pencils and use a different color for each trip.

A better answer is to have the needed sections of charts photocopied. Most copy centers have the large paper machines used for copying blueprints. The entire chart does not have to be copied. As I make the run often, I have whited out the Omega lines and added a heavy-lined latitude and longitude grid in 1-degree increments to chart 403, which covers Newfoundland to the Caribbean. A chart table-size 12- by 16-inch copy covers the U.S. East Coast to Bermuda. A 12- by 20-inch section gets you from Bermuda to the Caribbean. At a couple of bucks a pop, it is not a major calamity if the chart gets wet or blows overboard (provided you have spare copies, of course).

On black-and-white copies of coastal charts, it is useful to fill in with colored pencil those areas that are too shallow for your boat. In the middle of the night, you're more likely to be alerted by a red area than by hard-to-read numbers.

Length of Degree of Longitude   TIP 193

Although a GPS can provide you with this information, I find it handy to have a table of longitude length for making plotting sheets and guesstimates on east–west passages. *Bowditch* has the exact figures from which this table was developed, but it is a big, heavy book. I've listed 2-degree increments and avoided high latitudes where nobody in their right mind would want to go.

Chart Table Cover   TIP 194

The last thing you want to do to your beautifully varnished teak navigation table is to poke it full of holes with divider points. To protect it, cover the chart table with a piece of the special linoleum-like product used for covering drafting tables. Small holes from dividers "heal" themselves, and the surface is resilient to dropped objects. The material is available in tan and light green from drafting supply houses, but with the change to CAD (computer-aided design), drafting table cover is becoming harder to find.

LONGITUDE LENGTH BY LATITUDE
(TIP 193)

Latitude	Length of Degree of Longitude
0°	60.01 nm
2°	60.03 nm
4°	59.9 nm
6°	59.7 nm
8°	59.5 nm
10°	59.2 nm
12°	58.8 nm
14°	58.3 nm
16°	57.8 nm
18°	57.1 nm
20°	56.5 nm
22°	55.7 nm
24°	54.9 nm
26°	54.0 nm
28°	53.1 nm
30°	52.1 nm
32°	51.0 nm
34°	49.9 nm
36°	48.7 nm
38°	47.4 nm
40°	46.1 nm
42°	44.7 nm
44°	43.3 nm
46°	41.8 nm
48°	40.3 nm
50°	38.7 nm
52°	37.1 nm
54°	35.4 nm
56°	33.7 nm
58°	31.9 nm
60°	30.1 nm
62°	28.3 nm
64°	26.4 nm
66°	24.5 nm
68°	22.6 nm
70°	20.6 nm

Datums · TIP 195

I got a call from an owner who had sailed to Trinidad saying something was wrong with his GPS. He said he was in a harbor, but the built-in chart on the GPS showed he was a mile inland. It took a long time to explain chart datums, at very expensive international phone rates.

I fell prey to complacency on one trip to the Caribbean. I entered our destination waypoint from a detailed chart, as we needed to stay about a half mile off an unlit island. On the last night out, the crew woke me to report that there appeared to be a large object directly ahead of us. I turned on the radar and saw that the object was the island. (Fortunately, there was enough moonlight for the island to be visible to the crew.)

In checking, the detailed chart was not the same WGS-84 datum as the GPS was using. Also, the last survey date on the chart was 1895.

On Closing with Ships · TIP 196

Merchant ships generally travel in the low 20-knot range. The *Queen Elizabeth II* was going 34 knots when she ran aground off Nantucket a few years ago.

As shown earlier, the formula for viewable distance to the horizon in perfectly clear conditions is

$$nm = 1.144 \times \sqrt{h}$$

in which nm is nautical miles and h is height of eye in feet.

Let's assume that a person standing up in a sailboat is 10 feet off the water. This puts the horizon at 3.6 miles. Most people think the horizon is farther away. The largest guess I've had given to me was 50 miles. In reality, because the area of a circle is pi × radius squared (πr^2), offshore you are in a 40.7-square-mile "world."

To get the visible range of an object, one takes the sum of the observer's horizon and the same formula applied to the height of the object.

Let's take a ship 50 feet tall, in waves, with perhaps 30 feet visible:

$$1.14 \times \sqrt{30}$$

is 6.24 miles. Added to the 3.6 miles calculated above for a person whose eyes are 10 feet above the water, the ship will be visible at 9.9 miles.

Let's assume the vessels are on reciprocal courses, with the ship traveling at 22 knots and the sailboat at 8 knots. This yields a closing speed of 30 knots. Therefore, the time between the moment a ship first becomes visible on the horizon and impact occurs is one-third of an hour, or 20 minutes.

If the ship were a liner like the *QE2*, with a height of 150 feet, her range would be 14 miles, so we'd have a total of 17.6 miles. The liner's speed of 34 knots + 8 knots for the sailboat yields a closing speed of 42 knots. This gives a little more time—25.7 minutes—for evasive action.

OK, you say, the chances of being on exactly reciprocal courses are slight. Let's look at a merchant ship approaching on a 30-degree angle from our bow.

For the mathematically inclined, the formula for closing speed is the square root of the sum of your speed squared and the other vessel's speed squared, minus twice the product of both vessels' speed multiplied by the cosine of the crossing angle:

$$c = \sqrt{a^2 + b^2 - (2\,ab \times \cos C)}$$

This is the formula for two sides and the included angle of a triangle in plane geometry. Yes, we should use spherical geometry, as the Earth is round, but that's a whole lot more complicated!

Now that you are totally confused, for our merchant ship example the closing speed of an 8-knot vessel and a 22-knot vessel at 30 degrees is 15.5 knots. Therefore you have 40 minutes, assuming the same visibility.

Remember that such calculations are predicated on perfectly clear conditions—no haze, no fog, and 20/20 vision on the part of the observer.

Thermometer · TIP 197

Having a means to measure water temperature is very desirable to determine entrance into the Gulf Stream or other ocean currents denoted by a marked temperature differential, not to mention eddies off the stream. A RadioShack remote thermometer with a probe on a wire can be taped in contact with a metal through-hull fitting.

For better response, however, I affix the probe and wire to a line with a fishing sinker on the end and drop the probe down a drain (such as a cockpit scupper) so it is immersed in water, but does not extend below the bottom of the boat. The temperature change at the west wall of the stream is usually dramatic and rapid. On my last passage to Bermuda, the fastest talker on board could not call out the 0.1-degree increases as we entered the stream.

Binoculars　　　TIP 198

Do not buy any magnification greater than seven power (7×), unless buying the current generation of image-stabilized binoculars, in which case you can go up to about 10 or 12 power. For light gathering, get lenses as large as possible. One of the ways to ensure seasickness is to look through high-powered binoculars during rough conditions.

GROUND TACKLE

Anchors　　　TIP 199

Anchor sizing is very dependent on wind loading. As mentioned previously, the effect of high winds is exponential, and doubling of wind speed quadruples load.

To get an idea of wind loading, multiply the height of the bow by the boat's maximum beam (both dimensions in feet). Multiply that product by 1.67 to account for a low cabinhouse, mast, standing rigging, etc. If the vessel has an unremovable dodger or a large cabinhouse, add its frontal area to the equation. Because a vessel will never stay straight into the wind but sails back and forth on the end of an anchor, multiply the final frontal area by 2.

Use the table below to get an idea of what your ground tackle must withstand. It's easy to understand why many boats beached after hurricanes are still attached to their mooring anchors.

The numbers constitute wind loading for dry air and have no allowance for the force of waves hitting the boat.

One can never have enough anchors. If I were going to select an inventory of anchors for most conditions, I would choose one each of the following:

- **plow**—one size larger than recommended by manufacturer for size of vessel. This is the working anchor, used on all-chain 300-foot rode with a power windlass.

- **lightweight (Danforth) type, high tensile**—of size recommended for vessel in normal, not storm conditions, with about 40 feet of chain and 250 to 300 feet of rope rode.

- **three-piece fisherman type**—Luke or ABI, with assembly instructions, secured well in bilge of vessel, with 300-foot rode that can double as drogue deployment line. Used for storm or rock anchor.

- **very large Fortress**—aluminum anchor, stored disassembled, with the bolts that hold it together well secured to anchor. Storm anchor for soft bottoms. If space is at a premium, you can skip a rode for this anchor, but if at all possible it should have its own rode of 40 to 50 feet of chain and a 300-foot rope rode.

WIND LOAD ON ANCHOR OR MOORING LINE

Area (sq. ft.)	Wind Pressure			
	30 Knots	60 Knots	80 Knots	100 Knots
1	3 lb.	13 lb.	22 lb.	32 lb.
50	150 lb.	630 lb.	1,115 lb.	1,600 lb.
150	450 lb.	1,890 lb.	3,345 lb.	4,680 lb.
200	600 lb.	2,520 lb.	4,460 lb.	6,480 lb.

Anchor Chain   TIP 200

There are over twenty specifications for chain, all with slightly different dimensions. The chain manufacturers' standards have changed, so there are the old and new standards to consider. If you want to buy chain to duplicate what fits your windlass, be sure to take at least 4 feet of the present chain with you when shopping. By comparing a long length of one chain to another, the subtle differences in link length will become evident. Look carefully at the grade of the chain, as the same physical size can vary by 300 percent in strength.

Chain is not as strong as people think. The working load limit of ⅜-inch BBB chain is 2,650 pounds. High-tensile chain is stronger, with ⅜-inch at 5,400 pounds. As the links are longer on high-tensile chain, it does not work as well on some windlass gypsies. Occasionally one can find ⅜-inch BBB chain to high-tensile specs, which is the best of both worlds.

Shackles for Anchors and Chain   TIP 201

There is no point in using a 2,000-pound safe working load (SWL) screw-pin shackle to affix an anchor with 4,000 pounds holding power to ⅜-inch chain. But it is amazing how yachtsmen tend to pick shackles predicated on what fits easily, rather than examining strength.

Galvanized screw-pin shackles are frequently imported from Third World countries with lax manufac-turing standards. The cost difference is slight to buy brand-name shackles from a reputable manufacturer. All screw-pin shackles should have the pin moused with Monel wire to prevent unscrewing. A dab of anhydrous lanolin (LanoCote) on the threads may facilitate disassembly.

Some people use stainless steel screw-pin shackles on ground tackle. This is a bad idea. Perhaps the worst application is using a stainless shackle to hold an aluminum anchor to a galvanized chain. While this battery will not light up Honolulu, given good conductive saltwater mud to live in, the anchor will be destroyed in a matter of weeks.

Avoid galvanized swivels that use clevis pins to connect the an-

Anchor swivels are generally frowned on as an unnecessary weak link in the ground tackle system, but they do help prevent twist. This one has screwpins with Allen heads; it's made by Suncor. (Tip 201)

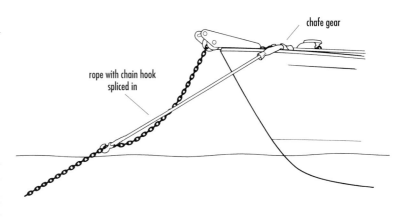

A chain hook tied or spliced to one end of a length of rope is used to grab the anchor chain near the water; pulled aft until there is slack in the chain, the rope is then made fast to a cleat or bollard. The natural stretch in rope has far more shock-absorbing effect than chain. (Tip 202)

chafe gear

rope with chain hook spliced in

chor to the chain. Galvanized cotter pins are not that strong and should not be replaced with stainless because of their electrolysis potential. The photo here shows a neat connection.

Bow Rollers and Chocks   **TIP 202**

While leading an anchor chain out over an anchor roller is very convenient, it is not a good idea to take all the strain of the anchor rode over the bow roller, which may deform it and will definitely make sleep very difficult. A 20-foot length of rope with a chain hook spliced to one end should be used to take the strain off an anchor chain, with the rope led through a bow chock (see drawing).

The procedure is to hook onto the chain, secure the other end of the rope on deck, and then pay out enough chain so the rope takes the strain. Be sure to use a lot of chafing gear on the rope. Sea-Dog now imports stainless steel chain hooks (see photo) that are an improvement over galvanized hooks, which may rust rapidly.

Boats tend to sail back and forth when anchored. An attachment point for the anchor low on the bow will help reduce this yawing. Yachts with a bowsprit frequently have an extra hole at the lower dolphin striker attachment point to which a chain hook and rope can be permanently fastened. If your boat sails a lot, consider having a fitting fabricated. Bed it well with 3M 5200.

Sea-Dog sells this cast 316 stainless steel chain hook that is ideal for an anchor chain snubber. Sea-Dog calls this item a "Clevis Grab Hook," and has sizes to fit ¼- to ½-inch chain. Pictured here is the ⅜-inch chain size, part #146710. Hall Spars & Rigging in Bristol, Rhode Island, sells this hook spliced to 20 feet of ⁹⁄₁₆-inch Caprolan nylon three-strand rope, which Practical Sailor *rated best at abrasion resistance. (Tip 202)*

CHAPTER 7

GALLEY TIPS

Chef Guillaume, aka Bill Seifert, ready to cook while anchored in St. George's Harbour, Bermuda.

Let's face it, long ocean passages can be boring. Aside from the occasional fish caught or bird sighted, the highlight of the day is often the meals. I always cook on any boat I'm on to be assured of decent food, and to escape the monotony of a passage. If it is wet and cold on deck, the meals get fancier, and therefore take more time to prepare (at least that's my excuse to be below in a nice, cozy galley). Carleton Mitchell's boat *Finesterre* won the Newport–Bermuda Race a record three times. His success has been attributed to hot meals for the crew regardless of the weather.

When one eats in a fancy restaurant, the food always looks visually pleasing, and the offerings are not what one usually eats at home. On boats, adding a dash of paprika or a sprinkling of parsley goes a long way toward the crew's perception that the food is going to taste good.

I used to laugh at my former wife who planned meals by the

color scheme of the food on the plate, but I must admit that I have taken to thinking more about color when planning menus. I try never to serve anything exactly like it comes out of the package. A sprinkle of dill weed or a little lemon juice perks up vegetables, for example. If the crew eats food different from what they have at home, there is no basis for comparison to what "mother used to make."

One can, however, get carried away. On the big boat I used to cook on, a favorite dessert among the twelve to thirteen crew was flaming crêpes. The popularity of the dish may have resulted from the owner's edict that no alcohol was to be consumed while racing. Frequently, a famous sailmaker or marine journalist would join us for long races. On one race, I first served the flaming dessert to the visiting star. He took the flaming plate and tossed it overboard, thinking there was a fire in the galley. This incident ended the flaming crêpes on *Tandem*.

I do make an effort in menu planning to include foods that keep the crew moving. Without the exercise of walking, a lot of people get constipated on boats. Fruits, fiber, and liquids help. I caution crew to monitor urine color. If it gets dark, increase liquid intake.

THE BEGINNING OF MY COOKING CAREER

Frequently I am asked how I got started cooking, and cooking on boats. My mother was very much the society woman—president of the DAR, PEO, WWC, AAUW, and a bunch of other initials I can't remember. My dad traveled a lot, and when my mother had to go to an evening function, she would leave me a TV dinner to heat up. This was the 1950s, and TV dinners were very basic and lacking in flavor and volume for a growing boy. Fortunately, we had a charge account at the local market, and I soon found that it took less time to grill a steak than heat a TV dinner and that it was easy to pop a potato in the oven to bake and make a tossed salad.

When I started crewing on an auxiliary sailboat at age fourteen, it turned out that I was the only person who could stand to be below with the smell of the alcohol stove, so it soon became my job to make coffee or soup. The owner's wife was not much into provisioning, so the skipper started to give me money to buy food.

I've had my share of disasters, like the time I made pork chops and greasy hash browns when the boat was in rough water, and everybody except me became ill and I had to steer all night (fatty foods don't sit well in rough weather; see page 155). Then there was the famous time that the boat rolled and a box of oatmeal spilled all over the wet cabin sole. The owner went below, slipped, and slid the length of the saloon on his aft end. It took thirty years before I cautiously brought oatmeal on boats again. One problem that I have not yet overcome is that people tend to gain about a pound per day when I cook on a passage.

Dan Spurr and I have made passages together, and he insists we include a few recipes. Some years ago I was cajoled into putting together a recipe book by the many requests of "Gee, I sure would like to know how to make that." This chapter concludes with a few recipes from my collection, beginning on page 157. Since my iron stomach means that even at sea I can be a proponent of that old saw, "life is short—eat dessert first," you'll find the desserts first.

PROVISIONING

Planning and Checklists TIP 203

I make a checklist of staple supplies and check the inventory on the boat before going shopping. This avoids the inevitable diet and menu problems that arise from having, for example, five bottles of ketchup but no mustard aboard. See the accompanying list of stores and supplies.

Provisioning Quantities TIP 204

While the length of any passage can be charted, the duration cannot. The winds may be on the nose, or worse yet, the boat may be dismasted and take a long time to reach port under a jury rig. Most offshore races require food on board for at least two to three times the expected passage time. I always provision for at least 50 percent more time than I expect the passage to

take, and tuck some cans or freeze-dried food away in case of calamity.

Happiness is being able to provision over several days or even a week. I like to buy canned goods and nonperishable items early, along with meat that will go in the freezer first, expecting it to be used last. Most boat freezers take at least a day to freeze a 6-inch stack of meat, so I try to layer the freezer and not load it fully all at once. Predicated on available stowage space on board, I continue provisioning, buying

CONSUMABLE STORES

Passage: _____

Produce	Dairy	Baked/Snacks	Beverages
lettuce	milk	whole wheat	Coca-Cola
cucumbers	coffee cream	rye	Diet Coke
peppers	whipping cream	pumpernickel	Pepsi
carrots	sour cream	English muffins	Diet Pepsi
celery	butter	pita or wrap breads	7-Up
cabbage	margarine	Triscuits	Diet 7-Up
fresh parsley	yogurt: plain	Saltines	ginger ale
tomatoes	yogurt: fancy	pretzels	club soda
radishes	eggs, whole	tortilla chips	tonic water
scallions	egg substitute	peanuts	fruit juice
baking potatoes	Cool Whip	peppermint candy	fruit punch
red potatoes	cream cheese	candy bars	beer
general-purpose potatoes	Swiss cheese	granola bars	beer, light
onions	mozzarella	popcorn	
apples	cheddar cheese		
oranges			
bananas, green			
bananas, ripe			
lemons			
limes			

STAPLE SUPPLIES

Yacht: _____

Passage: _____

Condiments	Baking	Cooking	Beverages	Sundries
vanilla	flour	mayonnaise	regular coffee	paper towels
ginger, ground	yeast	vegetable oil	instant coffee	toilet paper
nutmeg	sugar	olive oil	decaf instant	napkins
cinnamon	baking powder	Pam or equivalent	sugar substitute	paper plates
allspice	baking soda	maple syrup	iced tea mix	paper bowls
anise seed	Bisquick	preserves	lemonade mix	plastic glasses
thyme	brownie mix	raisins	Gatorade mix	plastic wrap
basil	honey	soy sauce	cocoa mix	1 qt. Ziplocs
parsley	molasses	teriyaki sauce	condensed milk	1 gal. Ziplocs
rosemary	chocolate chips	candied ginger	shelf milk	2 gal. Ziplocs
dill weed	walnuts	cider vinegar	tea bags, black and herbal	aluminum foil
dill seed	oatmeal	balsamic vinegar		garbage bags
caraway seed	baking cocoa	capers		dish detergent
paprika	coconut	dry bouillon		insect repellent
tarragon	cornstarch	sherry		pot scrubbers
dry mustard	confectioners' sugar	unflavored gelatin		Handi Wipes
garlic powder	brown sugar	mustard		dish towels
garlic salt	cornmeal	ketchup		facial tissue
coriander	Parmesan cheese	Worcestershire sauce		matches
curry powder		Tabasco sauce		Soft Scrub
chives, dried		lemon juice		Fantastik
cumin, ground		relish		Mr. Clean
pepper		pickles		Zud cleanser
celery seed		salad dressings		bleach
chili powder		barbecue sauce		toothpicks
salt				
horseradish				
oregano				

highly perishable fresh vegetables and fruit at the last minute.

Outside the U.S., more products are available in cans. Canned heavy cream and butter are wonderful, and do not take refrigeration space. Corned beef is universally available, but the flavor and gristle content varies. Buy a can of each brand and taste before stocking up. Various canned meats are available from Brinkman Turkey Farms, Inc. (see appendix 7).

Do not store aluminum cans in the bilge. In only a few weeks, your beer supply will be depleted from holes in the cans. Steel cans in the

PASSAGE QUESTIONNAIRE

Name: _____

Allergies to any foods: _____

Foods I dislike: _____

My favorite dinner is: _____

My favorite lunch is: _____

My favorite breakfast is: _____

Favorite canned beverages: _____

Favorite cold liquid made from powder (e.g., iced tea, lemonade, Gatorade): _____

Favorite hot liquid, other than coffee (e.g., cocoa, bouillon, special tea): _____

In the mornings, I take my coffee:

- ☐ Black

- ☐ Cream

- ☐ Sugar

My favorite juice (e.g., orange, pineapple): _____

I drink _____ glasses of _____ skim _____ 2% _____ whole milk per day.

Items on the proposed menu I don't like: _____

---

bilge must have their labels removed (in case of water damage) and will rust at the seals. I always identify cans on top with a felt tip marker, even if they are stored in a dry locker, so I don't have to pick up each can to identify its contents.

Flour and dried pasta frequently have insect larvae (see also tip 205). I package small quantities of each in zippered plastic bags with a few bay leaves added. While large sizes of any foodstuffs are more economical, better choices are smaller sizes that will be totally used before spoilage becomes a problem.

I strongly recommend Beth Leonard's *The Voyager's Handbook* (International Marine, 1998), which has excellent provisioning tips and lists.

Speaking of lists, I send a questionnaire (see above) and proposed menu to crew members before a passage, to determine their likes and dislikes, plus information on allergies and other possible health issues.

FOOD STORAGE

Cardboard Boxes   TIP 205

Do not bring cardboard boxes on board. Although the problem of insect infestation is most prevalent in warm climates, I have found cockroaches, silverfish, and other critters in cardboard boxes as far north as Nova Scotia. It's handy to transport groceries by taxi, cart, and dinghy in boxes, but always unload the boxes, inspect each item, and get the empty boxes as far from the boat as possible as soon as possible.

Plastic Containers   TIP 206

When buying plastic food containers, look for PET (polyethylene terephthalate) plastic, which is more vapor proof than other popular plastics. It's also recyclable.

When space is limited, store leftovers in zippered plastic bags rather than rigid containers; be sure to squeeze out all the extra air.

Preserving Fresh Vegetables   TIP 207

Barbara Gill turned off the refrigeration unit aboard *Sonnet* but is able to keep produce a long time. Barb sews the edges of white terrycloth towels together about two-thirds of the way up the towel to make a bag with a fold-over closure. She moistens the bag and places vegetables inside. Each day she rinses out the bag and remoistens them, keeping the bag in a cool place.

I have used Evert-Fresh green plastic bags with good success. These bags release the ethylene gas produced by vegetables but don't allow air in.

Cabbage and the Crunch   TIP 208

This often-maligned vegetable lasts a long time at room temperature. If the outer leaves turn black, leave them on unless they begin to rot.

Crunch is good. Crunch is fresh. When you want to add some crunch to a sandwich, peel off the bad leaves until you get to good ones. Unless the entire head is going to be used, peel off the outer leaves rather than cutting into the cabbage, which will hasten its spoilage.

When the cabbage is finally consumed or goes bad, fall back on canned water chestnuts to add crunch.

OUTFITTING THE GALLEY

Since I always cook on any boat I'm on, I have developed a list of the minimum equipment required for a passagemaking galley.

Safety considerations and modifications are covered below in the context of cooking in rough weather (see pages 154–55).

Bagging It

On the Tartan factory racing team's Tartan 44, we were very weight conscious. When Dazey came out with the Seal-A-Meal baggers, I bought one to be able to precook food and then toss it in a closed aluminum

MINIMUM GALLEY EQUIPMENT

one pressure cooker, 6-quart minimum	one potato masher, kind with round holes
one large pot with integral pasta drainer, 8-quart minimum Revere #2028 with #1558 insert or equal	one measuring cup, 2-cup capacity, plastic, flexible
	one measuring spoons set
two 3-quart or larger saucepans with heavy bottoms and lids	one combination grater, stainless steel
	one meat thermometer, instant-reading type
one 1-quart saucepan with heavy bottom and lid	one salad fork and spoon
one 12-inch-diameter deep frying pan	one baster
one teakettle, closed top, fill through spout only	one electronic timer
one coffee percolator, 8-cup minimum, preferably stainless	one serrated bread knife
	one large carving knife, 10- to 12-inch blade
one insulated cookie sheet, 12-by-14-inch minimum size	one medium knife
	one small knife
one 9-by-13-by-2-inch baking pan, preferably stainless	one rubber apron
	two mitt-type pot holders, 12 inches minimum length
one 8-by-8-inch or 9-by-9-inch baking pan, preferably stainless	two pot scrubbers
two 2-pound loaf-size bread pans, preferably aluminum	four sponges
	three dish towels
one large salad bowl to also serve as mixing bowl	six Handi Wipes
	one salad bowl for each crew plus three extras
one whisk, medium size, stainless steel	one 8-inch-minimum-diameter by 2-inch-deep bowl for each crew plus two extras
one large, heavy-duty cooking spoon	one plate for each crew plus two extras
one large ladle	one large coffee mug for each crew plus three extras
one plastic spatula	
one metal spatula, large	one fork for each crew plus four extras
one metal spatula, small	one spoon for each crew plus four extras
one high-quality vegetable peeler, stainless steel	one table knife for each crew plus two extras
one tongs, stainless steel	one steak knife for each crew plus two extras
one high-quality can opener	

pressure cooker filled with seawater to warm. My first cooking experiment was making an omelet at home by bagging raw eggs with shredded cheese. Because the eggs cooked from the outside in, the omelet was very good, and I found that with careful timing I could make them a little runny in the middle. I told Charlie Britton, Tartan's president, about the bagger, and he liked the idea of more time on the rail and less time below cooking.

Charlie came into my office a few days later and said, "Seif, I'm not so sure about your bagger. I tried it the other night, and I just made a mess."

"What did you do?" I asked.

"Well, I took a bread wrapper, dropped in a couple of eggs, then put it in boiling water. The bag melted and spoiled one of Linda's pans, and now she's mad at me, so I blamed it on you."

The $8,179.95 Bread-Baking Machine

The most convenient schedule for an Alden customer from Milwaukee was to leave work and fly to Rhode Island every three or four weeks to look at his boat under construction the following day. Rather than meet him at a motel for an evening meeting, I asked him to stay at my house. The owner found the food at Chez Seifert better than airline fare, and I would make a light late supper for him.

One day I programmed my automatic bread machine to make bread while I was at the office, and

the owner liked it so much that after dinner I reloaded the machine and got him to press the start button. He took the loaf "he baked" home to his wife and called the following day to tell me he wanted a bread-baking machine on his boat.

"No problem," I said. "The machine costs $179.95. Just be aware that you need to run the generator for 4 hours, 40 minutes while the machine goes through its cycle."

"That's a long time to run the generator," the customer asked. "Could you put in an inverter to run the bread baker?"

"No problem," I replied, "but with an inverter, we had better increase the size of the house battery bank to run it."

"Sounds reasonable," the customer replied.

"But with a larger house battery bank," I added, "we should increase the size of the 110-volt battery charger to charge the larger battery bank. And a larger alternator on the main engine for the house battery bank would be a good idea."

"All sounds reasonable," the customer answered.

When the change order came through, the customer computed that if he baked bread on board every day, his investment would be amortized when he was 128 years old.

COOKING IN ROUGH WEATHER

A proper seagoing galley is not as spacious as one would want when cooking in harbor. When it is rough, it is essential to wedge yourself in to have one hand for the pot and one for the spoon. On *Tandem* I installed four pad eyes in the galley and had a belt with four snapshackles on lanyards so I could be immobilized in the middle of the U-shaped galley without having to hang on. Yacht chandleries sell "cook's harnesses," and a lot of boats have eyes for them built into a bar in front of the stove. I much prefer to be harnessed to one side rather in front of the stove, which makes opening the oven door impossible.

Be sure the stove is gimbaled and ballasted so the whole unit is not top-heavy when pots are on the

burners and the oven door is opened. (See appendix 1, page 185.)

Rather than having hot food on top of the stove in open pots that might spill, I find it preferable to pop a roast into a high-sided pan with potatoes and perhaps some vegetables and put it all in the oven.

If the boat does not have an oven, use a pressure cooker with the top clamped on, but not under pressure unless you are in a hurry. I have wired the pressure cooker to the stove rails to hold it in place when the boat is jumping off waves. Crews think I'm a great guy to cook hot meals in rough conditions. I don't tell them that putting everything in a pot or in the oven is easier than trying to keep condiments and cold cuts corralled to make sandwiches.

One habit I have learned the hard way is to close any container immediately after use. You would not believe the slippery mess made by a spilled jar of mayonnaise!

Protective Apparel TIP 209

I bought a huge heavy rubber apron at a commercial fisherman's supply house in New Bedford, Massachusetts. The apron covers the front of me down to my toes. With the apron on, I don't have to worry too much about being burned by hot spilled food. I was alerted to this possibility because of what happened to Brigham Britton, the father of the founder of Tartan Marine.

Boots, as his nickname became, was heating a pan of water on the stove to make coffee one rough day. He had taken off his foulweather gear but still had his sea boots on. The boat lurched and the pan of water spilled into his boots. It was over a month before he could walk again.

Another essential item is a pair of 12-inch oven mitts, available from a restaurant supply house. Wear them, as it is very easy to touch the sides of a boat oven and get burned when using normal pot holders to retrieve things from the oven.

Oven Width and Height Limits TIP 210

We had thirteen on board *Tandem* for a Miami–Nassau Race. I had measured the length of the oven and convinced a butcher to cut a rib roast 14 inches long. Shortly after the midafternoon start, I was preparing the roast for the oven. To my horror, the roast was too high to fit. I poked my head up on deck and grabbed a winch handle. With a couple of blows to each rib I was able to crack them enough to flatten the roast to fit in the oven. When I was on the sixth rib, one of the crew came down from the rail to tell me that they had counted heads, and I was the only one missing, but they had to find out who I was beating up below.

A winch handle can also be pressed into service as a meat tenderizer (see pages 166 and 167).

Abdicating the Galley

Kelley Alexander was overqualified to be cook on the Alden 76-foot *Malabar XIV*, but she liked her work and was fanatical about keeping others out of the galley. Her father, judge of New York's highest court, gave Kelley a rough time about wasting her education and master's degree by "being a boat bum." Kelley stopped the criticism by showing her dad her brokerage statement and asking him if he knew anybody else her age who had saved as much money.

We were taking *Malabar* from Bermuda to Jamaica, making 13

knots on just the staysail. It had been blowing for a few days, and seas would occasionally break over the top of the dodger, 18 feet above the water. Just before noon, most of the ten-person crew was in the enclosed cockpit. Kelley came up and asked who wanted lunch. Having a cast-iron stomach, I immediately raised my hand, followed by a few reluctant others.

The galley on *Malabar* is forward of the mainmast, but from my position close to the companionway I could smell Kelley's cooking, so I gave a play-by-play account of the cooking. "Smells like Kelley is frying some chouriço [a spicy Portuguese sausage] . . . she just added some onions . . . there went a lot of garlic . . . oh boy, more olive oil!"

One by one, most of the crew unzipped parts of the cockpit enclosure and lost their previous meal. Kelley, who is half Polish and half black, appeared in the cockpit with a large bowl of sausage and peppers. Her complexion is normally a beautiful nutmeg, but this moment it was more of an olive drab. As she watched me devour lunch, she finally acquiesced and said that I was welcome to use her galley if I got hungry again before the weather improved.

SERVING AND CLEANUP

Plates, Glasses, and Coffee Mugs   TIP 211

If the weather is anything over dead calm, serve meals in large 2-inch-deep bowls rather than on shallow plates. I like the plastic bowls sold by Galleyware that have nonskid bottoms.

I number the coffee mugs and assign each person a number, so they do not have to be washed for refills. For cold beverages, I use heavy, plastic disposable glasses, with each crewmate's name inscribed with a marker, which saves thorough washing.

Washing Dishes   TIP 212

Most people use an inordinate amount of freshwater for washing dishes. The best way to preserve freshwater is to have a supply of pressurized seawater at the galley (see Conserving Freshwater, tip 155). The handiest faucet is a standard household spray nozzle on a hose. If your boat has a seawater anchor washdown pump, it is a simple matter to tee off the line and run a hose to the galley.

Unless I am in very polluted water, I use pressured seawater to wash residue off plates, pots, etc. Then I apply some dishwashing detergent (lemon Joy) to a wet Handi Wipe and scrub the surfaces. On the open ocean, I rinse off the soap with seawater, then give the dishes a quick freshwater rinse. When on

soundings, I use a little freshwater for rinsing, saving it by pouring from mug to mug and plate to plate. It is important to get all the soap residue off, as residual soap can cause diarrhea.

A very handy device for washing dishes on boats with two deep sinks is a slatted teak grating that fits close to the bottom of one side. The washed dishes can be placed on the grating and rinsed. The dishes can be left there to air dry without worry of sea conditions causing them to go flying around.

A great gadget for the galley is a pump-type soap dispenser. I prefer those made by Delta. Mounting is easily accomplished by drilling a $1\frac{1}{16}$-inch hole through the countertop. Having a ready supply of detergent available makes washing up a few dishes easier than opening a cabinet, grabbing a bottle, opening it, squirting out a little detergent, closing the bottle, and restowing. The Delta pump assembly withdraws from the top for easy refilling of the reservoir.

Garbage   TIP 213

On offshore passages, I am very careful that no food is deposited in the galley garbage can. It is perfectly legal, and environmentally sound, to dump food overboard when more than 25 miles offshore. I meticulously keep all plastics, and wash off any food residue with seawater before depositing in the trash. Cans are punctured and go over-

The addition of a simple teak grate turns a galley sink into a dish drying rack. (Tip 212)

board. Glass bottles are filled with seawater and jettisoned. Cardboard goes overboard after being ripped into small pieces.

After the experience of saving recyclable items on board, hauling them ashore, and then a few days later watching them and other garbage be dumped not more than five miles offshore, I only save nonplastic garbage when I'm traveling to place where I know it will be properly disposed of.

I sailed from Rhode Island to the Azores in 1996 (1,984-nautical-mile great circle route) and ended up with one nonsmelly garbage bag of washed-out Ziploc bags and all rigid plastic cut in small pieces.

RECIPES

Desserts

Triple Chocolate Bread Pudding

1–2 cups stale white bread cut in about ½-inch cubes

4 T. melted butter or margarine

8 ounces semisweet chocolate, cut into ½-inch-or-so chunks

Toss above together and divide into six to eight ovenproof ramekins or one casserole.

Combine

4 large eggs

1 cup sugar

½ cup unsweetened dry cocoa powder

2 cups chocolate milk

½ tsp. vanilla or rum

Beat eggs lightly, add other ingredients, mix until blended. Pour over bread mixture. Let stand at least ½ hour, pushing bread down into liquid as required.

Preheat oven to 350°F. Place ramekins in large pan, and fill pan with hot water until halfway up sides of ramekins. Bake 30 minutes until pudding is just set; a large casserole takes longer. Serve with whipped cream and shaved chocolate on top.

Yes Bars

When people taste these, they always ask: "Is there coconut in these?" or "Do I taste oatmeal in these?" or "Did you add . . . ?"

Therefore I picked an affirmative name.

Cream together

1 cup margarine, cut in chunks

1½ cups sugar

3 T. molasses

1 tsp. vanilla

2 large eggs

Add

1½ cups flour

1 tsp. baking powder

Process until smooth, then add

1 cup dry oatmeal, regular or instant

1 7-ounce package coconut

1 cup chopped walnuts

1 12-ounce package chocolate chips

Mix by hand to blend, then spread into a greased 9-by-13-inch pan. Bake about 35 minutes at 350°F.

Adult Pudding

I am indebted to Dick Meyers from Water Island, St. Thomas, for sharing the recipe for the pudding I had aboard his Morgan 46 in Tortola.

This sounds easy, and it is, but tastes like a lot of work went into it. Use Jell-O vanilla cook-type pudding mix—*not* instant. Substitute sherry for half the milk, but otherwise follow the package directions. This pudding is so rich that it is best served with a dollop of whipped topping. Dick also reports success using port wine, but I have not tried this variation.

Chocolate Chess Pie

Credit for the basis of this recipe, for which I was a finalist in a cooking contest in 1996, goes to Nancy Carter of the Alden 54 *Cloud Shadow*. It's definitely not low in calories, but good for a special occasion.

1 ounce unsweetened chocolate

1 ounce semisweet chocolate

½ cup butter or margarine

Melt above. If using microwave, be sure to use 50 percent power or less.

Add

1 cup white sugar

½ cup brown sugar

⅓ cup milk

3 T. Grand Marnier

3 large eggs, beaten

Mix until smooth. Pour into unbaked 9-inch pastry pie shell. Bake 55 to 60 minutes at 325°F until set. Cool, then chill before serving. Top with whipped cream and shaved unsweetened chocolate.

This pie takes less than 5 minutes to put together if a premade crust is used (I like Pillsbury's folded ones).

Date Chews

Combine

    1 cup finely chopped dates
    1 cup brown sugar
    ¾ cup whole wheat flour
    1 cup finely chopped walnuts
    1 tsp. baking powder
    2 eggs, lightly beaten
    ½ tsp. vanilla

Press batter into a greased 13-by-9-inch pan. Bake at 300°F for 30 minutes.

Let cool only a little and, while still warm, cut into squares. Roll squares into balls and roll in powdered sugar.

Molasses Spice Cookies

In Marblehead, Massachusetts, cookies like this are called Joe Froggers, after a famous cook who made them for sailors to take to sea. The ginger helps queasy stomachs.

Cream together

    ¼ cup butter or margarine
    1 cup sugar
    ¼ cup molasses

Add

    1 large egg
    1½ tsp. ginger
    1 tsp. cinnamon
    ½ tsp. allspice
    ½ tsp. salt

Mix well, then add

    2¼ cups flour
    2 tsp. baking soda

Mix only until blended.

If dough is too runny to shape into balls, refrigerate about an hour. Form walnut-sized balls, and roll them in sugar spread on a plate. Place balls 2–3 inches apart on a greased cookie sheet. Bake at 350°F about 12 minutes. Cookies should be a little soft. Let cool a few minutes on baking sheet, then remove to rack for cooling . . . if you can resist eating them warm.

Quick Caramel Coconut Frosting

This frosting perks up brownies made from a mix. Hot, it is good on ice cream.

Bring to boil in a saucepan

    1 cup water
    1 cup brown sugar

Reduce heat and stir frequently. Cook 10 minutes, then add

    ¼ pound butter (a little less is
    OK)

Continue cooking and stirring until frosting thickens, then add

    1 7-ounce package coconut
    (1½ cups chopped nuts
    may be substituted for co-
    conut)

Pour over cooled brownies. Be sure to wash pan immediately.

Bill's Mint Chocolate Chip Bars

One evening I got the hungries for Breyers Mint Chocolate Chip Ice Cream. Unfortunately, the grocery was closed, so I concocted these bar cookies from on-hand materials.

Cream together

    1 cup margarine
    1½ cups white sugar
    2 eggs (or one-half carton Egg
    Beaters)
    2–3 T. peppermint extract

Then add

    1 tsp. baking soda
    2¼ cups white flour

When mixed, add

    12 ounces chocolate chips
    (this is 2 cups)

Spread into greased 9-by-13-inch pan. Bake at 350°F for about 35 minutes.

Note: Bar cookies will not turn brown when fully cooked, but will feel done to the touch.

Bananas Foster

Bananas Foster is generally served over vanilla ice cream. If ice cream is not available, whipped topping works, as do the canned custards available outside the U.S. Barb Gill of *Sonnet* showed me the easy way to cook bananas if the dinner has been cooked on a grill: put unpeeled bananas on the grill and cook until the skin pops.

Per banana, combine in frying pan over low heat

    2 T. brown sugar
    1 T. butter
    1 ounce rum
    1 dash cinnamon

After sugar has melted, slice bananas into pan (if not cooked on the grill). Cook bananas, turning often until they are softened a little and coated. Pour bananas and extra sauce on ice cream or other dessert. If you want to be dramatic, add the rum at the end of the cooking; heat it a little, then ignite it.

Butterscotch Oat Date Nut Bars

This is a handy bar cookie to make because a mixing bowl is not required. The name practically is the recipe.

Preheat oven to 350°F. Melt over medium heat in a 6-quart or larger saucepan

- 1 cup margarine or butter
- 2 cups sugar
- 3 T. molasses (or use brown sugar and omit molasses)

Stir frequently to prevent burning. Mixture will bubble and look like lava. Remove from heat and let cool 5 to 10 minutes. If mixture becomes too cool, adding other ingredients will be difficult. If too hot, eggs will cook. Add

- 2 cups flour
- 1 cup oatmeal, uncooked, either regular or quick
- 2 tsp. double-acting baking powder
- ½ tsp. salt
- 2 tsp. vanilla
- 2 large eggs
- 1 cup chopped walnuts, or preferably pecans
- 1 8-ounce package chopped dates

Dough will be stiff and have somewhat of a toffee-like consistency. It is easiest to add everything except nuts and dates. Mix, then add remaining ingredients.

Press into a greased 9-by-13-inch pan. Bake about 30 to 35 minutes. Top should be springy, with tester just coming out clean.

Coconut may be substituted for dates and nuts for a more cost-efficient bar cookie.

Breakfasts

Eggs Guillaume

This is an easy version of the classic Eggs Benedict, and many people like it better. I traditionally make it on the last day of a passage.

The following ingredients are for each 1-egg serving; multiply as needed for 1–2 servings per person.

- 1 egg
- 1 slice turkey ham, ¼ inch thick, skin removed
- ½ can Campbell's cheese soup
- ¼ can white wine
- 1 dash Worcestershire, white if available
- ½ English muffin, toasted
- Pinch of parsley, preferably fresh, but dried is OK

Toast English muffin halves and set aside.

Warm turkey ham in oven.

Place cheese soup in a pot. Add wine. Warm slowly on stove top; you may have to whisk to blend. If only dried parsley is available, add a tablespoon or so. Add Worcestershire.

If a muffin tin is available, wipe each cup generously with butter, and carefully break an egg into each cup. Bake in 350°F oven for about 15 minutes until egg whites are set. If a muffin tin is not available, cut both ends out of the soup cans, remove labels, and wash cans. Place cans vertically in a pan of simmering water about 1 inch high. Put a little butter in each can and carefully break an egg into each can. Cook until the white is set, then run a knife around inside perimeter of can to break egg away from can. Lift can out of water and remove egg with slotted spoon.

Place a slice of turkey ham on English muffin half, then a poached egg, then top with sauce. If fresh parsley is available, use for garnish.

I frequently serve this with a tomato garnish: Spray a sheet of aluminum foil with Pam and place on a baking sheet. Place sliced tomatoes on foil. Sprinkle bread crumbs moistened with a little melted butter on top. Sprinkle with Lawry's seasoned salt. Place under broiler until bread crumbs are browned.

Birchermuesli

This is a great warm-weather breakfast, and is a lot easier to eat than to pronounce. Add toast or toasted English muffins as an accompaniment. The mix keeps several days in the refrigerator, but is usually eaten before spoilage becomes a problem. This recipe makes four generous servings.   (continued)

2 cups uncooked, quick-cooking oatmeal
1½ cups milk; shelf milk is OK

Combine above and let stand 15 minutes to overnight, the longer the better. Then add
3 T. sugar
2 T. lemon juice
2 medium apples, peeled and coarsely grated down to, but not including, core

Combine above and add to oatmeal mixture. Then add
¼ cup raisins; golden is preferable, but dark are OK
¼ cup dried apricots, diced (if apricots are not available, increase amount of raisins)
1 8-ounce can pineapple tidbits or mandarin orange segments; drain, but reserve liquid (these canned ingredients can be replaced with a package of frozen fruit, thawed and drained, or a canned tropical fruit salad)
1 8-ounce can green grapes; drain and cut grapes in half
2 nectarines or peaches, peeled and cut in chunks

Slice 2 large bananas into reserved pineapple or mandarin orange liquid. Toss gently to coat banana slices and then discard liquid. Add
½ pint whipping cream, whipped, or a small container of Cool Whip

Fold all together and refrigerate until serving time. If you like, add ½ cup toasted almonds, slivered. If you happen to have fresh strawberries, cut up about a dozen and toss them in.

Gingerbread Pancakes
Dissolve
1 tsp. instant coffee powder in ½ cup hot water

Let cool a little if ingredient below is thawed. If not thawed, add immediately to hot water. Add
1 6-ounce can frozen unsweetened apple juice concentrate
1 egg or equivalent egg substitute
2 T. applesauce

Mix together, then add
1 cup whole wheat flour
1 tsp. baking soda
¾ tsp. ginger
½ tsp. cinnamon
⅛ tsp. allspice
⅛ tsp. salt—*do not omit*

Spray griddle with Pam. These pancakes may be difficult to cook, as they are already brown, so you may want to time each side. Serve with a dollop of low-fat lemon yogurt—not syrup.

Bran Muffins
This recipe makes a large batch, but the batter keeps four weeks or more in the refrigerator. The batter may smell fermented, but still

bakes nicely. The batter may also be frozen.

In a large bowl, mix together
1 15-ounce box Raisin Bran cereal
3 cups sugar
5 cups flour
5 tsp. baking soda

Add
4 large eggs, beaten
1 quart buttermilk
1 cup salad oil
1 cup raisins
20 dried apricots, snipped in small pieces (optional)

Bake in a 400°F oven in foil muffin cups about 12 to 15 minutes, until nicely browned on top.

One time when we had these on our boat, the Newport harbormaster came on board for his morning Bloody Mary. His dog Brecken jumped on board our boat and snatched a muffin off the cockpit table and gobbled it down, foil muffin wrapper and all. Carole quickly offered to pay for an operation on Brecken, but the harbormaster laughed and said not to worry, adding that Brecken eats lobsters, shell and all.

Be sure to label the container of this muffin batter. For one Bermuda Race, I made a large batch and used half of it on the way down. The owner's wife came on board in Bermuda, opened the container, smelled it, and threw it away. The return crew was muffinless.

Coffee Cake

This cake is amazingly tasty, has almost no fat, and is easily transportable.

    3½ cups flour
    3 cups sugar
    1½ tsp. salt (optional)
    1½ tsp. baking soda
    1 tsp. cinnamon
    1 tsp. nutmeg
    1 tsp. vanilla
    2 large eggs
    ⅔ cup water
    1 cup applesauce
    2 cups canned pumpkin (one
        can)
    1 cup chopped walnuts or
        pecans
    1 cup raisins, light or dark

Mix dry ingredients. Mix liquid ingredients enough to beat eggs slightly, or pre-beat them lightly. Add nuts and raisins.

Grease and flour four 13-ounce empty coffee cans (the former 1-pound size before inflation hit coffee). Divide batter into the four cans, and place cans upright on a baking dish.

Bake 1 hour 15 minutes at 350°F.

Let cool on rack, then place plastic tops over the can openings. This coffee cake keeps a week in the can at room temperature, indefinitely in the freezer. To serve, run a knife around the perimeter of the can if coffee cake does not slide out. If contents are really stuck, cut out the bottom of the can with a can opener and push the coffee cake out.

Dates may be substituted for the raisins. Whole-wheat flour works with this recipe.

Quick French Toast Batter

Here's the quick and easy batter I use offshore for French toast. The fractions are proportions, so use about two-thirds Egg Beaters to one-third orange juice.

    ⅔ Egg Beaters or other pre-
        pared egg product
    ⅓ orange juice
    splash Cointreau, sherry, or
        light rum

Beat lightly.

Fowl Sausage

This is my name for the dish, *not* a comment on it!

    1 small apple, peeled and
        grated
    ½ pound ground chicken or
        ground turkey
    ¼ tsp. black pepper
    ¾ tsp. sage
    ½ tsp. fennel
    ½ tsp. coriander
    ½ tsp. salt (optional)

Mix together, shape into patties. Fry in a nonstick skillet sprayed with Pam or equivalent on both sides until browned. If the chicken or turkey does not have much fat, you may have to add just a little butter or margarine to make them brown.

Hash Browns

Chef Forrest Childs of the Glen Oaks restaurant in Big Sur, California, showed me how to make decent hash browns.

Wash potatoes; it is not necessary to peel them except to remove spots of tar, etc. Place potatoes in a pot. Fill pot with half seawater and half freshwater. Bring pot to boil, then shut off the fire. Any time after about 20 minutes, remove the potatoes and grate *thinly* on a hot griddle that has been greased with half butter and half oil. The layer of potatoes on the grill should not be more than ¼ inch high.

Sprinkle with chopped onion. Turn when the bottoms are brown and add just a little more butter, which will speed browning the second side. Turn the potatoes onto the serving plate. Sprinkle with paprika and parsley. Serve with a dollop of sour cream.

Dinners

Easy Au Gratin Potatoes

I invented this dish one night when I forgot to put potatoes in to bake and had less than a half-hour before dinner. Proportions are not all critical.

Peel six to eight potatoes. Cut into ½- to ¾-inch cubes. Boil in water until cooked but still firm. I find that if I start the water to boil when I start peeling, things work out about right. Drain potatoes and rinse pot to remove starch. Return potatoes to pot.   *(continued)*

Add

- 4–8 ounces Velveeta, cut in ½-inch chunks
- 1 small onion, minced very fine
- 1 pint sour cream
- 1–2 tsp. pepper, white if available
- 3–5 T. parsley

Warm over low heat, stirring gently to melt the cheese.

Colcannon

This dish tastes a lot better than the ingredients sound.

Place in a pot of boiling water

- 1 medium head cabbage, shredded
- 4 large potatoes, cut in ¾-inch cubes

Boil about 10 minutes, until cabbage is still a little on the crisp side. Drain and place back in pot. Add

- ½ cup cream
- ¼ cup butter or margarine

Mash this up, but leave it a little lumpy. Add and mix in

- ½ cup scallions, finely chopped (if not available, finely chop a small onion)
- 1 tsp. salt
- ½ tsp. pepper
- ¼ tsp. nutmeg (more if the nutmeg is not pungent)
- ¾ cup grated cheddar cheese

Place in a greased 2-quart casserole. Sprinkle on top

- ¼ cup grated cheddar or Parmesan cheese

Dot with about 2 T. butter.

Bake in a hot (450°F or so) oven for 15 minutes, or until cheese on top melts.

Fruited Beans

This is a pleasant change from normal baked beans, and is guaranteed to get the crew moving. Dish is good either hot or cold.

Soak overnight (OK to use one-third clean seawater)

- 2 cups great northern or navy beans

Cook beans in their soaking liquid about an hour until tender, but not mushy. If part seawater was not used for soaking, add a teaspoon of salt before cooking. Drain, but reserve a cup of cooking liquid. Add to the cooking liquid

- 1½ tsp. dry mustard
- 1 medium onion, finely chopped
- ½ cup chutney
- salt and pepper to taste

Mix to dissolve mustard; add back to the beans. Pour about half the bean mixture into a greased 2-quart casserole. Prepare and mix together

- 2 medium apples, peeled and cut in slices
- 3 medium peaches, peeled and sliced, or use a small can of peaches
- ½ cup dried apricots

Put about half the above mixture over the beans. Add the rest of the beans and top with the remaining fruit mixture. Combine together

- ¼ cup honey
- ¼ cup molasses

Drizzle evenly over the top of the casserole. Cover casserole and bake at 325°F for an hour. Remove cover and bake another half hour. To make casserole look pretty, top with

- ½ cup yogurt

Bake about 5 minutes more.

Variations:

- Use canned beans, drained and rinsed. Dissolve mustard, etc., in sherry in lieu of bean cooking liquid.

- Use mincemeat in lieu of chutney.

- Use all canned fruit, like pears, peaches, and apricots. Cut down a little on liquid.

Caribbean Rice

Use fruit punch instead of water for making rice. Add a small can of crushed pineapple just before serving.

Orange Rice

Use orange juice instead of water for making rice. Garnish with thin slices of orange or finely chopped orange peel.

Dirty Rice

Add 1 to 2 cloves finely minced garlic to the water used for making rice. While rice is cooking, brown 1 pound ground beef and 1 large chopped onion. Drain off fat, add to cooked rice.

Breakfast Rice

Brown 1 pound sausage meat. Pour off fat. Add to 3 cups cooked rice, with a little sour cream to bind it all together.

Potpourri of Wild Rice

Cook ½–¾ cup wild rice according to package directions. Cook 1 cup white rice according to directions. In 1 or 2 tablespoons of butter, sauté
    ½ cup chopped scallions
    ½ cup sweet red pepper, finely
      chopped

Reduce heat and add remainder of butter. When butter is melted, combine rices and vegetables.

This dish may be made ahead and rewarmed in a covered casserole in the oven.

Creamed Spinach

I first had this at Nan Webster's house on Martha's Vineyard, and ended up finishing the bowl. This recipe multiplies easily.

For two servings:
    1 package frozen chopped
      spinach
    2 ounces cream cheese
    1 tsp. dried chives

    garlic salt to taste; start with 1
      dash

Defrost spinach and drain in a strainer. A more fun way is to pick up handfuls of spinach and squeeze out the water.

Place ingredients in a large frying pan. Heat over medium-high burner, stirring constantly until cheese melts. You may have to add some milk or cream to get desired consistency.

Vegetable Sauce

Be sure the owner does not see you making this, because it tastes like it took a lot of work.

Mix together
    1 cup mayonnaise
    2–3 T. balsamic vinegar

Serve on broccoli, asparagus, etc.

Spicy Corn Bread

This is an interesting combination of sweetness and tang from green chilies.

Cream together
    1 cup butter or margarine
    1 cup sugar

Add, one at a time
    4 large eggs

Add
    1 4-ounce can green chilies,
      seeded and chopped fine if
      not using a food processor

    1 16-ounce can cream-style
      corn
    ½ cup shredded Monterey
      Jack cheese
    ½ cup shredded mild cheddar
      cheese
    1 cup flour
    1 cup yellow cornmeal
    4 tsp. baking powder
    ¼ tsp. salt

To make it easier, I cream the butter and sugar in a food processor, add the whole chilies, and chop them while blending in the eggs. Then I add the flour, baking powder, and cornmeal, processing to just blend in, then add the rest of the ingredients with a quick shot to blend. On boats without a food processor, I do it the old-fashioned way, which tastes the same—it just takes longer.

Pour into greased and floured 8-by-12 or 9-by-13-inch pan. Place in preheated 350°F oven, then reduce oven heat to 300°F. Bake 50 minutes to an hour, until golden brown on top. Cool on wire rack.

Irish Soda Bread

Bakes well in a boat oven if an insulated cookie sheet is placed under the pan containing the bread.

Mix together in a large bowl
    2½ cups flour
    2 tsp. baking powder
    ½ tsp. baking soda
    1 tsp. salt

To save washing measuring cups, place in a 2-cup measuring cup
    ½ cup sugar   (continued)

Add
    ¼ cup vegetable oil
    1 large egg

Mix above together to beat egg a little and add to dry ingredients. Add
    1½ cups sour cream or a 12-ounce can of evaporated milk

Mix it all up, then add and mix in
    1 cup raisins
    3 T. caraway seeds

Pour into a greased 9-inch round or square pan.
    Bake at 325°F to 350°F for 45 minutes to an hour, until golden brown.

Low-Fat Variation
Replace vegetable oil and sour cream with 2 cups plain nonfat yogurt. Use ¼ cup egg substitute in lieu of egg.

Grilled Bread
If you're lucky enough to have a cooktop or range that has a grill component, you can try this recipe, the result of a recent cooking experiment that turned out well. Basically, you put bread dough on the grill. Yes, you read that right. After the first rising, punch down bread dough and refrigerate. When ready for a quick, tasty appetizer, roll out some of the bread dough about ¼ inch thick. Coat both sides with nonstick vegetable oil spray such as Pam.
    Over medium heat, toss the flattened dough right on the grill rack.

Close lid. After 3–4 minutes turn the dough over. Top with herbs, grated cheese, vegetables, or whatever.
    Close lid and cook 3–4 minutes. You will get a consistency about halfway between bread and a cracker, and a very good flavor, especially if you put some wood chips on the grill.

Beer Bread
This bread is made with a leavening agent more commonly found on boats than yeast.

Mix together
    4 cups flour
    2 T. baking powder
    2 tsp. salt
    ¼ cup sugar

Add
    1 12-ounce can beer
    1 large egg, beaten (optional)

Mix until just combined. Put in a greased loaf pan. Bake at 375°F for 1 hour 10 minutes, or so.

Variations
Add ½ cup grated cheese or 2 tablespoons any kind of seed — caraway, celery, etc.

Healthy Burgers
Actually, these are not totally healthy, just less unhealthy than the all-beef variety. Proportions are not critical.
    2–3 pounds ground beef
    1 pound ground turkey

1 egg or egg substitute
½ cup bread crumbs
1–2 T. dried bouillon powder diluted in a little hot water
⅓ cup parsley, fresh, or about 4 T. dried
1 tsp. black pepper
garlic powder to taste
very finely minced onion to taste

Shape into patties and grill. I like to serve on buns spread with mayonnaise, a slice of tomato, and a little red onion. The same ingredients also make a good meat loaf.
    Try replacing the egg with a little beer and the bread crumbs with grated carrot or apple for an even healthier burger.

Beef Wellington Par Guillaume
This is not as fancy as you will get in a good restaurant, but is easy to do on board.

Select a plump filet mignon. Cut a piece from the largest portion 13 inches long. Clean off gristle and fat. Save rest of beef tenderloin for stroganoff.
    Bring tenderloin up to room temperature. Defrost some sheets of phyllo dough, enough to cover the tenderloin with about 3/16-inch thickness of phyllo. Coat tenderloin with Grey Poupon mustard (we are on *yachts*, don't you know!), then wrap phyllo over the top. Use cut-off pieces of phyllo to make a fancy design on top of the roll.
    Bake in a 350°F oven for 30 minutes. Stick a meat thermome-

ter about 1½ inches into the end of the tenderloin. If the thermometer does not register 130°F, put meat back in oven for 10 minutes. Repeat as needed. When thermometer shows 130°F, stop cooking.

Be sure to show the crew the beautiful creation before cutting it into slices for serving.

Prom Chicken

Remove skin from boneless chicken breasts. Dip each breast in oil, as cholesterol-free as you want.

Mix on plate (proportions are approximate and dependent on number of breasts)
    1 cup seasoned bread crumbs
    ¼ cup grated Parmesan cheese
    1 tsp. garlic powder

Coat breasts both sides with the above. Form breasts into mounds with ends tucked under. Bake on cookie sheet in 350°F oven 30 to 40 minutes. Coating should just be starting to brown. Overbaking makes chicken too dry.

Note: To improve the taste of generic seasoned bread crumbs, add a little rosemary and tarragon and a generous amount of dried parsley.

Curried Leftovers

This is a low-calorie version. Good for the third night of the same meat.

Chop
    1 large onion
    1 cup celery

Open one 13- or 14-ounce can of chicken broth. Add a little chicken broth and the above to a large saucepan and sauté about 5 minutes.

Add ¼ cup flour to a small saucepan and make a roux with the remaining chicken broth. Cook until raw flour taste is gone, then add
    1 T. curry powder
    ¼ tsp. nutmeg
    dash cayenne pepper

Season sauce to taste. Combine roux and celery-onion mixture. Add
    2 medium tart apples, peeled and chopped into about ⅜-inch-square pieces

Add
    2–3 cups leftover cooked meat, cut in small pieces (chicken, turkey, pork, lamb all work well)

Cook on low heat until warmed through. You may have to add water if mixture becomes too thick. Serve over cooked rice.

One time a leftover portion of this migrated to the very back of the refrigerator. When I found it, mold had started to grow, and I called it "The curry with the fringe on the top."

Chicken Marbella

This dish sits well on tender tummies, and does not stay there too long—both desirable attributes offshore.

    3 to 4 *pounds* boneless, skinless chicken breast, cut in pieces the size of a prune
    1 T. finely minced garlic
    2–4 T. dried thyme or oregano
    1-pound package pitted prunes
    ½ cup or more pitted olives, either green or ripe
    1 3-ounce jar capers, with their juice
    1 cup old, stale white wine *and* ½ cup old, stale red wine to total 1½ cups (if you don't have stale wine, use 1¼ c. cheap white wine and ¼ c. red wine vinegar; 1¼ c. vegetable broth and ¼ c. vinegar can be substituted)
    1 cup brown sugar; or use white sugar with a generous dollop of molasses
    6 bay leaves

Mix sugar and liquid. If sugar does not dissolve, heat until it does. Combine with other ingredients. Marinate in refrigerator overnight. I put it all in a Ziploc bag and turn it occasionally. Place in a casserole. Bake at 350°F for 45 minutes to an hour, stirring after 20 minutes. When chicken is white all the way through, it is done. Do not overcook. Serve over rice.

Coating Mix

Commercial coating mixes (Shake and Bake) are very expensive. I make my own by combining:

  1 cup bread crumbs
  ½ cup white flour
  ¼ cup cornmeal
  1½ tsp. garlic powder
  2 T. paprika
  1 tsp. black pepper

Depending on what I'm putting it on, I sometimes add some Parmesan cheese. The above works well on pork chops. I mix an egg with about 3 T. water to dip the chops in before coating, which makes the coating stick better.

Swiss Steak

Trim most of the fat from the edges of a 2- to 3-pound round steak. Cut the edges just a little in three or four places so the steak will not curl up when cooked. Mix together, then sprinkle on each side of the steak

  1 tsp. garlic salt
  ½ tsp. pepper
  1 tsp. paprika
  3 T. flour

Use a meat tenderizer or the corner of a winch handle to pound the flour mix into the surface of the meat. Heat a large frying pan and add a tablespoon or two of olive oil. If the steak will not fit in the pan, cut it in pieces. Sear the steak on both sides until nicely browned. Transfer to a baking pan.

Add to the pan
  1 10-ounce can beef bouillon
    or equivalent made with
    dry bouillon
  1 small can V8 juice
Place on top of the steak
  ½–1 cup finely minced onions
  1–2 cups mixed finely
    chopped carrots, celery,
    and green pepper

Cover the baking pan tightly with aluminum foil. Bake in a slow oven (about 300°F) for 2–3 hours. Be sure there is an insulated cookie sheet under the pan when this is made in a boat oven. Check at 2 hours. The steak should be just about falling apart, and there should be plenty of liquid in the pan. If the liquid is low, add more bouillon.

Remove steak from pan. Transfer the pan liquid and vegetables to a saucepan on a medium-high burner. Mix about ¼ cup flour with an equal amount of water, adding the water gradually while stirring to make a heavy paste that will thin with the addition of more water without forming lumps . . . if your grandmother was a good woman. While whisking the pan juices, add the flour-and-water mixture slowly. When about half is added, let the juices cook for a minute or two while whisking. If the gravy does not get thick enough for you, add a little more flour-and-water and cook longer.

Serve the gravy over mashed potatoes. I usually serve Swiss steak with a green vegetable such as broc-

coli, green beans, or asparagus.

Note: Under *no* circumstances should the extra flour-and-water be poured down the galley sink. Pour it overboard.

Pretty Chili

This chili is low-fat and different.

Sauté and break up meat, cook until all pinkness is gone
  1 pound ground turkey or
    chicken

In a large pot, cook
  1 can vegetable broth
  1 large eggplant, peeled and
    cut into ¾-inch squares
  1 large onion, peeled and cut
    into ½-inch squares
  2 stalks celery, cleaned and
    chopped into ¼-inch
    pieces
  1 large green pepper, cut into
    ½-inch squares

Cook until the eggplant is a little browned or tastes cooked and the onions are tender. Combine cooked turkey or chicken with above in large pot. Add
  3 T. chili powder
  3 medium garlic cloves, finely
    minced
  1 16-ounce can stewed tomato
    slices or quarters, with
    liquid from can
  1 16-ounce can black beans,
    rinsed and drained
  1 16-ounce can white beans,
    rinsed and drained

If you like more soupy chili, add an additional can vegetable broth. If you like more spicy chili, add cayenne pepper and ground cumin, starting with ½ teaspoon of each and tasting before more is added. Simmer until warm.

Low-Fat White Pizza
This creation was inspired by the tasty white pizzas served at the Sambuca restaurant on St. Maarten, Netherlands Antilles.

Use ready-made pizza dough or make enough white bread dough for one loaf, let it rise once, then punch down and roll out.

Place in food processor bowl
12 ounces nonfat mozzarella cheese, shredded
1½ cups nonfat cottage cheese
2 T. fennel seed

Process above to chop fennel seed and achieve a smooth consistency.

Pat out pizza dough on a 15-by-10-inch baking pan. Spread with above sauce. Top with any (or all) of the following

1 6-ounce jar artichoke hearts, cut in small pieces
1 small eggplant, peeled, cut in slices ⅜ inch thick, quickly sautéed in vegetable broth
1 medium green pepper, cut in slices ½ inch square
1 medium sweet red pepper, cut in slices ½ inch square
1 small onion, cut in slices ½ inch square (or substitute a bunch of scallions)

1 4-ounce can pitted black olives, sliced
10 ounces fresh mushrooms, sliced and sautéed in vegetable broth
or
1 8-ounce can sliced mushrooms, drained, rinsed several times, marinated a minimum of 15 minutes with dry vermouth

Bake pizza in a 400–425°F oven for 20 minutes or so, until crust is firm.

Roast Turkey
For the last 50,000 miles, my traditional dinner for the second night underway has been a roast turkey. On boats without refrigeration, a frozen turkey has thawed enough to cook by then. On boats with refrigeration, I end up needing the room in the freezer for bread. Be sure to keep the turkey in an insulated bag while it thaws.

John Rousmaniere, writing in *Yachting* magazine, attributed our not doing well in a race to the numbing effects on the crew of a turkey dinner I prepared with two kinds of cranberry sauce. Even if Rousmaniere disagrees, turkey is kind on the tummy, there is a lot that can be done with the leftovers, and it is certainly cost efficient.

Take a tape measure when buying a turkey. To fit in most boat ovens, the bird cannot be more than 9 inches high. When I have been unable to find a low fowl, I have had to cut out the backbone prior to roasting, which is a laborious task, generally involving the ship's hacksaw and a winch handle.

Chef Forrest Childs of Glen Oaks restaurant in Big Sur, California, taught me how to cook a bird with succulent breast meat: Stuff a few cut-up oranges and apples in the bird and roast upside down, with the breast down so the juices baste the breast meat.

The Alden 54 built for Dr. Graham Guerriero for "summer" delivery was launched just before Thanksgiving. Graham came out to spend the holiday on his boat. I reversed the normal Thanksgiving ritual, and the poor invited the rich to Thanksgiving dinner at my house. As he is a surgeon and was the guest of honor, I asked Graham to carve. He inquired if the bird had Blue Cross, but then started slicing the breast at right angles to the breastbone, rather than parallel to the long axis of the breast, as I had always done. I asked him what he was doing, and he patiently explained the muscle structure of a turkey breast. By cutting across the grain of the meat, rather than parallel to it, the breast meat is more tender and juicy. Ever since, I have carved turkey this way, and the crew is amazed at how I always pick a good bird.

For dressing, I use Stove Top, adding sautéed onions, mushrooms, and celery. I try to make gravy from the pan drippings, but if it is rough, they slosh around the inside of the oven and I have to break out canned gravy.

Salad Dressings

Commercially prepared salad dressings are very expensive and full of fats and tropical oils. Use no-cholesterol, low-fat oil like canola for oil in these dressings. Use light mayonnaise in dressings that call for it. In Europe, salad dressing is always oil and vinegar, which gets boring.

Tomato Dressing (basic French)

    1 10-ounce can condensed
        tomato soup
    ¾ cup sugar
    ½ cup cider vinegar
    ½ cup oil
    ½ tsp. salt
    ½ tsp. black pepper
    ½ tsp. paprika or more to taste

Combine above, pour in jar. Add garlic clove cut in half.

Sweet-and-Sour Celery Seed Dressing

This dressing is especially good with fresh spinach, sliced hard-boiled eggs, and a little cooked, crumpled bacon.

    1 medium onion, minced
        finely
    1 tsp. spicy brown mustard
    ⅓ cup white vinegar
    ⅔ cup sugar
    ¾ cup oil
    1 tsp. celery seed

Mix ingredients in blender or food processor to pulverize onion.

Bleu Cheese Dressing

    1½ cups mayonnaise
    ½ cup sour cream
    ¼ cup milk
    1 T. finely minced onion
    1 T. lemon juice
    ½ tsp. Worcestershire
    dash Tabasco sauce
    dash garlic salt

Mix; then fold in 4–8 ounces crumbled bleu cheese.

Green Goddess Dressing

    ⅓ cup sour cream
    3 T. minced fresh parsley
    2 T. anchovy fillets or 2- to
        3-inch squeeze of anchovy
        paste
    1 T. snipped chives
    1 T. lemon juice
    1 T. white wine vinegar
    1 clove crushed garlic
    salt and pepper to taste

Mix in blender or food processor. Fold in

    ¾ cup mayonnaise

W hat is the ideal boat for offshore sailing? If there were one answer, everybody would have the same boat. The subject could take up this entire book. One book I highly recommend reading is *Desirable and Undesirable Characteristics of Offshore Yachts*, edited by John Rousmaniere.

DESIGN

Stability Issues

Capsize screening values generally end up with 30 feet as a minimum length. For comfort offshore, I like a minimum of 40 feet. Tests conducted at the Southampton University in England determined that a boat can be rolled by a wave height equal to 55 percent of its overall length. Therefore, the longer the boat, the better.

One also has to look at displacement. A light boat is not going to be as happy carrying all the food, stores, and spares for a world cruise as a vessel on which these items constitute less than a double-digit percentage of displacement. While naval architects build in a safety margin, increasing displacement adds to righting moment and therefore to stress on the rig.

Also, a heavy boat has more resistance to wave-impact capsize. The famous research scientist and naval architect Tony Marchaj asserts that a heavy-displacement boat may have as much as five times the capsize resistance as an ultralight-displacement boat of the same length overall.

You Can't Always Get What You Want

Most people say: "I want a boat that sails well."

The next breath is: "We need lots of storage space, and do not want to be confined in a small cabin."

While these attributes are not mutually exclusive, one does have to buy a larger vessel. A lot of people think 40 feet is about the limit a couple can handle. Twenty years ago this was true. But with the modern conveniences of roller-furling sails and power winches, the parameters have expanded. My favorite rig for a boat under about 55 feet is a cutter (or double-headsail sloop), with all sails roller furling. Over 50 feet, split rigs reduce sail size. I prefer a true ketch, with a permanent mizzen backstay.

Rather than traipsing all over the country to sail various boats and then waiting for good conditions, one can easily compare sailing characteristics by looking at IMS certificates for boats under consideration. U.S. Sailing (formerly U.S. Yacht Racing Union, North American Yacht Racing Union; see appendix 7 for contact information) can provide copies of IMS certificates for a modest fee. The certificate lists velocity expected on various angles to the wind in wind speeds from about 6 to 20 knots. The number will always look small for beating or dead running, but bear in mind that it represents velocity made good, rather than boat speed through the water. Wind angles are to true wind, rather than apparent wind angle, which is affected by boat speed. Certificates may list seconds per mile, which is easily converted to knots by dividing by 3,600.

The question of whether to pinch or foot going upwind is answered by an IMS certificate because it lists the optimum true wind angle for going upwind in the range of wind velocities. Of even more interest to cruisers is the optimum run angle, which is greatly affected by wind strength. An Alden 44 will make the best time on a run sailing 50 degrees higher than dead downwind in 6 knots of true wind; but at 20 knots, only 5 degrees deviation from course is required. (See the Polars on Passages, tip 185, for more information.)

Listed on an IMS Certificate is the displacement of the vessel, which will be very close to actual weight. Most boat manufacturers list displacement at a datum waterline rather than at the actual flotation plane. While displacement on an IMS certificate is generally greater than advertised, it is measured with all tanks dry and no stores on board. Remember that 60 gallons of diesel and 200 gallons of freshwater add a ton to displacement, and that's before food, clothing, spare parts, and, oh yes, crew.

A useful number is "sink," which is commonly known as "pounds per inch immersion." Current IMS certificates give the weight necessary to cause a vessel to float $\frac{1}{100}$-foot lower, but this is easily converted to inches (see Overall Effect of Adding Weight to a Vessel, tip 173).

Another important number is the limit of positive stability (LPS), which is the angle at which the vessel will roll over rather than come back up. Offshore racing regulations call for a minimum of 120 degrees; that is, the boat will go 30 degrees past horizontal and still come back up. The limit of positive stability assumes the vessel has a perfectly flush deck, and ignores the additional buoyancy from having its cabinhouse immersed or the loss of buoyancy from cockpit wells.

For a broad overview of boats, U.S. Sailing publishes *Performance Characteristics Profile of the North American IMS Fleet*. Nearly 700 production boat models are listed, with draft, sail area, displacement, limit of positive stability, righting moment, and the general-purpose IMS rating. (In IMS ratings, a smaller number indicates a faster boat.) Also included are very useful comparative ratios for evaluating performance, including length–beam, displacement–length, sail area–wetted surface, and beam–depth.

Once you have purchased a vessel, the best way to enhance performance is by spending $130 for a custom Performance Package from U.S. Sailing. The package includes polar diagrams and lots of tables, customized for your genoa size, propeller, and use of spinnakers.

THE PROPERLY BUILT YACHT

Frequently I am asked, "What would you do if you were, (A) buying a new boat, or (B) outfitting a previously owned vessel for offshore cruising?" This section includes some of my thoughts on what I would do. Obviously, some specifications are not applicable for an existing vessel, but the ideas presented here may pertain to refits. Equipment specifications include products that I have used with success but should not be construed to be the only suitable choice.

Fiberglass Hull and Deck Construction

I have managed aluminum vessels and seen firsthand all the problems that develop. Steel is a good material for hulls that take abuse, but is maintenance intensive and heavy for pleasure boats. Properly built ferrocement can be a good hull material, but is virtually impossible to insure, and the deck must be made from another material. Wood, even cold-molded, has its drawbacks in strength-to-weight considerations and rot potential. Properly executed fiberglass-reinforced plastic (FRP) has the fewest drawbacks. I use *fiberglass* loosely, including in the term all composite construction.

Several years ago there was much ballyhoo about compliance with American Bureau of Shipping (ABS) scantlings. After a number of failures of hulls built to its specifications, ABS stopped offering certification. I am familiar with one very expensive brand of alleged offshore cruising yachts that continued to satisfy ABS rules even after removing half the structural fiberglass in its hulls.

Fibers

The question of cored hulls and decks comes up often. The core material (balsa, foam, honeycomb, etc.) separates the fiberglass skins like the middle part of an I-beam. When the panel is bent, the fibers on the convex side are in tension and those on the concave side are in compression. Exotic materials such as carbon fiber and Kevlar are very strong in tension, but no better (or in some cases worse) than standard fiberglass in compression. For these materials to be effective, the axis of the fibers must correspond exactly to the direction of loading—not the easiest task in a rounded hull.

Fiberglass comes in several grades, the most common being E-glass and S-glass. *E* stands for electrical grade, and *S* for structural. Until ten years ago, most fiberglass boats were built with E-glass, and there is nothing wrong with this material. The configuration of fiberglass is important. Configuration

can be classified in three categories: chopped strand, woven, and linear continuous fibers.

Production boats are built in female molds with a highly polished interior surface. Gelcoat (basically resin with a pigment added) is first sprayed into the mold. Usually chopped strand goes down next, either as hand-laid mat or sprayed by a chopper gun that delivers chopped fiberglass strands and resin simultaneously. Thickness is built up with alternating layers of chopped strand and woven or linear fabrics.

The norm for woven structural glass used to be 24-ounce woven roving, which has bundles of fiberglass strands about $\frac{5}{16}$ inch wide that are woven through each other. The problem with this material is that the surface it makes is far from flat, and it takes a lot of resin to fill the spaces in the weave. Strength is also lost as the fibers go up and down in the weave. Woven roving has been replaced by linear fibers running at various crossing angles to each other and stitched together to hold configuration until locked in place with resin. The terms *biaxial* and *triaxial* refer to the numbers of layers of linear fibers.

To facilitate the molding process, the linear fiber sandwich often has a layer of mat on one side. A commonly used material is called 1808, which has two 9-ounce layers of linear fibers stitched to ¾-ounce mat.

Cores and Skins

Modern boats have thinner skins thanks to higher-modulus (read

stronger) materials, which saves weight. While stiff and strong, their impact resistance may be inadequate. A skin needs thickness to spread impact loads over a large area. One can easily plunge a knife through one sheet of paper, but trying to impale a phone book is difficult. To increase impact resistance, some scantling rules add additional layers of material below the waterline. This is fine for powerboats, but less desirable for boats under sail whose thin-skinned topsides are immersed and therefore vulnerable to catastrophic damage in the event of a collision.

The major difficulty with cored construction is bonding the skins to the core. Vacuum-bagging used to be high-tech, but is becoming more commonplace. The usual procedure is to lay the outside laminate in a mold, and then put the core material down in a layer of slow-curing resin. Plastic sheeting is laid over the core with air channels under it. A vacuum pump withdraws air, forcing the core down on the resin layer. When the resin hardens, the plastic is removed and the inside skin is laminated over the core. The amount of vacuum used is critical—too little and the core will not bond to the outer skin, too much and resin will be pulled into the core, resulting in a poor bond of the outer skin to the core. I was involved with a purportedly high-quality 50-foot boat that suffered from the latter malady—poor bonding of the core to the skin—and which the manufacturer refused to repair.

The high-tech molding method these days is resin infusion molding where all fiberglass is put into the mold dry and a vacuum pulls resin into the fibers. This method is supposed to result in perfect fiberglass parts, but I have observed large blisters in hulls formed via this process. One trade name of resin infusion is SCRIMP.

There is a lot of debate about core materials. Balsa is twice as strong in compression as most foams, but is also twice as heavy. Balsa will rot if water gets into it, but foams turn into mush. Laboratory panels of end-grain balsa show little migration of water. But regardless of grain orientation or core material, water can migrate great distances between the core and skin if the bond between them is broken. I have observed water migration from an improperly installed bow thruster tube extending back 30 feet through the laminate on a vacuum-bagged hull with poor bonding of skin to core.

Some foam coring materials exhibit a property called *creep*. When initially tested, the panel is rigid. But if the testing pressure is left in place overnight, the panel will sag.

Some foams are thermally sensitive and should not be used in decks, especially if the deck is not white.

Localized reinforcement with high-tech fibers (Kevlar, carbon, etc.) is becoming popular, but must be very carefully engineered. Because the yield strengths of materials vary, bending may fracture an unhomogeneous laminate. Think

of a spinnaker with a wire running down the middle: the spinnaker will blow out on each side of the wire. An early use of carbon fiber was the reinforcement of rudderstocks. This was a disaster because the bond between the carbon and the other materials broke when bent, and neither material was strong enough to carry the entire load. The photo shows a Kevlar–carbon laminate spinnaker pole, broken by progressive failure.

The (Costly) Ideal

If I had an unlimited budget to build a new fiberglass cruising boat, all laminating would be done with vinylester resin, which is much more impervious to water than polyester resin. Because bilge water may be present inside a hull, vinylester resin on the inside lam-

inate prevents inside-to-outside osmosis.

On my ideal boat, all structural fiberglass would be linear fiber, with the ply axis oriented parallel to stress. The hull under the waterline would be solid glass, stiffened by a large fiberglass grid floor system made from hollow inverted U-shaped channels heavily glassed into the hull (in boatbuilding terms, *floors* are the structural members under the sole).

For new boat construction, I'd cut limber holes in the floor system and then fill all low spots in the bilge—other than the central sump—so that any water below drains to the sump and does not form puddles. The best way to do this is to elevate each of the four corners of the hull (e.g., port bow, port stern) at least 5 degrees from level, and pour a thin-viscosity, slowly cat-

This broken Kevlar–carbon fiber pole is typical of early failures caused by the inappropriate combining of fibers.

alyzed filler material into the lower corner, using enough liquid to create a smooth path for water to reach the sump when the boat is level. I have also done this procedure with a vessel afloat, filling 55-gallon drums with water on deck to artificially change the plane of flotation, but the job is much easier at the early stages of construction.

Doing this job on an already built boat, I once poured in a little too much filler. It ran into the sump. I had to leave the vessel for a short while. The bilge pump dutifully pumped the filler, which solidified in the pump, strainer, and all the hoses, necessitating replacement of all.

I would use balsa coring above the waterline on my ideal boat, with additional layers of laminate forward of maximum beam. Transition from cored to uncored areas would be gradual to dissipate stress.

The deck also would be balsacored, except in areas of hardware mounting where the core would be replaced with resin and high-strength filler.

Most importantly, I would hire a *qualified* person to monitor the layup process, not an out-of-work yacht captain. Even in the most sophisticated shops, what happens in the lab does not always get carried out on the shop floor.

When buying a used boat, you should hire a technically competent surveyor, not just somebody who popped a couple hundred dollars for a moisture meter. As a prophylactic measure, have underwater surfaces stripped to clean gelcoat and the proper film thickness of vinylester resin applied. Vinylesters are harder to work with than epoxies, but are more impervious to water. If bottom paint is subsequently stripped from the hull, be sure the vinylester coating is not ground off.

Steering

For a cruising boat, wheel steering is almost mandatory. Transferring motion from the wheel to the rudder can be done in various ways, the most common of which is stainless steel cable connected to chain that goes around a sprocket on the wheel axle. The other end of the cable is dead-ended on a quadrant on the rudderstock. Cable is usually led via sheaves, but may be encased in conduit where straight runs are not possible.

If your boat has cable-pedestal steering, be sure you know how to remove the compass to get to the sprocket. Generally, only two very small screws hold the compass in place, and the others hold the compass together. Any movement of the latter will cause fluid to leak out.

Before working on anything inside the pedestal, stuff a large towel down the hole, as small parts will fall to the bottom of the pedestal, requiring removal of the pedestal for retrieval. There is a trick to removing a steering axle, so ask the manufacturer for instructions.

Before going offshore, check that the sheaves in the steering system are properly aligned so the cable does not rub on the side wall of the sheaves. It is amazing how many boats leave the factory with misaligned sheaves that very rapidly increase friction and wear.

Cable should be set up tight enough so it will not jump the sheaves when the helm is moved violently. Tangency guards are available that fit over the sheaves to prevent the cable from jumping off, and should be installed at least on the idler sheaves under the pedestal where the cable makes a 90-degree turn.

In specifying equipment for the Tartan 41, I did not like the occasional clunking noise made by the Nicopressed eyes on the ends of the cables passing each other inside the pedestal. Sparkman & Stephens always sea-trialed each new model. At the dock, Rod Stephens was doing his normal test of hanging a 1-pound weight 1 foot out on a steering wheel spoke to be sure the weight caused the wheel to turn. He turned to me and said, "Bill, did you deviate from any of our specs on the steering?"

"Yes, I did. I replaced the Nicopressed eyes connecting the chain to cable with swaged eyes to eliminate interference as they pass each other," I proudly answered.

"Who did the swaging?" Rod asked. "We did," I replied. "Bet your swaging machine is oriented north-and-south," Rod said.

I thought a moment, and said, "Yes, it is. How did you know that?"

"Because the swages are a little magnetic and cause the compass to change as the wheel is turned."

Needless to say, a deflated project engineer replaced the cables in the first boat and reverted to specification.

Modern racing boats use a simpler steering system that has a lot going for it: a drum on the steering wheel axle around which high-tech rope is wrapped. The rope leads through low-friction sheaves to a quadrant, eliminating the chain and stainless steel wire rope and their attendant connections. Because modern high-tech rope has better strength characteristics and almost as low stretch as wire rope, these systems work well. Remember high-tech rope if your wire cable breaks and you do not have a replacement.

Rudder Failure

Loss of steering can happen in many ways (see photo). Carrying a set of cables already attached to the chain makes changing a broken cable relatively easy. In running the new cables, use a straightened-out coat hanger or other stiff wire pushed up through the holes from the underside of the steering mounting area as a messenger to which the new cable is attached. Be sure the exact middle of the chain is engaged on the sprocket.

Most rudderstocks are stainless steel and have bars or a plate welded on over which the foam and fiberglass blade are constructed. These welds can break, leaving one with a rudder blade flopping around independent of the stock.

Some rudders are built with a hole in the top aft corner through which lines can be rigged for steering control. A good project when a

The bottom part of this skeg-hung rudder was sheared off—up to the bottom of the rudder's internal metal structure—in a collision. Fortunately, there was enough left to provide sufficient steering to make port.

vessel is hauled is to locally reinforce the rudder on the aft upper corner and then drill a hole and epoxy in a bronze pipe nipple. For boats up to 55 feet or so, ¾-inch IPS (nominal pipe size) is adequate. Grind the ends of the nipple flush with the rudder skin. Fill the nipple hole with expanding foam and paint over it. Hope you never have to use it. If you do, punch out the foam and run your lines through the nipple.

Without a hole, a large heavy-duty C-clamp can be affixed horizontally to the rudder for slow-speed maneuvering in calm water. Be sure the lines coming off each side of the clamp lead forward to help hold the clamp on the rudder. If possible, use blocks of wood be-

tween the clamp pads and the rudder to spread the loads.

Grounding or collision with underwater objects can bend a rudderstock. One Alden 46 owner was motoring into a harbor at 1.2 knots when he hit a rock with the rudder. He was amazed that the rudderstock, 4 inches in diameter by ⅜ inch wall thickness, bent, despite being supported on a skeg at the bottom. The post bent enough to jam the rudder hard over, causing loss of steering. Several powerboats were required to get the boat to a dock. The owner, a metallurgist, computed that the force of his boat stopping from 1.2 knots was four times the strength of the massive 150-pound rudderstock. He has been very careful since.

An emergency rudder can be made by clamping a spinnaker or whisker pole to a large piece of plywood, such as the lift-out panels in berths. You need several U-bolts and U-shaped pieces of wood such as those shown here.

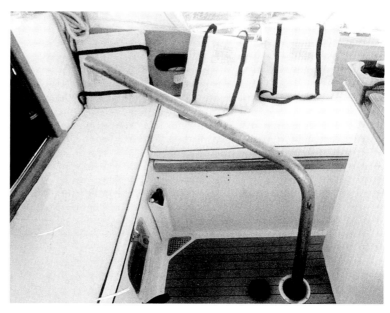

The emergency tiller on this Hinckley looks stout enough, but two strong men were unable to steer the boat with it underway. We had to rig lines from the tiller to the cockpit winches, which involved all sorts of extra blocks to get a good lead. We found that if we trimmed the sails to give just a touch of weather helm, only the windward winch needed to be tended constantly.

Emergency Steering

A Marion–Bermuda Race requirement, and a very good idea on any vessel, is to have a plan and parts for fashioning steering totally independent from the vessel's rudder.

The most common jury rig is to use the spinnaker pole as a stern sweep, but this works only in calm water. The easiest way of making a blade for the sweep is to use a berth top affixed to the pole with several U-bolts. Threaded rod can be used to make U-bolts. For spinnaker poles 3 inches or less in diameter, Jamestown Distributors sells ½-inch-diameter-by-3-inch ID galvanized U-bolts. Matching steel backing plates are inexpensive. Be sure to precut U-shaped pieces of wood to go between the pole and the berth top; these must be sufficiently thick to allow for the engagement of nuts, lock washers, and backing plates on the berth top side opposite the pole (see top left photo).

Alternatively, electrical suppliers have bronze U-shaped ground clamps in larger diameters that can be used to fasten a spinnaker pole to a flat panel of plywood.

Provision must be made to prevent rotation of the spinnaker pole, as the force of the water will cause the sweep to turn horizontally. A large crowbar can be used through the spinnaker pole jaw, provided the crew steering are quite strong. Light jaw castings may fracture, however, so the crew should be prepared for failure. In addition, the blade will try to float, requiring the helmsperson to exert force to keep the blade down.

When thinking about emergency steering, remember that the forces involved are very large. We are lulled into complacency by the mechanical advantage of steering with a wheel. The 14-inch quadrant used on boats of around 40 feet LOA provides the same power as a tiller 15 feet long! (See top right photo.)

Deck Hardware and Fittings

Metal Type and Backing Plates

On my ideal boat, all fabricated stainless steel is type 316L, mechanically and electro-polished. The slight extra cost of 316L over the commonly used 304 is worth it in the long run for its increased resistance to corrosion and surface oxidation (rust).

Where deck hardware is mounted through cored areas, the core should be replaced with chopped fiber and epoxy resin extending at least 1 inch around the fastener holes.

Backing plates must be installed for all hardware. To dissipate loads, backing plates should be set in a filler of vinylester or epoxy resin and a high-strength thixotropic material so that the backing plate forms a continuous void-free bond with the underside of the deck. Avoid the common practice of using bedding compound between the underside of deck and backing plates. Compressible bedding compound does not evenly spread loads to the deck structure, and over time may compress, causing loose fasteners and leaks. For work in the field, polyester body putty (such as Bondo) may be substituted for a proper bonding agent, but much more preferable is a vinylester putty such as that made by 3M.

Stanchions

Stanchions should be 30 inches high, with a minimum wall thickness of 0.125 inch. Unfortunately, the standard is 24 inches high. Lifelines set at that height hit most people at the knees, which could contribute to someone going overboard if the back of their knee contacts the upper lifeline. A nice touch found on a few yachts is to have the upper lifeline replaced with stainless steel tubing. To keep cost and complexity down, I'd only

do this from the stern pulpit to the midship boarding gate.

Chocks

Chocks should have rollers turning on bronze oil-impregnated bearings, and be serviceable from the deck. There should be a fairlead from the midship chock to the primary cockpit winches to facilitate docking with a spring line. Fore-and-aft placement of midship chocks is critical for easy docking. With the aft chock properly positioned, powering ahead on a spring line makes a vessel parallel park. Most chocks are too far forward, and powering on a spring line brings the bow in first. This can be counteracted somewhat by turning the rudder away from the dock. I have never been in a docking situation where I could not get a boat alongside a dock as long as I could get a spring line secured ashore.

My best docking exhibition was on a brand-new Alden 50 whose owner insisted on going for a sail on a blustery day. On returning to the harbor, we found boats had been moved and the only space available was 55 feet of dock starting at the shore. The wind was 40+ knots blowing directly over (at right angles to) the dock. The longest line on board was a spinnaker after guy, which I rigged from a cockpit winch through the midship chock and then to the bow. We brought the boat in perpendicular to the dock, directly into the wind. A crew jumped off the bow and made the spring line fast to a cleat on the dock near the shore end. As soon as for-

ward power was taken off, the boat blew out and hung parallel to the dock by the single midship line. Powering ahead and in on the spring line brought the boat closer to the dock. Then I eased off power so that slack in the spring line could be taken in. We also couldn't travel too far forward. It took several of these maneuvers, but eventually we got the boat docked without damage to her or the Alden 54 docked ahead. (See also Spring Lines, pages 215–16, and Docking, pages 215–17, in appendix 6.)

Removable Wood

Wherever possible, wood used on deck should be removable to facilitate varnishing. All wood on deck should be sealed on all sides prior to installation. If epoxy is used rather than varnish, an ultraviolet filter is best added to the epoxy, and only unexposed surfaces should be epoxy-coated. No bedding job is perfect, and if the unexposed, mounted side of wood is not sealed, water will get under the film at its edge and begin lifting the coating on the exposed areas.

Hatches

The strongest deck hatches I have found are Bomar cast Almag 35 with extra ribs extending under the Lexan glazing (any transparent material used for windows). Bomar cast opening ports also are rugged.

Stainless Steel Fasteners in Aluminum

All fasteners in deck hardware and rig involving stainless and aluminum are removed and coated with Duralac or Tef-Gel prior to commissioning. These dissimilar metals are most often found where stainless steel screws are used to hold hardware to the aluminum mast. Because of their differences in voltage potential, the less noble aluminum begins to corrode. Unlike brown rusty steel, however, corroding aluminum makes a sometimes-hard-to-see pile of white powder.

Winches

In the case of a winch failure, cockpit winches on my ideal boat would be configured so that each genoa sheet can be led fairly to the winch on the other side of the cockpit.

Speaking of failures, one day I got a panic call from an owner who told me he thought one of his $10,000 cockpit winches had broken because it turned both ways. I asked him if anything had been done to the winch recently. "Yes," he replied, "a couple of weeks ago I greased the winches." The next time I was on board I disassembled the winch and removed gobs of grease from the pawl pockets, replacing it with light oil. The winch worked perfectly. When lubricating winches, more grease is not always better.

Scuppers

Cockpit scuppers should drain all areas below bridge deck level in less than 90 seconds. Cockpit scupper hose runs should be as straight and short as possible to prevent clogging by debris.

At extreme angles of heel, the vertical scupper hose may back up water into the cockpit, but is less likely to accumulate crud. A sobering experiment is to intentionally block cockpit scuppers and fill the cockpit with water, noting the decrease in freeboard and timing how long it takes to empty.

Electrical Systems

Wire

All wire should be marine strand tinned copper. The best wire has irradiated thermoset insulation, which does not melt and offers more protection from abrasion, solvents, and ultraviolet light than conventional insulation. One good source for irradiated wire is the Berkshire Electric Cable Company.

I like to size DC (direct current) wiring for a 3 percent voltage drop or less. A table of recommended wire sizes based on the length of run is in the West Marine catalog. Remember that length is the total of positive and negative wire lengths from the device to the battery. Large-draw items that are not used for long periods of time, such as windlasses, can have a 10 percent voltage drop.

Troughs — It is very convenient to run wiring in plastic wire troughs with snap-on covers. I like separate troughs for AC, DC, and electronics wiring. Closed conduit should be avoided due to the potential for water sitting inside and causing degradation of the wires. If closed conduit must be used, provide drain holes. Do not bundle wires with ties inside the troughs, as it can cause heat buildup and make wire replacement more difficult.

Arrange wiring so that vibration from the engine and other sources is not transmitted to the wiring. I always try to secure wires very close to their termination so no stress is placed on the wire-to-terminal juncture. When not run in troughs, wire is supported at least on 18-inch intervals using screw-in-place mounts to hold the wire ties.

Color Coding — Wiring should follow the ABYC color coding standard (E-9, Direct Current Electrical Systems on Boats), with yellow used for DC negative. Each wire should be identified with a wrap-on wire marker or marking on its jacket with a permanent ink marker within 6 inches of each connection, and at 4-foot intervals along the wire run. A wiring diagram should include marking codes and connection of every wire.

Terminals — All terminals should be manufactured from tinned copper (use a magnet to check). All terminals should be installed with a double-crimping-type ratchet tool that will not release until the terminal is crimped to proper pressure (see photo with tip 124). Care must be taken that the terminal is inserted in the tool so crimping occurs on the split top portion of the terminal. Cost of a proper crimping tool (*not* a cheap combination stripper and crimper) will be quickly amortized. All terminals should be ring-type. Spade and quick-disconnect terminals should not be used due to the possibility of boat motion causing disconnection. When equipment comes with a spade connection built-in (engine senders and Par pumps are notorious examples), I compress the female spade to the male spade as tightly as I can, and then be sure the wire is arranged to hold positive pressure on the connection.

Terminals on tinned wire do not require soldering. Terminals on nontinned wire leads are soldered after crimping, with care taken that solder does not flow along the wire past the terminal, which will result in stiffening of the wire.

Battery lug terminals are frequently not well done, as proper crimping tools are very expensive, and less expensive models that work by hitting a die with a hammer are difficult to use in confined spaces. To ensure the least possible resistance, I mechanically crimp terminals on large wires with a Nicopress tool and then hold the terminal in the flame of a torch until solder flows into the terminal; I continue feeding in solder until all of the voids in the terminal are filled. Wire is held nearly vertical with the terminal over the flame as the solder is flowed in to prevent the solder from wicking along the wire and stiffening it.

In-Line Fuses—About 90 percent of electrical problems I have found with equipment having in-line fuses have turned out to be the fuse holder. Where equipment must be protected by fuse, such as low-amperage-draw electronics, a more reliable fuse block should be installed. I like to install a fuse block with extra positions to hold spare fuses of the correct amperage for the equipment, and install a clear polycarbonate cover to retain fuses during extreme vessel movement.

Butt Connectors—A bane of electrical installations is the use of butt connectors to connect equipment to the supply wiring of the boat's electrical system. Because the only way to replace the equipment is to cut the wire, eventually supply wiring becomes too short. It is much more practical to use barrier terminal strips. One must be careful to check that the terminal strips are chrome-plated, nonferrous metal (use a magnet). Terminal strips are sized to amperage, that is, #6-32 machine screws, maximum 20 amps; #8-32, maximum 30 amps; #10-32, maximum 75 amps. Junctions above these amperages should be made with stud-type terminals. When it is impossible to install a proper junction, I have used ring terminals on each end of the wires and held them together with a small nut and bolt. This is a much more secure junction than a butt connector. Do not put a stainless steel washer be-

tween the terminals, because stainless is not a good conductor of electricity.

After connections have been made and tightened, I spray them with two coats of CRC Heavy Duty Corrosion Inhibitor (#06026). Check all electrical connections for tightness after one month and then after twelve months of vessel operation, and respray with CRC.

Panels—To minimize shock hazard and prevent misinterpretation of wiring color codes, the electrical power distribution panels for the DC and AC electrical systems should be separate (black is hot for AC wiring and frequently negative for DC wiring). This has only recently become a code requirement, and many boats have combination panels. On these panels I have frequently made covers for hot AC wiring connections from split clear plastic hose held in place with wire ties. It's not always pretty, but better than getting zapped by AC.

The 72-Inch Rule—ABYC standards require that overcurrent protection be provided within 72 inches of the origin of any power, whether AC from shore, generator or inverter, or DC from batteries and alternators. This protection is preferably by circuit breaker, but high-amperage fuses are acceptable, provided a large inventory of spares is maintained. I like to spec the double-pole breaker for the shore power at the inlet at 5 amps higher than the main shore power breaker on the panel, so hopefully the more easily accessible panel breaker will trip first.

Because alternators may be damaged if run with output disconnected, I recommend placing a breaker or an overcurrent device in the field circuit running to the alternator.

Drip Loops — Where any wire enters a vessel — from deck feedthrough, pulpit connection of running lights, or any other manner — a drip loop is provided in the wire below decks so that any water traveling along the wire will drip from the wire before reaching any connections (see the photo with tip 110).

Lights

While fluorescent lighting has the best lumen-to-power consumed ratio, fixtures with proper electrical shielding of ballast are very expensive, and the styles are limited. Halogen bulbs do get very hot, but provide a lot of light. A good source of halogen lighting fixtures is A&B Industries (ABI); see appendix 7. Port and starboard interior lights should be on separate circuits or split fore and aft. Power distribution wiring to lighting is oversize to allow for the adding of more fixtures in the future without the necessity of replacing the existing wire.

It is very convenient to have lights on the deck and mast controlled from a waterproof breaker panel located in the cockpit close to the helm (Paneltronics #9952205 is a suitable eight-breaker panel). Suggested circuits include the navigation lights, steaming light, spreader lights, foredeck light, masthead light, tricolor light, masthead strobe light, and compass light. A fire drill on the foredeck in the middle of the night is not the best time to have to go below to turn on the spreader lights.

While it is a little heavy on power draw, very nice "mood" illumination can be installed by mounting tubular (also called "rope") lighting behind valences. Vista (appendix 7) makes tubular lighting used on the exterior of semi-trucks that can be cut to length and conformed around curves.

It's also very handy to have lights installed in each hanging locker, controlled by a refrigerator door switch that activates the light when the locker door is opened.

More of a necessity are lights installed in each deck locker, with manual control close to the top of the locker. This sure beats holding a flashlight in your mouth while digging through the locker contents in the middle of the night. All lights inside lockers are on their own circuits so you can see if one has been left on by simply checking the ammeter on the electrical distribution panel.

Batteries

I like two battery banks composed of 6-volt golf cart batteries, with each bank of adequate amperage to handle twenty-four hours' consumption while underway. A se-

lector switch lets you toggle between banks. Normal operation is to keep the switch in the Both or All position. Recharge daily to at least 90 percent of bank capacity. Shallow cycling increases battery life, but if one bank fails, the switch allows taking that bank off line.

For most redundancy, on my ideal boat the main propulsion engine would have two dual-output alternators, with breakers on the field wire to allow one alternator to be used at a time, with the other kept as a spare to be instantly put on line by turning on the field breaker. The alternator in use is changed on a weekly basis. The separate starting battery for the main propulsion engine is charged from one of the two alternator outputs. The switch allows starting the engine from the house battery bank (see drawing with tip 103).

The auxiliary generator or genset should have a separate starting battery, but a concealed switch may be installed to allow the generator to be started from either the ship's bank or the main engine starting battery.

Isolation Transformer

The AC shore power system on vessels traveling outside the U.S. should have an isolation and stepdown transformer capable of operation on either 50 or 60 Hz. Taps are provided on the transformer to permit inputs from 208 to 250 volts to be regulated to 115 volts.

Even vessels not going foreign benefit from an isolation transformer because it protects the boat from stray current found in most marinas. One Alden 54 I manage was eating about 20 pounds of zinc a season. After an isolation transformer was installed, the zincs began to last for several years each.

Extremely quiet, epoxy-encapsulated (called *potted*) transformers are manufactured by the Olsun Electrics Corp.; see appendix 7.

Battery Chargers

Due to advances made in battery charger technology, ferroresonant (they hum) models should be replaced with solid-state designs that electrically isolate AC ground and neutral from DC negative. If going abroad, the charger should operate from either 50 or 60 Hz. Battery charging output should be at least 40 percent of house battery bank capacity to allow for rapid recharging.

If gel-cell batteries are installed (not recommended), battery charger capacity must be increased, because the lower voltage required to charge gel-cell batteries increases recharge time.

On my ideal boat, the battery charger provides both bulk and float charge rates, and has an adjustable output finishing voltage to accommodate subsequent installation of different battery types.

The charger would have individual outputs to all battery banks and monitor the banks individually. The Promatic series by Professional Mariner satisfies these criteria and has the added advantage of accepting any AC input voltage from 90 to 270 and any frequency from 45 Hz to 440 Hz.

Yacht owners without a step-down transformer may consider a change-over switch to allow AC input to the charger to be hooked directly to non-U.S.-standard shore power, bypassing the vessel's shore power system, provided the charger can accept 220-volt, 50 Hz input.

Plumbing

Sanitation Hose

Odor permeation is a problem with toilet and holding tank hoses. Most resistant is rigid PVC pipe, which is therefore suitable only for straight runs. Next by a wide margin, according to *Practical Sailor* tests, is SeaLand Technology's OdorSafe hose. This hose is not very flexible and in less than tropical heat can be difficult to bend and force over hose barbs. Gentle warming of the hose helps.

All fittings would be Shields 800 fiberglass-reinforced series, which are made to fit 1½-inch hose. Under no circumstances should gray PVC commercial insert adapters be used because the barb is larger than 1½ inches diameter.

All hoses must be double-clamped with all-stainless steel clamps, and the screws opposed 180 degrees.

The best vented loops I have found are Forespar glass-filled Marelon, which have a gentle curve and a smooth interior for the least restriction of effluents.

Toilets

All toilets should be mounted so that the rim of the bowl is at least 2 inches above the static waterline; otherwise, the failure of a valve or vented loop could allow water to siphon into the boat, and if the boat is unattended it could sink.

If the toilet seat will not stay up at 35 degrees of heel, install shock cord or a hinged retainer. Yeah, this is a guy thing, but when underway one hand is frequently needed for hanging onto the boat while the other is occupied with the task at (in?) hand. Install adequate handholds near the head for use on both tacks. I do not allow crew to urinate over the side and would rather clean up a head than try to find a man overboard.

If the boat is equipped with two toilets, they should be on opposite sides to facilitate use while heeled over. Rebuild kits for toilets are augmented by replacements for all rubber and leather components, and all springs.

In *Practical Sailor* evaluations, the best head is usually a Blake or Wilcox-Crittenden Skipper, model 1550-C, the latter mostly because of its large joker valve that makes it hard to clog. Most of the yachts I manage have Wilcox toilets and I've rebuilt them many times. For awhile in the 1980s and early 1990s, Wilcox toilets were manufactured in a Third World country with very poor quality control. Check carefully for porosity in the castings. Here are projects I've done on Wilcox toilets:

- Disassemble toilet; remachine all mating surfaces to be smooth, without grooves.

- Grind the exterior of components to a smooth surface, then plate with marine chrome.
- Replace screws in the toilet seat assembly with stainless steel, as the standard screws rust quickly.
- Grind off lettering on the joker valve to allow a proper seal.
- Replace the bronze bolts that fasten the pump unit to the base with stainless steel bolts.
- Replace the drain plug with a stainless steel Zerk-Lock fitting to permit greasing of the leather without the hassle of disassembly.
- Replace the hose between the pump and bowl with hose running to a vented loop located above the static waterline.
- To keep the seat from twisting sideways when the boat is heeled (possibly dumping the occupant!), install plastic blocks on the underside of the seat to chock it into the rim (see photo with tip 79).

On all toilets, sanitation effluent hose should run from the toilet to a vented loop located above the waterline and then to a Y-valve such as a Whale #MSDV5606. While all Y-valves are likely to clog, this valve is least prone to and is easy to disassemble for cleaning.

One output from the Y-valve discharges waste overboard and the other runs to a polyethylene, heavywall (⅜ in. minimum) holding tank, with a minimum size of 10 gallons per berth.

To empty the holding tank offshore, install a SeaLand Technology #317-301200 or similar electric diaphragm pump that can be run dry without damage. Output from the pump runs through a vented loop located above waterline and then to a seacock and through-hull.

Through-Hull Fittings

Rather than use proper cast bronze through-hull fittings, a lot of boats are built with a pipe nipple screwed into the seacock and ground flush with the exterior of the hull. This installation is not strong, and likely to leak.

Flush through-hulls are easy to install if a boss to receive them has been molded into the hull, but are time-consuming to install on existing vessels.

For general use I like Perko series #322 through-hulls bedded with 3M 5200 and screwed into Perko #805 series seacocks, with minimum thread engagement length equal to the pipe diameter. Where through-hull fittings are installed through a cored hull, the inside skin and core must be removed at least 2 inches around the perimeter of the fitting. Replace the core with epoxy resin reinforced with chopped fiber and West System #404 high-density filler. The area should be covered with a laminate equal to or exceeding the thickness of the original inside skin. The successive layers of glass should overlap the filled area and previous layers by 2 inches for a total overlap of at least 6 inches (see drawing).

Intake through-hulls for engine cooling, pumps, etc., are located as close to centerline as possible so that they remain immersed when the boat is heeled 40 degrees. In-

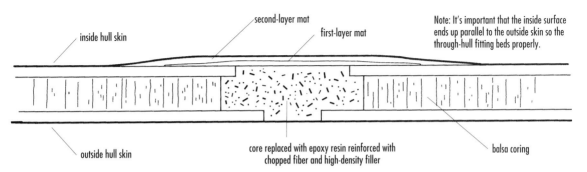

When installing through-hulls in cored hulls, the core must be removed and filled with a mix of epoxy resin and chopped fiber as shown here. The next step is to drill for the through-hull.

takes for heads are located at least 3 feet forward of discharges. Except as required by equipment manufacturers, exterior scoop-type strainers are not desirable. When required, scoop strainers should be Groco ASC or SC series, which are easy to remove for cleaning and painting.

Tanks

The ideal material for potable water tanks is Monel. Alternatively, 316 stainless steel may be used. If well supported, rotationally molded polyethylene is an inexpensive water tank material but is virtually impossible to repair if a crack develops.

Diesel tanks may be fabricated from aluminum, but Monel is preferable.

My waste tanks would be polyethylene or fiberglass, the latter constructed with vinylester resin.

Tanks should be internally baffled, with a 6-inch-minimum-diameter inspection port over each

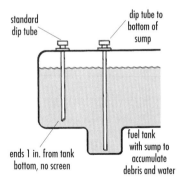

standard dip tube

dip tube to bottom of sump

ends 1 in. from tank bottom, no screen

fuel tank with sump to accumulate debris and water

A shallow sump in fuel tanks and a second dip tube allow pumping out of dirt and sludge, the most common cause of engine fuel filter clogging in rough weather.

baffled compartment. Metal tanks should have the area around inspection ports reinforced by adding an interior flange at the perimeter of the baffle opening to increase thickness to at least ¼ inch.

Tanks are fitted with a sump at the lowest point (despite not being permitted by all regulatory bodies), with a withdrawal tube running to the bottom of the sump to facilitate removal of detritus (see drawing). When configuration does not permit a sump, a 1½-inch IPS threaded flange should be installed in the tank top over the lowest part of the tank, with a suitable pipe plug supplied so that a suction pipe can easily reach the low point of the tank.

Having a means to suck the very bottom of the tank is especially important on diesel fuel tanks so that water can be removed. Algae only grows on the interface between water and fuel, and if there is no water, there can be no growth.

Standard withdrawal tubes are removable and run to within 1 inch of the tank bottom. Strainers are *not* fitted to the bottom of the withdrawal tubes.

Tanks are installed with 6-pound-density closed-cell foam, blown in place under the tank, with channels left open for drainage of any liquid. Tanks are secured in place with sufficient reinforcement to support the filled tank's weight even when the boat is inverted.

Tanks can be removed from the boat through the companionway or other hatch.

Pipe fittings screwed directly into aluminum fuel tanks must be stainless steel, using Tef-Gel on the threads. Other fittings are sealed with RectorSeal #5. Fittings on water and waste tanks may be Marelon or glass-filled nylon.

Diesel fuel tanks have a return at the opposite end of the tank from the withdrawal fitting to dissipate the heat from returned fuel. The return is through a tube extending to within 2 inches of the tank bottom to prevent foaming.

Freshwater Tanks—A return fitting on potable water tanks allows a valve to be installed at the farthest shower from the water heater so cold water can be returned to the tank rather than wasted.

Potable water tanks have separate withdrawal tubes for the pressure water system and hand pump system. If this is not possible, install a shut-off valve in the line running to the hand pump to prevent the pressure water pump from sucking air through the hand pump.

Water obtained in many ports in the world is not suitable for drinking, but is satisfactory for showering and cleaning. It is therefore handy to have segregated systems so that one tank has quality water for drinking and the other has questionable local water or even rainwater obtained from deck catchment devices for cleaning.

The primary system for non-potable water has hot and cold water plumbed to conventional mixing faucets in the heads, showers, and galley. The secondary system for drinkable water has a separate selector valve for tank source and can be connected to one cold-only faucet at each sink. The secondary system has a pressure pump, but foot or hand pumps could be used.

Vents—Potable water tanks preferably vent to a spigot at the galley sink. Fuel tank vents are installed in the cockpit, above the scuppers, and the hose extends as high as possible from the vent fitting and is fitted with a vented loop.

It is convenient to have a way to wedge a container under the fuel tank vent to catch overflow while refueling.

Holding tanks vent through the hull at the waterline, with hose running to a vented loop located above the waterline with the boat heeled 40 degrees.

Avoid dips in vent lines that could trap liquid and prevent flow of air into tanks. The sound of in-rushing air when a deck fill cap is slowly unscrewed is indicative of a poorly designed or blocked vent system.

Fuel Supply

Two Racor #500MA strainers would be installed for each diesel engine (propulsion engine and generator). Valves would be installed to route withdrawal through either filter, with positive closure of the fuel supply to the other filter.

Each Racor filter should be equipped with a vacuum gauge. The owner may elect to install a PAR/Jabsco #45710-0000 pump, piped to transfer fuel between tanks through

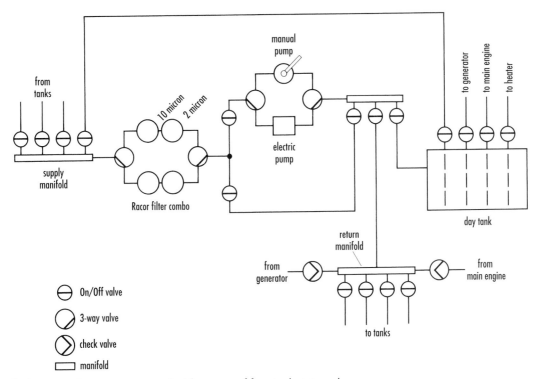

This fuel system allows one to pump fuel from any of four tanks into a day tank that supplies the main engine, genset, and possibly a heater. Note the Racor filters.

a Racor filter. Vessels with a large number of diesel fuel consumers may consider installation of a day tank, with fuel filtered before reaching the day tank (see drawing previous page).

Power Bilge Pumps

The main electric bilge pump would be a diaphragm type, connected to an Ultra bilge pump switch. Though expensive, the Ultra Pumpswitch Sr. and Jr. switches are the most reliable switches available and are worth the extra cost.

I prefer that the pickup for the bilge pump be oversized hose without a strainer on the bottom of the hose. The pickup runs to an easily accessible engine intake-type strainer, and then to the pump. The bottom of the pickup hose has notches cut in it so it cannot suck itself tight to the hull interior. Pickup hose for any bilge pump must be readily removable from the bilge.

The secondary bilge pump is a centrifugal type, located higher in the bilge, also controlled by an Ultra switch with an alarm connected in parallel to the pump wiring so that the alarm sounds whenever the pump is running. The secondary pump has the highest capacity available (yet owners should be aware that its actual flow rate may be one-half to one-third of that advertised due to lift height and flow restrictions).

At least two manual bilge pumps are installed, one operable from below decks with all hatches and ports closed, and one operable from the cockpit. Edson diaphragm pumps are recommended only in bronze.

To prevent back-siphoning through the pump to the bilge, all bilge pumps discharge through a vented loop to a through-hull fitting located above the waterline with the boat heeled. Under no circumstances should bilge pump discharges be teed into cockpit scupper hoses because in extreme conditions, when the cockpit is filling with water, the scuppers are needed to quickly drain the cockpit. Adding bilge water to the cockpit water only slows draining.

Miscellanea

- The water heater would have an air-purging valve in the hose returning engine coolant to the engine in order to facilitate complete filling of the engine cooling system.
- The shower mixers would be the pressure-compensating type to eliminate temperature fluctuation as the water pump cycles. A valve is installed at the hot water inlet of each shower mixer and is plumbed to divert freshwater back to the tank until hot water flows through the piping.
- The best tank gauge I have found is the Hart Tank Tender system, which works much more reliably than systems relying on internal tank floats.

Interior

Joinerwork

For new yacht construction, I like American cherry (*Prunus serotina*) for interior wood, kiln dried to 12 percent moisture content or less. Lumber must be selected for brown heartwood. Yellow sapwood is discarded or used in joinerwork that isn't visible. If possible, lumber is quarter sawn.

Cleat stock (wood pieces used to reinforce joints) should be Honduras mahogany (*Swietenia macrophylia*). Cleat stock is ⅞ inch square with the outside corner radiused to ¼ inch.

Where possible, screw joints put screws in shear rather than tension.

Any interior woodwork that may have to be disassembled for access to any part of the vessel should be fastened with oval Phillips, Fearson, or square-head screws of silicon bronze plated with statuary bronze. No bungs would be used. Stainless steel screws are preferred, as they are stronger; heads would be painted brown to blend with the woodwork. Joinerwork is constructed as modular as possible so whole units can be removed for access.

To prevent warping, no boards wider than 4 inches would be used unless lumber is ripped with a thin kerf blade, finger-jointed on a shaper and epoxy-glued back together.

All high-pressure laminate would be ¹⁄₁₆-inch countertop grade and laminated to a plywood platform in a laminate press because non-pressure-bonded contact cement may eventually bubble. While color selections are limited, it is preferable to use high-pressure laminate that has the same color throughout its thickness.

Four coats of Interlux 9297 sanding sealer would be applied to all exposed wood surfaces prior to installation in the boat. Application should be across the grain with a foam brush. If coats are applied not more than twelve hours apart, sanding is not necessary between coats. In preparation for finish coats of varnish, sanding sealer must dry forty-eight hours and then be thoroughly sanded with #220 or finer-grit paper in a random-orbit sander. Building up and filling the grain with sanding sealer is done only on interior wood areas not subject to a lot of sunlight, as the material does not have ultraviolet filters and may eventually break down.

All joinerwork corners should be rounded, preferably made with corner posts epoxied in place.

The chart table and galley would be padded at kidney height.

All fiddles must be a minimum of 2 inches high, with clean-outs at corners. Athwartships galley countertops have removable fiddles at 12-inch intervals.

Bulkheads

All bulkheads must be glassed (tabbed) to the hull or deck with trapezoidal-shaped high-density foam at least 1 inch thick fitted between the outboard edge of the bulkhead and the interior of the hull. The small dimension of the trapezoid should equal the bulkhead thickness; the large dimension of the trapezoid against the hull is at least three times the bulkhead thickness. The purpose of the foam is to absorb the shrinking of fiberglass as it cures and to avoid hard spots in the hull.

The veneer on plywood bulkheads must be removed because glassing to plywood provides better adhesion. After the bulkheads are glassed in place and the resin has completely cured, through-bolts and large fender washers should be installed through the glass laminates and the bulkhead to strengthen the joint.

In new boat construction, Peel Ply is applied (to retard curing) to the inside skin of the hull as soon as all laminations are complete (but not cured, called "green") to improve secondary bonding. All secondary bonds on my boat would be made with vinylester or epoxy resins because they are stronger than polyester resins.

Chainplate-carrying bulkheads and any others exerting forces that tend to separate the skins of a cored laminate would be installed by removing the inside skin and core for at least 12 inches on each side of the bulkhead. Trapezoidal foam would be used as described above, and the bulkhead glassed to the outside skin. The area would then be filled with resin mixed with chopped fiber and high-density filler to the level of the inside skin. Overlapping layers of glass would be applied to the bulkhead and inside skin, with an overlap of at least 12 inches onto the uncut interior skin.

Galley Stove

The stove should gimbal through at least 35 degrees on both tacks; gimbaling action must not cause chafe on the LPG supply hose. A stainless steel bar should be fitted inboard of the stove, positioned so that the burner knobs can be operated with the stove gimbaled. The oven door would have a positive lock. Adjustable fiddles clamp pots in place over the burners. For extreme conditions, a stainless steel spring, fastened to the stove top on either side of the pressure cooker, holds the pot in place.

Iceboxes

Refrigeration and freezer boxes would be molded from fiberglass, with a white gelcoat interior surface. All corners and edges should be generously rounded to ease cleaning.

The area into which boxes are mounted would be lined with heavy-duty aluminum foil or, better yet, metallic Mylar foil, and the edges sealed with Mylar foil tape.

Drain pipes are rigid PVC to avoid crushing by the expanding foam used for insulation. The drains end in a valve with space under for a pan. Without a valve, cold air will escape.

Insulation space must be at least 6 inches to the inside of the hull or engine compartment, and a minimum of 4 inches elsewhere.

Half-fill the box with water or a similar weight before 2-pound-density expanding foam is poured into the insulating space; the weight will keep the box from becoming dislodged as the foam expands. Drain channels must be provided in the foam so any condensate drains to the bilge. Doors or lids should have standard refrigerator gaskets for airtight seal. Foam tape is not used, as it readily breaks down.

Berths

Berths should be a minimum of 28 inches wide and fitted with Textilene lee cloths extending at least 22 inches above the top of the cushions. The lee cloths should be made with a hem on the bottom for insertion of a 1-by-¼-inch aluminum strip and are fastened through the strip, preferably with bolts and large fender washers (see art with tip 82). Lines for lee cloth lead at least 30 degrees outboard of the berth's inboard face. If a rollover is feared, leading lines to an additional set of pad eyes installed even farther outboard, and lower, lowers the lee cloth and angles it over the berth occupant.

Berth cushions are made of 2-inch firm foam glued to 2 inches of medium-density foam with 1 inch of soft foam on top. Sheets are not fitted, because Third World laundries will shrink them. If a fitted look is desired, use clips— Taylor #823, West Marine part #589317— designed to hold tarpaulins in place, with shock cord between sets of clips.

While it is expensive, the best material for cushion covers is Ultrasuede. For the saloon, at least one and preferably two sets of slipcovers are provided. One set of slipcovers is patterned cotton (to avoid showing stains). Prior to sewing, the cotton fabric is washed by commercial laundry to cause shrinkage. Cotton covers are for use in warm areas. For offshore passages, a set of slipcovers made from Sunbrella or other water-resistant fabric prevents water from soaking into the cushion foam when somebody sits down in wet foul-weather gear.

The boat's name would be printed in large letters with indelible laundry marker on all sheets, pillowcases, and slipcovers. The boat's name also would be included on all clothing sent to a laundry. Boat name is marked on foul-weather gear, safety harnesses, etc. It is handy if pillowcases, towels, etc., have embroidered numbers and each crew is assigned a number.

Fiddles

Shelves inside lockers have high removable fiddles manufactured from clear polycarbonate to facilitate viewing contents. Lockers with a lot of athwartships depth have pad eyes and shock cord with hooks to hold contents from movement as the boat heels.

Windows

Fixed cabinhouse windows would be ½-inch-thick light gray- or green-tinted polycarbonate (Lexan is a popular brand name). Windows would be mounted with stainless steel frames inside and outside. The frames would be fastened through the cabinhouse sides with ¼-inch bolts and ¼-inch stainless steel barrel nuts on the inside. The outside frames would be a minimum of ⅜ inch thick, with tapped holes for Lexan storm covers or shutters. The cutouts for windows must allow the polycarbonate glazing to expand at least 5 percent, which it will do from even the heat of a closed-up vessel (see drawing; see also photo with tip 26).

The bedding between windows and frames is GE Ultra Glaze, and is applied so it doesn't fill the gap between the ends of the windows and their cutouts. Windows and their frames should be designed to allow at least ⅛ inch thickness of bedding on each side of the window. Polycarbonate windows even-

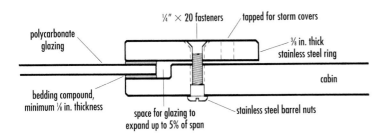

When installing lenses in window openings, be sure to allow for polycarbonate (such as Lexan) to expand. Note the tapped holes in the exterior frame for storm shutters.

tually deteriorate. A longer-lasting material is monolithic tempered safety glass, minimum ½ inch thick. If safety glass is used, the design of storm shutters should allow them to be bedded as replacement windows in the event the window glass is fractured.

Door Hardware

Automatic door latches, ABI part #2039CH, would be installed on all large passageway doors. Under no circumstances should doors be held open with nonlatching devices, because a door may be grabbed as a handhold and come adrift. Spring-type supports would be installed for cabinet doors that are likely to be opened underway when both hands are needed for other purposes (e.g., galley lockers or the door to the toilet paper holder in the head).

Rig

Spars

Until the price of carbon fiber comes down and compatibility issues with metal are resolved, as well as difficulties grounding carbon masts, I prefer masts made of #6061-T6 aluminum. All welding on aluminum must be done with a pulsed arc welder to avoid overheating the metal and resulting in loss of temper.

The spreader brackets should not be welded to the mast. Compression tubes are fitted inside the mast at the spreaders to dissipate loading.

The masthead would be a four-sheave design, with two sheaves for-

ward and aft (see Masthead Sheave Arrangement, tip 34). Rollers are fitted along the side sheaves for chafe protection. The sheaves are as wide as possible with flat grooves.

The spinnaker halyard blocks would be on cranes with replaceable stainless steel bails on the cranes for block attachment. Spare bails are provided.

All shroud tangs would be the double-plate type with the wire terminal sandwiched in the middle. The tang clevis pins would be as short as possible so that they are in double shear rather than bending mode. External tangs are preferable to shroud attachments inside the mast, because in the event of a standing rigging failure they are easier to jury rig.

All hardware installed on aluminum must be insulated with thin dielectric material extending ⅛ inch past the perimeter of the hardware. All stainless steel fasteners must be generously coated with Tef-Gel or Duralac. Only shear-loaded hardware should rely on tapped fasteners. Where possible, stainless steel RIVNUTs would be used in lieu of tapped holes. Hardware under tension may be mounted with solid-center Monel pop rivets.

Wire runs for lights would be PVC schedule 40 pipe conduits installed inside the mast, with one pipe running to the top, and one to an exit location for the spreader light and steaming light wires. The lengths of PVC pipe would be joined by solvent-weld couplings. PVC conduits would be secured to the mast at 4- to 5-foot intervals with

¼-inch stainless steel U-bolts. Pop rivets should not be used to secure conduit because the rivet causes chafe on the wiring inside the conduit. Metal tubing should not be used for wiring conduits in masts, as it is electrically conductive and if it comes adrift will cut through wires.

Standing Rigging

Wire—I prefer Dyform type 316 stainless steel 1×19 wire with Sta-Lok or Norseman terminal fittings. Swaged ends eventually corrode internally and must be carefully done with a rotary hammer swaging machine.

Turnbuckles—To facilitate jury rigging, I like double-jaw turnbuckles with either bronze screws and stainless steel barrels or vice versa to prevent the galling that occurs with stainless on stainless. Turnbuckle threads should be well lubricated with anhydrous lanolin (LanoCote or equivalent) prior to tightening. Holes for cotter pins to stop turnbuckles from unscrewing should be tapped for machine screws of suitable size (see photo with tip 43). It is much easier to unscrew a bolt than straighten a cotter pin bent 180 degrees, and machine screws do not require wrapping with tape. Stainless steel should never be wrapped with tape. Standing rigging turnbuckles are tensioned only on leeward side when sailing, or with vessel artificially heeled by heaving down with spinnaker halyard tied to a fixed object.

Running Rigging

All genoa and mainsail halyards would be braided ropes with Technora or Technora-Spectra cores. Conventional Dacron double braid would be used for spinnaker halyards where stretch may add shock-absorbing effect.

The primary genoa halyard would be rove over the forward starboard sheave and exits the mast on the port side through a stopper to a winch. The halyard has a stainless steel thimble and screw-pin shackle for attachment to the roller furling's upper swivel. There is no point in suffering the weight, length, and expense of a snapshackle for a halyard that is seldom released. A Flemish eye in the bitter end facilitates reeving with a messenger line.

The secondary genoa halyard would run over both the forward and aft sheaves on the port side and be external. The halyard would have a snapshackle on one end and an empty eyesplice on the bitter end. The winch is on the port side of the mast. If needed, the stainless steel screw-pin shackle can be placed in the eyesplice and the halyard used as an emergency main halyard.

The primary mainsail halyard would be rove over the aft starboard sheave and exit the mast on the starboard side through a stopper to a winch.

The staysail halyard would be the same specification as the primary genoa.

The spinnaker halyard block would have a wide sheave. A screw-pin shackle would fasten the block to the crane and be safety wired with Monel wire. A spare shackle would be provided. The halyard would be external to minimize chafe at the mast entrance and exit boxes. Chafe protection is provided on the spreaders where the loaded halyard passes.

The spinnaker halyard would be long enough to reach the primary winches in the cockpit, and suitable pad eyes would be installed for a fair lead. The spinnaker halyard shackle may be tied to the halyard with a bowline around an oversized stainless steel thimble, and the rope seized to the thimble on each side to keep it in place on the thimble. There are two good reasons to do this: spliced spinnaker halyards can hang up in masthead blocks; and a tied-in shackle facilitates end-for-ending halyard to spread wear.

Mainsheet

The most cost-efficient blocks are made by Garhauer Marine. The mainsheet blocks on my boat would not swivel and would be affixed to through-bolted bales on the boom.

Bales would have $\frac{3}{16}$-inch sheet nylon or equal washers between the bale and boom, and have a cross-bar so the block cannot get stuck between the bale and boom. The sheet would be Technora or a Technora-Spectra blend. To facilitate end-for-ending, the sheet would be tied to the block becket rather than spliced.

Roller-Furling Lines

Roller-furling lines should be high-tech cordage with strength equal to 80 to 90 percent of the genoa sheet's maximum loading. The common practice of using a larger, conventional rope furling line with core removed (so it doesn't fill and jam the drum) is not recommended because this practice reduces the strength of the furling line when the genoa is reefed and likely to be highly loaded.

Genoa Sheets

These should be made from high-tech cordage to reduce size and weight. Selection must be made carefully, as some high-tech lines are stiff and will not work well in self-tailing winches. Strength is computed so that the maximum load is 20 percent of $0.00431 \times$ sail area in square feet squared $\times$ maximum wind velocity in knots squared.

APPENDIX 2. *Cruising Paperwork*

ESSENTIAL PAPERS AND DOCUMENTATION

Replacing documents in a foreign country can be very difficult. Take along copies of all necessary papers, and whenever possible use the copies rather than the originals.

Following are descriptions of the documents that are required or helpful.

Proof of Yacht Ownership

While federal documentation is nice, and gives one great protection under the law, it is not mandatory for visiting foreign countries. I have had a copy center make double-sided copies of the official documentation certificate on the same cream-colored 80-pound stock as the original, and the copies are difficult to discern, except that the annual stickers do not stand out.

When traveling to a vessel by air, I carry a copy of the documentation certificate with me in case my baggage is inspected for duty fees on the items I am bringing to the vessel. Having an official-looking documentation certificate helps prove the vessel is "in transit," which are the magic words to avoid duty.

Be sure that your mail-forwarding agent promptly opens the annual renewal on documentation, forges your name, and returns it to the proper address. If the documentation lapses while you are in a foreign country, paperwork can be very complicated . . . and expensive.

Cruisers report that offering only state registration to customs officials can be a problem in small Pacific islands, while U.S. Coast Guard documentation is never questioned.

Proof of Insurance

Some countries require insurance. Some major boatyards require liability coverage. I take along a copy of the binder page for my million-dollar umbrella policy, just in case.

Passports

Passports are mandatory for all persons on board. Before leaving the U.S., have extra pages added to your passport. Bring along extra passport photos, as some foreign consulates can renew passports. Some visas also may require passport-size photos.

Make multiple color photocopies of your passport's first pages, which have all the pertinent data. Keep the copies separate from your passport. In a third location, record passport number, date and place of issue, and expiration date.

Visas

To determine if the countries you are going to visit require visas, consult U.S. Publication #9517, *Foreign Entry Requirements*, available for a small fee from the Federal Consumer Information Center (see appendix 7). If your list is short, a passport office may be able to give you information over the phone.

Entry requirements may be different for arrival by private pleasure yacht, so be sure to mention your mode of transportation. Some countries require the posting of a bond equal to the airfare for each crew out of the country, and you should be financially prepared to do this, as well as prove you have some financial means.

Cruising permits are required for some countries and areas within countries. Call the embassy or consular office of places you intend to visit before departure. In case a dispute arises later, always record the name of the person you talked to and the date of the conversation.

Customs Clearance

In the hustle of leaving the U.S., it is easy to forget to see a customs agent for form 1378, *Clearance of Vessel to a Foreign Port*. Most countries require clearance from your last port of call (commonly called a *zarpe*), so be sure to visit the authorities before departure. If your stay is brief, some officials will allow you to check in and out simultaneously, saving time with officialdom.

Crew List

A laptop computer and a small printer are very handy for producing crew lists, as some countries require multiple copies. Each crew list should include the vessel name, documentation number, tonnage, home port, mailing address, and a place to fill in the last port of call. The captain should be designated to collect passports and paperwork from crew and present them collectively (in some ports *only* the captain may process paperwork). Each crew member should be identified by full name, date and place of birth, passport number, date and place where issued, and status, that is, captain, able-bodied seaman, cook, etc. Exceptions are countries that require posting of a bond for yacht crews, but not yacht passengers, in which case a yacht has one captain and the rest are passengers.

Yellow Card

"Yellow card" is the common name of the World Health Organization International Certificate of Vaccination. These have to be obtained from a public health office and can involve some paperwork. Call the local public health office to find out the current status of vaccination requirements for the countries you plan to visit. Ask for the proof of vaccination they require before visiting your health facility to get the actual shots. And call the health facility beforehand to be sure they have the necessary vaccines on hand.

For more information, see the Health section in appendix 3.

Driver's License

If your state allows renewal by mail, be sure to take along the forms. I have an international driver's license obtained from AAA (Automobile Association of America), required in some countries by auto rental companies.

Ship Radio Station License and Operator's Licenses

While it is no longer a requirement in the U.S. that every VHF radio be licensed, appropriate licenses for all radios on board may be required in some countries. The present U.S. FCC (Federal Communications Commission) ship licenses are valid for ten years at a fee of $75.

Logbook

Maintain a cruising log in a book with nonremovable pages. Every day or two, note your location. Be sure to include departures and arrivals in ports, and crew changes with method of crew transportation—for example, "Jennifer Jones departed 12 August, Iberia Airlines flight #807 to Madrid, then transfer to flight #345 to New York."

If you are anchored at night, be sure to note frequently in your log that the anchor light is on. Unless you are in a designated anchorage area (of which there are few outside the U.S.), you are liable even if a recklessly operated boat hits you while you are anchored and not properly lighted. Being able to prove that you are diligent about your anchor light can be advantageous. I like to keep a separate deck log (see tip 183).

Equipment List

Record the model and serial number of all installed and loose electronics and items of value such as cameras, portable radios, and recorders carried on board. You may be asked for a list in some foreign ports, and having to take the navigation station apart to get the serial number of permanently installed electronics while the customs inspector waits is never convenient. Leave a copy of the list with your U.S. contact, in case replacement parts are needed; the serial number of the display may be required to order a new knotmeter paddlewheel, for example. Even though they may not ask for it, send a copy to your insurance company with your policy number prominently displayed.

Prescriptions for Medication

Ask your doctor to include the generic name and as much information as possible about each prescription, preferably typed rather than in physician's handwriting. Also ask about the shelf life of the drugs: some simply lose their effectiveness; others decompose and after time could become injurious.

In your logbook, note the date of any drugs that must be replaced. Keep copies of the prescriptions on board as well as with a friend in the U.S. Make a full inventory of your medical kit, including both prescription and over-the-counter preparations. You may have to declare the drugs in some countries. Leave all drugs in their original containers, even vitamins. In general, more drugs are available without prescription outside of the U.S. Brazil is a good place to restock, because drugs are cheap and prescriptions are not required for most types.

While it is a heavy book, the *Physician's Desk Reference* (Medical Economics Co., www.medec.com), commonly abbreviated *PDR*, is a good source of information about drugs. This volume is updated annually, so ask your doctor to save his outdated one for you. *Health Information for International Travel* is available from the U.S. Government Printing Office (www.access.gpo. gov/). *The Merck Manual of Medical Information* (Merck & Co., www.merck.com/) is a well-laid-out, general-purpose reference. The book *Where There Is No Dentist*, by Murray Dickson (Hesperian Foundation, www.hesperian.org), and a small kit put together by your dentist can save a lot of pain.

Upon Arrival

Money

Obtaining local currency has become much easier with the worldwide proliferation of ATM machines. I carry at least two credit cards, each with a $10,000 limit.

One must use credit cards judiciously, however. I was in Lisbon, Portugal, during the summer of 1996, and was withdrawing the maximum per day on each card to build up cash to pay for fuel. After the fourth day, I found one card no longer worked. It took some expensive telephone calls to determine that my bank's computer had decided the card must have been stolen and had invalidated it. Before leaving the U.S., find out what triggers your bank's computer to refuse a card. Also obtain the name and title (as bank personnel change frequently) and direct telephone number of the person who reviews what the computer rejects.

The advent of ATM machines has a negative side. A lot of foreign banks no longer make cash advances on a credit card larger than the ATM limit. To get a wire transfer of money, you need the routing number of the bank where the money will be picked up and your passport number. Before departing the U.S., talk to your bank to determine its requirements for making a wire transfer. Be sure to get a phone or fax number that is not an 800, 855, 866, 877, or 888 number, as most toll-free numbers will not work internationally. Be prepared to wait for the wire transfer. To get $2,500 transferred from the U.S. to a small bank on the island of Gomera, in the Canary Islands chain off Africa, took six business days in 1996.

Telephones

Before leaving the U.S., sign up with a call-back company. Call-back companies do what the name implies: you call them, enter the phone number from which you are calling and a code, and then hang up. Within minutes the company calls back and you are connected to a U.S. Watts line on which you can place calls for a lot less money than foreign telephone companies charge. Some foreign telephone companies are advanced enough to block calls to call-back companies, and even block access to the AT&T USA Direct access numbers.

Be sure to compare rates, as prices vary widely.

A must-have gadget is a tone dialer. These are available from RadioShack for less than $25, and generate the same tones as a U.S. touch-tone telephone. Foreign telephones do not interact with U.S. tones, and being able to make selections from a voice mail list can save a lot of long-distance charges.

Dealing with Foreign Officials

As in the U.S., a lot of public-service jobs are assigned through patronage rather than proficiency. Always treat officials with great respect, as most of them are on ego trips. Do not joke about local customs or anything else.

Fly a quarantine flag when you are within 20 miles of shore. I like to buy a separate yellow Q code flag so the vessel's code flag set does not have to be disturbed. Proceed to the port of entry without stopping, even if the beach you are sailing past looks inviting. Some ports have designated quarantine anchorages; others have wharves for entry clearance.

It is not uncommon to have to deal with different officials for health, immigration, customs, and agriculture. Only the captain should leave the vessel to deal with officials, and the crew must remain on board without visitors until the yacht is cleared in.

It is not uncommon for fresh vegetables and produce to be confiscated, so I always try to eat what's left before coming into port. Also, everyone on board should clean up, and the vessel's interior should be straightened. Until you know the local customs, dress conservatively in long pants and a shirt.

If you carry firearms, not declaring them can cause confiscation of the vessel and land you in jail. On the other hand, some customs officials will impound firearms and conveniently "lose" them while in storage. Engraving the name of the boat in large letters on firearms will help. Keep receipts for the purchase of weapons and copies of U.S. carry permits. Some countries allow firearms to remain on board in a sealed locker, and having such a place available may be helpful. These same suggestions apply to prescription drugs and excess quantities of tobacco and liquor.

Graft

Yes, it is prevalent. Be sure to tell officials that you want a receipt for payments before handing over any cash or traveler's checks. Explain that you need the receipts because you are writing an article on the various fees in ports or some other such story to avoid the official thinking that you do not trust him. If at all possible, try to get in advance some of the currency for your next port of entry. You can be caught in the Catch-22 position of having to pay entrance fees in local currency but not being allowed ashore before the fees are paid to get local currency.

Rather than the customary cigarettes or liquor "gift" to an official, I like to have a quantity of boat shirts made up. These do not have to be Izod. A T-shirt printed with a drawing of your boat and words like "Friend of (boat name)" costs a few dollars when purchased in quantity. An official wearing one of your boat shirts off duty goes a long way toward preventing trouble with the local criminal element.

Kwikpoint Cards

These cards are rather extensive pictures of various items that one might want or need in a foreign country. Pointing to a picture of a hard-boiled egg is a lot easier than trying to look up the foreign words in a foreign language dictionary. The cards used to fold to pocket size. The "improved" 1997 version is larger and only fits a hip pocket. They also make good presents for other cruisers you will befriend. Kwikpoint cards are available from GAIA Communications.

Mediterranean Market Basket

An essential reference for shopping in Mediterranean countries is *The Mediterranean Market Basket*. The book has lists of food names and cooking terms translated into a bunch of foreign languages, as well as conversions. It is available for $20 from the Seven Seas Cruising Association (of which any cruiser ought to be a member).

Flags and Country Identification

Fly the courtesy flag of the country you are in from the starboard spreader. The U.S. flag identifies the vessel as being owned by what people think of as a "filthy rich American." The two boats I manage from Milwaukee indicate the hailing port as "Milwaukee, WI"—it's better for people in foreign ports to wonder if Milwaukee is a small town in the West Indies than to add "USA" to the transom.

Boat Cards

As a convenient way of exchanging addresses, many cruisers have "business" cards printed with boat name, sometimes a drawing, mailing address, ham radio call sign, etc. These are very cheap in black and white; a colored accent can be added with a marking pen on long passages when one is looking for a project.

Mail

Arrange to have someone in the U.S. whom you trust act as a mail drop. The person must be able to decide what mail to forward and what to pitch. It is very handy if the person also has access to your funds to pay bills, as the time lag for foreign mail can result in late payments and cancellation of credit.

Do not have mail forwarded to you until you arrive at a port. Many factors may delay or prevent your arrival. When you arrive at a port, talk to a local merchant and ask if you can have one package of mail sent to him or her. Sending mail to a large marina, port captain, or general delivery is a lot less sure than a place of business known to the local post office.

The U.S. Postal Service has reasonable rates on International Priority Mail. For outgoing mail from a foreign country, try to use DHL, UPS, Emery, FedEx, or some other rapid shipper. All offer flat-rate envelopes and service speed vastly exceeding most countries' mail systems. It is helpful to bundle correspondence and send it to your mail drop for the addition of U.S. postage and mailing. Remember that mail is a subsidized bargain in the U.S.; it's more expensive and much less reliable elsewhere. For individual letters, take along a micro letter postage scale, such as model MP4000 from Metal Products Engineering.

Security

As soon as possible after arrival, seek out other cruisers and ask about any trouble with locals. Chances are you will hear the worst-case scenarios. Problems vary from harbor to harbor. Do not assume that if it was safe to leave your boat unlocked in one place, it is safe everywhere else in the country. In some ports it may be necessary to hire someone to watch your boat when you are not on board.

Do not wear expensive clothes, jewelry, or watches on the street. I travel with two wallets. The main one stays hidden on board, and my shoreside wallet is stocked only with the money I plan to spend that day. One credit card is carried in my left shoe. If you rent a car, do not leave valuables in the car. A lot of locals get copies of rental car keys. I had $400 stolen from my pants locked in the trunk of a Toyota while swimming at a nude Caribbean beach.

ADDITIONAL PRECAUTIONS

Waiver of Liability

In this litigious society, having each crew sign a waiver protects both the vessel and the crew from each other. The document may also make people think twice about doing anything that might put another in peril. See sample, below.

Release of Claim Against Vessel

When I hire casual labor, I always have the person sign a release when I pay them. It is very easy for a local to tell the authorities that he has not been properly compensated for work, and the authorities are more likely to believe a resident than a "rich yachtsman." Without a re-lease, you have no proof of payments in cash. Your vessel can be impounded and the skipper jailed. If I have any doubts about a boatyard, I also get a release. It is prudent to warn the party that you are going to require a signed release when hiring them. I blame the requirement on the boat's insurance company, and most people believe that.

Waiver of Liability

Yacht: _____

Voyage: _____

Having volunteered to be a crew member on the above-named yacht, I understand the perils of the sea inherent in an ocean voyage. I have the training and experience necessary to undertake such a voyage and am in good physical health and without any impairment that could impact my ability to participate in such a voyage.

By executing this Waiver of Liability, I for myself, my heirs, successors, assigns, and legal representatives hereby waive any and all claims against the above-named yacht, her owner(s), and other crew (paid or volunteer) and agree to hold each and every one of them separately and collectively harmless from any and all loss, cost, claim, damage, or expense including, but not limited to, attorneys' fees, which I may incur or which may arise directly or indirectly as a result of or out of my participation in this ocean voyage.

Signature: _____

Date: _____

Printed Name: _____

Release of Claim Against Vessel

Yacht: _____

Official Number_____

I, _____, in consideration of the sum of _____, having been in hand paid this _____day of_____ in the year_____,
   I for myself, my heirs, successors, assigns, and legal representatives hereby waive any and all claims against the above-named yacht, her owner(s), and crew thereof. I agree to hold each and every party separately and collectively harmless from any and all loss, cost, claim, damage, or expense that may arise directly or indirectly as a result of my presence on above-named vessel.

Signature: _____   Witness: _____

Printed Name: _____   Witness Printed name:_____

Photographs of the Boat

Photos of the boat serve a number of useful purposes, from handy references to documenting equipment for insurance.

Inventory

Devote a roll of film to the boat, photographing the contents of lockers and especially the nav station. These photos may be helpful with the insurance company if the vessel is burgled.

Hull

When your boat is hauled out, take photographs of all underwater portions of the hull. Always include some portion of the vessel visible above the waterline as a reference. If they do not stand out, mark the transducer and through-hull locations with contrasting-color tape. This makes a good reference if someone has to go over the side for emergency repairs. You may think you can remember how it all looks, but the details may escape you, especially in a crisis. Besides, the diver may not be you (if you are lucky!).

I once hired a diver to clean the boat's bottom. Suddenly he spouted up to tell me that the keel was falling off. I showed him the picture taken the previous spring of the normal crack at the keel/hull joint and asked him if it was any worse. He calmly said, "Nope. Looks about like the picture. Guess it is not falling off."

Show the underwater photos to yard personnel hauling the boat so they can position the slings away from the knotmeter paddlewheel and prop shaft.

Sails

As mentioned in tip 46, it is very important to photograph the sheet leads and details of storm sails that are used infrequently.

I like to lie on my back on the deck and look up at sails that are new, making an effort to have the photo show the fore-and-aft location of the maximum draft. Several years later, if the process is repeated, stretch will be evident, and having "before and after" pictures will help a sailmaker to re-cut.

Power and Appliances

Basically, all of the connections to a boat are different in Europe and those parts of the world that use European standards. The best plan is keep the present inlets and change shoreside connections.

In Europe and many parts of the world, shore power is 220 volts AC, 50 Hz. Your boat must have a step-down transformer, which converts shore power to U.S. standard 110–120 AC volts, but cannot change the frequency to the 60 Hz commonly used in the U.S. Most motors will work on 50 Hz, but may run hotter and draw more current. Electronically controlled motors, like variable-speed drills, will not work and will be irreparably damaged by 50 Hz. Resistance devices such as lights, soldering irons, and toasters will work.

Before departing, call the manufacturer of your refrigeration system, watermaker, and any piece of equipment operating from AC current to check its compatibility with 50 Hz. Sometimes a dual Hertz motor can be substituted for a U.S. standard 60 Hz. If you have a computer on board, be especially diligent in checking the frequency of the power adapter. If available, I strongly suggest getting a car adapter to run the computer from 12 volts DC, as foreign power can have nasty surges that can wipe out a laptop.

A charger for the boat's batteries that works on 50 Hz current is essential. In general, older ferroresonant chargers are not compatible. The modern generation of solid-state chargers are not frequency sensitive. You may want to add an inverter to power those onboard devices that require U.S. standard 60 Hz. Some additional wiring may be installed to connect frequency-sensitive devices only to the inverter. Remember that any U.S. standard dual-plug electrical outlet can have the metal bus bar connecting the two outlets broken so that one outlet can be wired to the inverter and the other to shore power through the transformer.

The transformer should also be an isolation transformer to protect against galvanic corrosion as well as the risk of shock from stray AC currents sometimes present in marinas.

If your vessel has a step-down transformer, make a lot of pigtails with a female socket to fit the male plug on the cord that feeds the transformer and about a foot of wire to connect to the proper plug to fit the receptacle on shore. Shoreside power connections vary widely around the world, and if you cruise to a lot of countries you will end up with a large bag full of plugs to fit foreign outlets.

Help is on the way, as there is a new European standard for 16- and 32-amp service. Even if a qualified electrician attaches the foreign plug to your pigtail, use your own elec-

The bus bar connecting the two outlet terminals can be broken so that each can be wired separately—one to the inverter, the other to shore power through the transformer.

trical multimeter to be sure the hot wire from shore is connected to the proper side of your pigtail *each time* you plug into power. On a standard U.S. female 110-volt receptacle, the hot wire is the shorter of the two parallel slots.

While some foreign shore power connections do not have dedicated polarity, making it essential to check which wire is hot, I learned to always check before plugging in. One very rainy day, I decided to add an outlet to the shore power system on my Tartan 30, docked at a very nice yacht club in Mentor, Ohio. Not wanting to suit up in foul-weather gear to go out and disconnect the shore cord, I turned off the double-pole breaker for shore power inside the boat. As I was connecting the new outlet, I involuntarily threw my pliers across the cabin when I received a bad electrical shock. In checking afterward, I found the dock had been wired with power coming in on the green (ground) wire, which the master breaker did not interrupt.

American Boat & Yacht Council (ABYC) code requires that the green (ground) wire for shore power be connected to the vessel's ground, as is the negative side of the DC power. Devices like generators and inverters connect the white (neutral) and green ground wire together, so even if the transformer is wired to isolate the green and white wires, they may be reconnected by these devices.

Transfer switches for source of power—shore, generator, or inverter—are supposed to switch both

the hot and neutral. Be sure yours does. I once saw a boat that got the hot side of 220-volt power connected to the vessel's DC ground, which blew up every DC device on board and would have started a fire if not promptly disconnected. Not pretty!

Electrical wiring on boats appears to be straightforward and relatively simple, which is why the major cause of fires on boats is electrical problems. If wiring is not properly done, one can very quickly get in a world of trouble. The ABYC periodically conducts seminars on boat wiring that are open to the general public. While they may be overly technical, I strongly recommend you attend one if you are going to do a lot of wiring on your boat.

Television and VCRs
European TVs use a different scanning rate than American sets. Wait to buy a European TV and a new VCR in Europe.

Cellular Telephones
European cell phones are different from those in the U.S. and are actually better, as one number follows you all over Europe.

Water and Plumbing

As with electricity, European water connections may be different. Some look like U.S. standard hose thread, and to which a U.S. female hose end (particularly one made from plastic) sometimes can be screwed on. Gardena-type quick-

disconnects also are common. Carry at least six 1-foot lengths of ⅝-inch inside diameter hose with a U.S. standard male hose connection on one end and four using ¾-inch ID hose.

Another handy gadget is a rubber adapter made to connect dishwashers to home plumbing. These devices connect different sizes of hose and come in handy when clamping on metric hose.

Before filling tanks, find a liveaboard in the harbor to ask if the water is drinkable. In Portugal, shoreside water is very good. Next door in Spain, nobody drinks it.

If your boat has aluminum tanks, do not add bleach to purify the water. The chlorine will react with the tanks and form white deposits that clog filters and pumps, in addition to slowly eating the tank.

Propane

If your cooking fuel is anything other than propane, change the stove to propane before leaving. Buy at least three spare pigtails with POL fittings attached. (A POL fitting is the left-hand-thread, bullnose fitting that screws into the tank, West Marine part #319780.) You will end up cutting off the small end fittings at the opposite end of the hose from the POL and replacing them with various foreign adapters secured with hose clamps. Pick up a bunch of hose clamps that fit the pigtail hose. West Marine also has a U.S.-to-European adapter, part #356248.

Stamped into your propane tank will be the empty (tare) weight and the full weight in pounds. Convert these to kilograms (multiply by 0.454) and write these numbers on the tank with an indelible felt-tipped marker. Also mark the tank with your boat name. Draw an arrow around the POL inlet on the tank to remind both you and the refiller of the POL fittings' left-hand threads. If you do not accompany your tank to the station, it may be helpful to send the tank out for refilling with the pigtail attached.

There is a very good chance your tank will get refilled with butane rather than propane. Most stoves will work satisfactorily on butane, which burns hotter than propane. Check with your stove manufacturer to confirm butane compatibility, and if necessary purchase smaller burner orifices.

Paper Goods

Be sure your paper towel holder is the type with a rod that runs through the roll, not the type that clamps onto the ends of a roll. European paper towels are 2 inches shorter than the U.S. standard of 11 inches, so a clamp will not work. European toilet paper also is shorter, but most holders have a central rod, so a shorter roll works.

Nuts and Bolts

If your boat was built in the U.S., all threaded fasteners will be SAE standard, generally coarse thread. Common designations are 10-24,

¼″ × 20 (¼-inch diameter by 20 threads per inch), ⁵⁄₁₆-18 (⁵⁄₁₆-inch diameter by 18 threads per inch), and so on (see Tools and Maintenance, chapter 5). The first number refers to diameter, the second to threads per inch. Smaller fasteners are usually fine thread, 6-32 and 8-32 being common. Electrical devices may use fine thread 10-32. Stock up with threaded fasteners and nuts before departing. The rest of the world uses metric fasteners.

Finish washers are handy to convert flathead bolts to holes that aren't countersunk, but they are not very strong. If the application puts a lot of tension on the bolt head, double up on finish washers and use a conventional flat washer under the two finish washers.

Also very handy to have are lengths of stainless steel threaded rod from which long bolts can be manufactured on board. Before cutting threaded rod, screw on several nuts. After the cut is made, file the cut end with a slight bevel; unscrewing the nuts will then rethread the cut end. Jamestown Distributors is a good source for cost-effective threaded stainless steel rod.

Metric thread may look very similar to SAE thread, but don't use metric fasteners in SAE tapped holes or nuts. The results will be galling and poor strength. Head styles are sometimes different on metric fasteners, but nuts all look the same. Before departing, spread out all of your SAE threaded nuts and give them a light coat of paint to identify them as SAE thread. Take along an empty box with lots

of compartments to hold the metric fasteners you will eventually end up buying.

In general, screws are not as critical as bolts, and metric sizes can be substituted.

Maps

While charts are necessary for navigation, they do not go inland very far and may not mention towns and geographic areas used for reference in weather broadcasts. Ordinary road maps are very handy and compact. Most embassies can provide maps of their countries if asked. For long-range planning, the *National Geographic Atlas of the World* is helpful. Bartholomew makes good maps of the world and eastern and western Europe. For the Mediterranean Sea, use Freytag & Berndt's maps of the Mediterranean.

Health

Consider joining the International Association for Medical Assistance to Travelers (IAMAT). It is a nonprofit organization that advises travelers of health risks and immunization requirements for 200 countries. IAMAT publishes a directory of English-speaking doctors in 125 countries, with phone numbers. These doctors agree to a set payment schedule for an IAMAT member's initial visit. Risk charts are provided for malaria, schistosomiasis, Chagas' disease, and other things you really do not want to know about but should. IAMAT has offices in Canada, New Zealand, Switzerland, and New York in the U.S.

Docking Equipment

Almost all docking in Europe and other parts of the world is done in what is referred to as a *Med moor* in which the stern is near a quay. Some harbors provide a mooring chain to hook up to the bow, while others require the vessel to set its own anchor.

Mooring chains are always grubby, and a selection of chain hooks should be carried covering ⁵⁄₁₆- through ⁵⁄₈-inch chain. I like to affix the chain hook with a screw-pin shackle to a 30-foot length of rope the same diameter as the normal mooring lines for the vessel, with an oversized galvanized thimble spliced in one end. You will also need two additional mooring lines of the same specification and two 6-foot lengths of chain for the stern. The quay will have either rusty steel bollards or rusty steel rings that will chafe through docklines in a short time.

Because there will probably be boats close to yours on both sides, at least six and preferably eight fenders are necessary.

For tips on docking under power, see appendix 6.

The ramp with which to board a vessel lying stern-to is called a *passarelle*. One day, the couple who owns one of the yachts I manage was having a ferocious argument about what kind of passarelle to buy. The husband wanted one that was lightweight and easy to stow. The wife wanted one that was wide and stable with handrails both sides. Finally, they resolved that if they had me buy a passarelle, they both could be mad at me and not at each other. After a day shopping in Mallorca, I purchased a folding aluminum unit, 3.5 meters long unfolded, with removable handrail stanchions on one side. This seemed to satisfy both of them.

I did make an error in mounting the pivot socket on the taffrail. I made a tight-fitting hole for the socket and did not fit a massive backing plate below. Because there is considerable leverage on the one pivot socket, the teak on the taffrail cracked.

This boat has a split backstay, so I drilled a hole in the triangular joining plate and affixed a block for the halyard that is necessary to hold the outboard end of the passarelle up off the quay. Having the passarelle lifting line close to the stern is handier than using a spare main halyard and having to go to the mast to adjust it.

The subject of what spare parts to carry is purely subjective, predicated on the length of passages and availability of air freight service to intended destinations.

A word on air freight: Before ordering parts from a foreign port, check the local phone book to determine which air freight companies have local offices, then call the companies to determine how they handle customs and duty. Some companies do all the paperwork and deliver parts to you. Others will just notify you that freight has reached the country, and you have to hire an agent and pay duty to get the shipment. After you are comfortable with the local services, or at least understand what may be involved, specify your choice of air freight company to the person from whom you are ordering parts.

Regardless of how many spare parts you carry, chances are you will never have all you will need. The following pages are for reference and reflection on outfitting.

Main Propulsion Engine

Biocide to add to fuel at each bunkering.
Complete set V-belts, highest available horsepower rating. Two sets recommended.
Cross-reference listing from auto parts store of other manufacturers' belts.

Water pump impeller and gasket for pump. Three recomended.
Spare set of screws for water pump cover plate.
Fuel filters, primary. Six recommended.
Fuel filter on engine. Four recommended.
Oil filter. Six if not cross-referenced to NAPA or equal filter.
Engine oil, enough for two changes.
Oil filter wrench, checked for operating clearance on vessel.
Hand pump for changing oil, with tubing long and small enough to reach bottom of fuel tanks.
Oil sample bottles.
Antifreeze or water pump lubricant for closed cooling system, minimum 2 gallons.
Radiator cap for closed cooling system.
ATF or other fluid specified for the transmission.
Injectors. Complete set with washers or gaskets.
Complete gasket set with copper compression washers.
Thermostat and gasket.
Complete set of hoses, including raw-water intake.
Section of exhaust hose, nipples, and hose clamps for joining.
Zincs. If engine uses them, buy at least six generic.
Fuel solenoid shutoff switch, if engine has one.

Electric fuel pump, if engine has one.
Mechanical fuel pump, if engine has one.
Pivot bolt and locking bolt for alternator with locking bolt long enough to go through threads on alternator and have separate nut in case built-in threads strip.
Spare complete alternator and voltage regulator if separate from alternator.
Oil pressure switch, replacement for each. N/C (normally closed) will indicate as shorted with an electrical tester and engine off; N/O (normally open) will indicate no continuity with engine off.
Set of high-pressure fuel lines from injector pump to injectors.
Fuses for engine panel.
Lightbulbs for engine gauges.
Mechanical oil pressure gauge installed.
Set of throttle and shift cables, plus the right forks and clevis pins.
Stop cable, if engine has one.
NPT pipe plug, ⅛ inch (to replace broken oil pressure sender/switch).
Shaft stuffing box packing (Drip-Free recommended).
Aerosol belt dressing.
Cutless bearing for prop shaft.
Drivesaver prop shaft coupling or equal, if vessel has one.
Ignition switch, extra keys for stan-

dard and spare switches.

Starter solenoid.

Starter motor, complete.

Replacement keys for prop shaft to engine coupling and propeller.

Complete parts list for engine and shop manual, if available.

Account with credit card number on file, and good relationship with parts source for engine.

Rigging and Deck Hardware

Cotter pins for rigging clevis pins and turnbuckles on lifelines.

Large screw-pin shackles, at least two with pins the same diameter as the shroud turnbuckles.

Pawls and extra pawl springs for winches.

Dogs and knobs for deck hatches and opening ports.

Screw-pin stainless steel shackles to replace snapshackles.

Length of high-tech, low-stretch rope long enough to replace any halyard on board.

Messenger line: mast height × 2. Pack so it will not get cut up.

Small lengths of light line: ¼- to ⅜- inch diameter, about twenty pieces 3 to 10 feet long (check your rigger's scrap bin).

Nylon seizing twine and sailmaker's needles.

Monel seizing wire.

Sail repair kit (see tip 50 for list).

Two spare winch handles.

One or two large blocks of adequate size and strength to accommodate spinnaker halyard.

Spare steering chain and cable as-

sembly, if boat has this type of steering.

Two (at least) 6-foot lengths of anchor chain; use for tying up to rusty bollards or rigging replacement.

Two docklines with metal thimbles spliced to one end to use with chain above.

Chafing gear for anchor, docklines.

U-bolt wire clamps sized to fit standing rigging, if it is wire.

Norseman-type ends for standing rigging wire, one each wire size, if standing rigging is wire.

Length of 1×19 wire equal to longest stay or shroud on boat, and of same diameter.

Three Norseman-type ends for above, six spare cones.

If standing rigging is rod with special rod ends at the mast or spreaders, get a rod end with an eye or jaw fitting attached to facilitate re-rigging with wire if rod breaks—and you are lucky enough not to lose the mast.

Nicopress tool, wrench operated, adequate for all wire sizes used on board.

Nicopress fittings, sized to wire on board, including wire under vinyl-clad lifelines, which is generally 3⁄16 inch upper and ⅛ inch lower on U.S. production boats.

Heavy-duty thimbles for all Nicopressed wire sizes.

Wire cutters, *not* bolt cutters, ⅜ inch capacity, for shortening wire halyards, lifelines.

Zippers and extra sliders for all canvaswork on deck.

If boat has internal halyards, about 2 feet of bicycle chain to use on end of messenger to re-reeve halyards.

Shock cord and end fittings.

Grommet installation kit: punch, crimping dies, lots of ½-inch ID solid brass grommets. In a pinch, grommets and lashing can fix a lot of things. Check grommets with a magnet to be sure they are not brass-plated steel.

Spare set of battens, if mainsail has battens.

Complete set of sail slides for luff and foot, if mainsail uses slides. If plastic, replace with metal before going offshore.

Bicycle or air pump, with needles, for inflating fenders.

Replacement for canvas fasteners, especially the turn-the-stud type.

Lubricants

Heavy water-pump grease.

Grease gun, extra Zerc-Lock fittings, extra grease cartridges.

Winch grease.

3-in-One oil or equal.

Super Lube aerosol.

Corrosion Block.

Aerosol silicone.

Never-Seez compound or equal.

Aerosol carburetor cleaner; good de-greasing agent.

Zipper lubricant.

Note: WD-40 omitted on purpose, because Corrosion Block is better at freeing things; also, WD-40 is *not* a lubricant and will wash out other lubricants.

Bedding, Pipe Sealants, and Adhesives

3M 5200 (small tube).

Silicone sealer (small tube).

#2 Permatex (tube).

RectorSeal #5 (small can for all pipe joints, better than Teflon tape).

CRC corrosion inhibitor.

Contact cement, flammable type (small cans for sail repair with dry fabric).

Krazy Glue or equivalent (small tubes).

Loctite red thread-locking compound.

West System epoxy large repair pack plus two refills.

5-minute epoxy in dispenser tubes (at least three).

Tape

High-quality duct tape, minimum of three rolls.

Nylon filament strapping tape, rolls totaling at least 100 feet, minimum ¾ inch wide.

Colored electrical tape, useful for coding things.

2-inch-wide clear packing tape.

Double-sided tape made for holding Velcro down.

Plumbing

Washers or seal sets for every faucet on board.

Package of garden hose washers.

Tailpieces for sinks and extra nuts.

Complete spare pressure water pump.

Extra pressure switch for pressure water pump.

Replacement pump or rebuild kit for any other power pumps on board.

Propane solenoid.

Propane regulator.

Plumbing nipples and couplings to replace solenoid in propane system.

Plumbing nipples to connect propane solenoid to regulator.

Rebuild kit for toilet.

Hose, one length equal to longest run of each size used on boat, except perhaps engine exhaust.

Diaphragms for all manual bilge pumps, and valve kits.

Packing for rudderstock.

Senders and gauges for fuel and water tanks, if Hart Tank Tender is not used.

Extra baskets for all strainers and filters.

At least two each of the following nipples, in red brass:
¼-inch NPT×close
¼-inch NPT×2 inches (measures just under ½-inch OD)
⅜-inch NPT×2 inches (measures about ⅝-inch OD)
½-inch NPT×2 inches (measures about ¾-inch OD)
¾-inch NPT×3 inches (measures just over 1-inch OD)

Stainless steel tubing, 1½ inches OD×6 inches.

Stainless steel tubing for any hoses on board larger than 1½ inches ID.

Spare hose for shower.

Hose clamps to replace at least half of those on board.

Replacement ends for garden hoses.

Male and female garden hose thread to ½-inch IPS adapters.

Power bilge pump switch.

If vessel is plumbed with Qest or equal nut and tubing system, take lots of spare nuts and a few couplings to repair splits in tubing.

Muffler wrap kit sold to repair a leaking car muffler is a good high temperature repair.

Toilet bowl waxes, at least six, useful for temporarily stopping leaks.

O-rings for deck fills.

O-rings or gaskets for all strainers.

Electrical

Fuses, at least five of each used on board (check back of electronic equipment for built-in fuses).

Circuit breakers of same type as used on panel. Most 12-volt panel needs will be satisfied with
1 10A
1 20A
1 30A
1 50A

Switches, replacements for all switches on deck lights, windlass, winches, etc., with rubber boots.

Complete spare knotmeter transducer.

Extra paddlewheels and axles for knotmeter transducer.

Spare sets of zincs for underwater use.

Lightbulbs for
Navigation lights, deck level; note that bow and stern may be different.

Masthead tricolor light.

All interior lights.

Flashlights: note that two- and three-cell flashlights use different bulbs.

Compass.

Spreader lights: Replacement bulbs often can be found at auto parts stores.

Complete spare VHF antenna, same as installed one, with at least 25 feet cable, PL-259 on end.

Extra PL-259 connectors, plus other types used on various equipment and antennas.

Crimp-on electrical terminals; you can never have too many.

Electrical wire ties, at least 100; black is more UV-resistant.

White electrical tape; use marking pen to identify wires; can also be used for on-deck taping.

Assorted electrical wire, minimum 100 feet #12 tinned stranded copper.

Small butane soldering iron and spare butane cartridges.

Rosin core small diameter electrical solder, rosin flux.

If vessel has wet-cell batteries (i.e., not gel-cell), carry

Hydrometer to measure each cell's specific gravity.

Distilled (not spring or mineral) water to add to batteries.

Replacement solenoids for all on board. Check engine, power windlass, power winches, powered mast, and all high-draw pieces of equipment.

Dinghy and Outboard Motor

Inflatable-boat repair kit with extra tubes of glue and fabric.

Spare locking wire pennant made of old lifeline wire with the Nicopressed eye at each end, minimum length 15 feet.

Lots of spare locks, most helpful if keyed alike.

Extra set of oars.

Spare inflation pump.

Spare inflation valve, if inflatable.

Spare fuel line with pump bulb.

At least two changes of spark plugs.

Six shear pins.

Kit of all ignition components.

Extra starter cord and recoil starter assembly.

Water pump.

Complete carburetor.

Oil to add to gas, if two-cycle engine.

Plastic fuel container, about 3 gallons, in addition to remote tank. Lash on deck when full. Yes, I know I said not to lash things on deck, but even having gasoline on board a diesel-powered boat may cause an insurance claim to be denied. Do not put in locker, as heat may cause escape of vapors that are more explosive than dynamite. When tank is empty, leave it open upside-down for a day before stowing in locker.

Interior Hardware

At least two spares of each type of hinge used on board.

Longer screws (if joinerwork permits) to reinstall hinges after original screws pull out.

At least two spares of each type of locker closure—elbow catch, ball stud catch, etc.

In Vessel's Canned Goods Locker

One medium-size sail bag with two manual can openers inside it. If the boat must be abandoned, stuff canned food in the bag and take it to the life raft.

Safety Gear List

Life raft, inspected annually. Add boat name, telephone contact on raft, additional retroreflective tape.

Handheld watermaker, either packed in raft or in abandon-ship bag. Note: Even if not used, handheld watermakers must be periodically serviced by renewal of the preservation fluid, a process commonly called *pickling*. This is much easier to do if the watermaker is *not* packed inside the liferaft.

Lots of small flashlights, one in each crew's pocket at all times after dark.

Safety harnesses for entire crew, preferably automatic inflating type with re-arming packs.

Pouch on harnesses containing personal strobe, whistle, dye marker, all held in with tethers.

Tether for strobe long enough to hold over head, whistle in mouth.

Two tethers for each harness with carabiner hook on one end, center-jointed snapshackle at other end.

Jacklines in cockpit so one can clip on before leaving companion-way, then slide aft to steer.

Jacklines on side decks running from stemhead to stern cleats.

Lifesling with added retroreflective tape, boat's name. End of line secured to vessel.

Yellow horseshoe or other throwable flotation device with added retroflective tape and sea anchor.

Automatic activation strobe light attached to horseshoe.

Flag, at least 10 feet off water on weighted pole, attached to horseshoe with 25 feet of floating line. Add retroflective tape to flag and pole.

Thick plywood storm shutters, adequate in size to cover fixed windows on one side of vessel, with strongbacks and bolts. Foam tape for waterproofing them.

Pad eyes or other hardware outboard of wheel or tiller to be used as lashing points when hove to.

Knife on pedestal in cockpit, another handy at mast.

Fire extinguishers.

CO_2 fire extinguisher, minimum 10 pounds.

SOLAS flares: eight red parachute, six red handheld, four white handheld, packed in waterproof container(s).

Three SOLAS orange smoke generators packed in waterproof container.

1-million-candlepower (or more) spotlight with adequately long cord to use it forward of mast, and at least two spare bulbs.

If vessel has a MOM (man overboard module by Survival Technologies), carry a re-arming pack for it.

Lots of Cyalume light sticks, some in abandon-ship bag.

At least two strong buckets with lanyards; get horse buckets from farm supply company.

Drogue, either Jordan Series of small cones or Galerider with

adequate rode. Blocks and securing points to lead rode from cockpit winches to stern.

Storm trysail with separate track strongly secured to mast (or spare mainsail).

Photographs of sail hoisted.

Storm headsail with area not more than 30 percent of foretriangle.

At least three anchors, one of which should be a large fisherman type, with separate rodes for each. Note: One rode can double as drogue warp.

Jim Buoy anchor trip line and marker #1204, one or more. Primary use is marking an anchor that has to be abandoned, which is frequently the best way to untangle a boat that has dragged into your vessel.

Take two-and-a-half times more emergency food or provisions than what you expect to consume on a planned passage, because if you are dismasted or have other major failure, your passage could take a lot longer than expected.

Emergency water, separate from yacht's tanks: at least 1 gallon per person per 500 miles.

Diving mask, fins, snorkel (dive mask good on deck in heavy rainstorms).

Boarding ladder, midship mount, bottom rung at least 21 inches underwater. Nonskid on rungs if not teak.

Football helmet with face guard for going up mast in heavy weather.

High-quality bosun's chair with downhaul ring on bottom.

Covers for all deck Dorade and other vents.

Abandon-Ship Bag

5-watt handheld VHF radio with extra batteries in waterproof packing.

Hand-operated watermaker (if not packed with raft).

Handheld GPS with spare batteries in waterproof packaging.

Signal mirror.

Space blankets.

50 feet ⅛-inch nylon cordage.

Two 6-foot 50-pound-test (minimum) wire fishing leaders with several lures (pack in a plastic container in bag). Also, stainless steel fishhooks.

Prescription medications necessary for life of any crew.

Diaper rash ointment.

Collapsible radar reflector.

Sunglasses.

Sunblock.

Small piece of plywood for cutting fish on.

Pair of heavy gloves for handling ⅛-inch line and wire leader.

Roll of Shop Towels or other strong, reusable paper towels in waterproof packaging.

Cyalume light sticks, at least twelve, packaged to avoid breakage.

Twenty 1-gallon reclosable plastic bags.

Survival rations. Visit any life raft repacker and get the outdated ones from commercial rafts.

As much water as will fit in bag, in 1-pint plastic bottles.

Passports for all crew in reclosable plastic bag.

$1,000 in U.S. cash or traveler's checks.

Roll of duct tape.

Small medical kit with waterproof dressings.

Phenegrine suppository seasickness medication.

See/Rescue streamer, 18 by 40 feet, West Marine #448433.

Sky-Alert Parafoil kite, West Marine #260201.

Sponge.

Yacht Outfitting Safety Equipment

Permanently installed preventer system from end of boom(s).

Floorboards secured adequately to hold in place during rollover.

Locker catches housed to prevent contents from opening latch.

Fiddles or shock cord inside lockers to retain contents when a locker is opened while the boat is heeling.

Positive stop on all athwartship drawers so they cannot come all the way out.

Heavy equipment stored below affixed to strong securing points.

Mast heel secured to mast step.

Handholds installed to allow movement inside vessel at 90 degrees heel.

Engine installation adequate to hold it in place during rollover.

Batteries well secured.

Separate engine starting battery, kept offline and reserved for emergency starting.

Diagrams of
    Through-hull locations.

Safety and medical gear storage.

Tools and spare parts storage.

Emergency tiller, tested underway.

Alternative to rudder for steering the boat.

Seacocks on all underwater connections.

Cockpit volume verified that drainage time is less than 90 seconds.

Stanchions through-bolted to sockets, sockets through-bolted with backing plates.

Lift-out panels in berth tops and elsewhere secured with strong stops.

Navigation lights to international standards.

Tricolor light with strobe at masthead.

At least two halyards capable of raising any sail.

Minimum of two manual bilge pumps, one operable from deck, one belowdecks, with as much capacity as possible. Remember that a smaller boat has less internal volume and will sink faster.

Power and manual bilge pumps have vented loop high above waterline.

Permanently mounted or hoisted radar reflector as least 25 feet above water.

Nonskid tape on plastic hatches forward of mast.

Guards for midship and forward cleats.

These are lists of things to do for one of the yachts I manage that is frequently left for long periods of time.

Layup

Deck

Deflate inflatable boat, wash with freshwater, dry, stow.

Run outboard in freshwater. Run it out of fuel, clean exterior, stow. (Do *not* run outboard unless it is in water.)

Double docklines. Spray with insecticide.

Add hose and/or chain at shore end to docklines for chafe protection.

Wrap headsail tightly, then by hand turn the furler to wrap the genoa sheets around the sail. Add a stainless steel screw-pin shackle to the drum to prevent it from turning. For longer term or in high-wind areas, remove genoa.

Do the same procedure for the staysail. Rig line from staysail clew to shroud to put tension on staysail so it does not vibrate.

Be sure zinc is hung over side of boat.

Install covers for toerails, handrails, Dorade boxes.

Rig fender board with rubber bumpers as primary hold-off from dock.

Stow Lifesling, horseshoe, crew-overboard flag below.

Furl mainsail in as far as possible, if boat has mainsail furling. If Hood Stoway system, install flute stopper in main track with plastic buttons outside and fabric in cavity.

If no furling, secure mainsail with sail ties and cover, or preferably remove and stow below.

Be sure brake on steering wheel is on. If a lot of wash is likely to be encountered, tie off wheel to the pad eyes outboard of wheel.

Lock forward and aft deck hatches.

Clean plastic in windows, then remove bimini and dodger canvas; stow below.

Be sure all halyards are tied off from mast.

Reduce tension on backstay to 1,200 pounds on gauge.

Lock life raft to vessel.

Lock whisker pole to mast and anchor in place if not stowed.

Install air vents for lazarette and sail locker.

Stuff sponge in end of boom to prevent birds from nesting.

Install hidden companionway locking device.

Interior

Inspect lockers for traces of spilled food; clean up.

Leave roach killers in food lockers.

Be sure all food that is not canned is in Ziploc bags.

Defrost and clean refrigerator and freezer. Leave tops open and secured.

Clean under shower gratings in both heads. Clean shower pump strainers.

Pump heads dry, then fill with freshwater and pump out.

Leave Bounce fabric softener sheets around interior to prevent closed-up-boat smell.

Place aluminum foil on top of hatch screens and close screens to keep sunlight out of interior.

Hide GPS units under a berth, not in chart table. Same for the watermaker in the abandon-ship bag.

Prop berth cushions upright for air circulation and prevention of mildew underneath.

Close curtains to keep sun out of vessel.

Pump water through soap dispensers; leave apart.

Wash bilges with freshwater; dry thoroughly.

Mechanical

Change engine oil. Check generator hours and change oil if over 100 hours or vessel will be laid up for longer than three months.

If holding tank has been used, pump out, add 2 gallons bleach, let sit for a day, then fill with freshwater, let sit for a day, then pump out totally.

Pickle watermaker (see page 204). Leave a big note that it must be flushed before using again.

Check propeller shaft stuffing box to be sure it is not leaking.

Check centerboard stuffing box to be sure it is not leaking.

Check that cellular phone has been shut off at central office. Unhook antenna from phone to prevent possible damage from lightning. Leave note that it is unhooked.

Disconnect VHF antenna at base of mast to prevent lightning damage. Leave note on VHF. Also, tape over VHF breaker.

Remove knotmeter impeller. Install dummy plug. Clean impeller.

Close all seacocks except cockpit scuppers. Leave a big note that they are closed.

Run freshwater through main engine by sticking pickup hose from emergency bilge pump valving into a bucket of freshwater (see tip 154).

Disconnect inverter by turning off switch under aft berth. Tape over AC inverter switch.

Shut off propane at tanks. Leave a note on galley switch.

Disconnect shore power. Shut off master battery switches.

General

Hire someone reliable to visit vessel at least weekly to check
Docklines for chafe.
Bilge for water.
Battery charge status.

Commissioning

Following is a checklist used for commissioning one of the yachts I manage. Your boat might not have all these toys, but the list can be used as a reference for making your own.

Deck
__ Genoa roller furling operates.
__ Staysail roller furling operates.
__ Mainsail furling operates.
__ Mainmast winches operate.
__ Whisker pole trigger operates.
__ Windlass operates both directions from deck switches.
__ Windlass operates both directions from cockpit switch.
__ Deck washdown forward operates. Valve for freshwater/seawater OK.
__ Winches for mainsheet and outhaul operate.
__ Stoppers for above work.
__ Primary cockpit winches operate in all three speeds.
__ Secondary cockpit winches work both speeds.
__ Hydraulic backstay pumps down.
__ Boom vang raises with no pressure, pumps down.
__ Centerboard goes up and down.
__ Lazarette and sail locker hatches work; are dogged securely.
__ Life raft unlocked.
__ Crew-overboard pole installed, connected to horseshoe.
__ Horseshoe installed, connected to light, battery in light checked, drogue checked.
__ Lifesling installed, pennant connected.
__ Jacklines/preventer system installed.
__ Knife installed on pedestal.
__ Anchor/chain either deployed or stowed with cover on chain pipe.
__ Swim ladder: either in place or stowed in sail locker.

Mechanical and Plumbing
__ Main engine starts, runs for an hour. Check
　__ Oil level.
　__ Oil pressure:
　　__cockpit ___.
　　__engine room ___.
　__ Coolant level.
　__ Transmission level.
　__ Racor fuel filters checked.
　__ Temperature:
　　__cockpit gauge___.
　__ Transmission shifts both forward and reverse.
　__ Belts tight.
　__ Engine visually checked for leaks.
　__ Stuffing box checked for leakage.
　__ Alternator output checked, both alternators.
__ Generator starts, runs for an hour. Check
　__ Oil level.
　__ Oil pressure.
　__ Coolant level.
　__ Temperature.
　__ Visually inspected for leaks.
　__ Alternator output checked.

__ Refrigeration.
　__ Engine drive operational.
　__ AC system operational.
　__ Intake strainer checked.
__ Air-conditioning pumps water, strainer clean.
　__ Aft unit operates.
　__ Forward unit operates.
__ Espar heater operates.
__ Power bilge pump operates, strainer cleaned.
__ Forward shower sump pump operates, strainer clean.
__ Aft shower sump operates, strainer clean.
__ Holding tank pump operates, tank empty.
__ Pressure water operates, strainer clean.
__ Emergency power bilge pump works.
__ Cockpit manual bilge pump works.
__ Edson manual bilge pump under galley sole works.
__ Aft head works.
__ Forward head works.
__ Aft sink drains.
__ Forward sink drains.

Autopilot
__ Reservoir level checked.
__ Pump checked for leakage.
__ Ram, plumbing checked for leaks.
__ Control panel on helm causes wheel to turn.
__ Control panel at nav station causes wheel to turn.

Watermaker
__ Intake strainer clean, seacock on.

__ Filters, primary pump checked for leaks.
__ Membranes visually checked for leaks.
__ Valve manifold checked for leaks.
__ Operates for an hour, makes potable water.

Washer-Dryer
__ Washer works.
__ Dryer works. Lint trap cleaned.

Electrical
__ Shore power works, each outlet tested.
__ Inverter works.
__ Microwave operates.
__ Dome lights work.
__ Wall swivel lights work.
__ Mood lighting works.
__ Navigation lights operate.
__ Spreader lights work.
__ Steaming light works.
__ Tricolor light works.
__ Anchor light works.
__ Strobe light works.
__ Courtesy lights work.
__ Compass light works.
__ Cockpit supply to GPS works.
__ Cockpit searchlight plug works.
__ Propane solenoid operates.
__ Propane system holds pressure for one hour with solenoid on.
__ Burners on stove work.
__ Oven works.
__ Broiler works.
__ Propane grill works.

__ Propane tanks checked for gas level.
__ Engine blower works.
__ Interior fans operate (five).
__ Battery water level checked.
__ House bank.
__ Generator starting.
__ Main engine starting.
__ Battery charger causes voltage increase in all three battery banks.
__ Bow thruster works in both directions.
__ Tank gauges appear to work.
__ Wind generator outputs.
__ Ammeter works.

Electronics
__ Radar operational.
__ VHF operational.
__ SSB operational.
__ Handset works.
__ Audio output jack works.
__ GPS #1 works, batteries checked.
__ GPS #2 works, batteries checked.
__ Garmin 210 GPS works.
__ Stereo works.
__ Radio.
__ Tape.
__ CD.
__ Cockpit speaker plugs operate.
__ Instruments work.
__ Knotmeter impeller removed, cleaned, reinstalled, operation verified.
__ Depth-sounder operates, both stations, no alarms.
__ Wind direction works, both stations.

__ Wind speed works, both stations.
__ Compass works, nav station.
__ Cellular phone works.
__ Fax machine, computer printer works.
__ Cordless phones work.
__ Handheld VHF operates, battery charged.
__ TV works.
__ Electronic barometer works.
__ Satellite global communications Inmarsat M unit operational.
__ Voice line.
__ Fax line.
__ Data line.

Interior
__ Deck hatches open, all dogs work.
__ Opening ports open, stay open, dogs operate freely.
__ Cabin sole boards lift up.
__ Locks on sole boards work.
__ Drawers and lockers open, relatch.
__ Tools checked and oiled if necessary.
__ Electric drill recharged.

Miscellanea
__ Inflatable boat holds air.
__ Outboard works.
__ All flashlights work.
__ Fire extinguishers checked for charge.
__ Strobes in safety harnesses checked for operation.
__ Abandon-ship bag out (if appropriate).

ailboats behave much differently under power than when sailing. Knowing how a vessel is likely to respond to the helm under power in varying conditions contributes greatly to a skipper's confidence. I have talked to single-handed transatlantic racers who said that storms encountered at sea are not as terrifying as docking at the end of the race.

Knowing and applying the following cardinal rules will put you on the path to becoming a seasoned skipper and help you weather situations that you haven't encountered before.

Cardinal Rule 1. *The bow tends to move with the wind and the stern with the engine.*

Cardinal Rule 2. *The person at the helm must know the direction of both wind and current and plan maneuvers to utilize their effects.*

The following discussion assumes that the boat has a right-handed propeller, as most do. Viewed from astern, a right-handed propeller turns clockwise in forward gear. Do not use the direction of engine rotation to determine the "hand" of a propeller, as some transmissions reverse that direction. If your boat has a left-handed propeller, exchange the words "port" and "starboard" in this discussion. Also, all references to helm position are made assuming the vessel is steered with a wheel rather than a tiller.

GOING AHEAD

In forward gear, a right-handed prop tends to suck water in on the starboard side and dispel it to port, thus moving the stern to starboard and the bow to port. (In reverse gear the opposite happens: the stern pulls to port.) This is called *prop walk*, or the *paddle-wheel effect*. As the speed of the boat increases, the lateral plane of the keel and rudder become more effective and the boat tracks straighter.

Because of prop walk, vessels with right-handed props turn to port tighter than they can to starboard. Boats with deep and narrow centerboards turn better if water depth permits the board to be all the way down, because the boat pivots around the board. Boats with wide centerboards that significantly increase fore-and-aft lateral plane turn better without the board. Fin-keeled, spade-rudder boats turn fastest. Boats with long conventional keels and keel-hung rudders usually take the largest area to turn.

Making a Tight Turn

To execute a tight turn to starboard, you must overcome the tendency of a right-handed prop to pull the stern to starboard. Put the wheel hard over to starboard (step 1). As soon as the bow starts to turn, move the transmission to reverse (step 2).

Keeping the wheel hard over, give the boat a good shot of reverse throttle. This will tend to pull the stern to port, accelerating the bow's turn to starboard (step 3). Also, the forward motion of the boat will be slowed, thus cutting the turning radius. When the bow has swung, reingage forward (step 4). See illustration.

A tight turn to port is easier, since prop walk will help rather than hinder the turn. In this instance, however, bursts of reverse throttle must be limited, since they will tend to walk the stern to port— the opposite of what you want.

BACKING

Backing is confusing. The boat does not respond well, and helm positions are opposite. Some skippers like to stand in front of the helm facing backward, because visibility is improved and the helm then works the same (relative to the helmsperson) as in forward. If you do this, be sure to keep an eye on what the bow is doing. While it may be easy to keep the stern in the middle of a narrow channel, the bow can blow off to leeward, possibly striking other vessels.

Because the rudder is out in front of a boat making sternway, forces on the rudder and helm are greatly increased. Be sure to keep a good grip on the wheel.

Backing Straight

When reverse is engaged, the stern pulls to port. Because speeds in reverse are generally slow and the propeller is in front of the stabilizing influence of the keel, boats tend to track poorly in reverse (i.e., don't

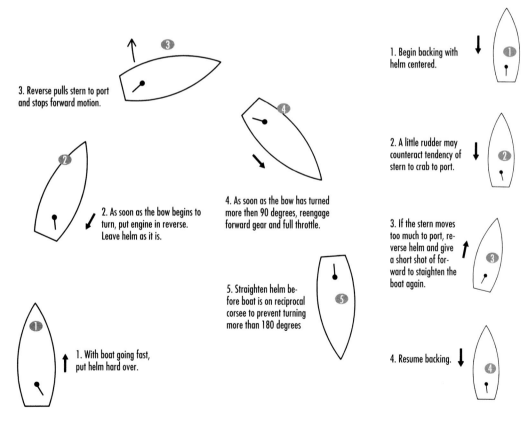

3. Reverse pulls stern to port and stops forward motion.

2. As soon as the bow begins to turn, put engine in reverse. Leave helm as it is.

4. As soon as the bow has turned more then 90 degrees, reengage forward gear and full throttle.

5. Straighten helm before boat is on reciprocal corsee to prevent turning more than 180 degrees

1. With boat going fast, put helm hard over.

1. Begin backing with helm centered.

2. A little rudder may counteract tendency of stern to crab to port.

3. If the stern moves too much to port, reverse helm and give a short shot of forward to staighten the boat again.

4. Resume backing.

You can make a tighter turn to starboard by using a short burst of reverse.

Backing straight.

go straight). This is not all bad, because such boats turn quickly in reverse. Perhaps you have seen a large sailboat backing out of a crowded marina. The skipper isn't showing off, just leading with the rudder in order to turn more quickly.

If sufficient space is available, get the vessel moving backward with the rudder amidships (step 1) or just a little to starboard (step 2), then take the transmission out of gear, which gives the rudder sole control over steering. As sternward boat speed decreases and the rudder loses effectiveness, another shot of reverse is needed. If the stern swings too far to port, a quick shot of forward power with the helm (and rudder) hard to port straightens out the vessel (step 3). Return the rudder to midships before resuming backing (step 4). See drawing previous page.

Wind from the port side tends to move the bow to starboard, making backing in a straight line more difficult. Conversely, a brisk wind from starboard moves the bow the same way the propeller in reverse is pulling the stern, facilitating straight backing (assuming there is sea room on the port side of the vessel). Backing straight into the wind is a lot easier than trying to back with the wind on the bow, as the bow will be rapidly blown off in the latter instance.

Backing to Port

Because in this situation the propeller pulls the stern to port anyway, almost in proportion to the amount of throttle applied, very little rudder is required to back to port.

Backing to Starboard

Backing a right-handed propeller boat to starboard is difficult. The best way is to get the vessel moving backward as fast as you dare (step 1), then take the engine out of gear and put the helm a little to starboard (step 2). Sometimes, a shot of forward power with helm to port is required to maintain the desired orientation. See illustration.

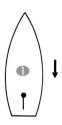

1. Get boat moving backward as fast as possible with the helm centered

2. Take engine out of gear, turn helm to starboard.

Backing to starboard.

DOCKING FROM ARRIVAL TO DEPARTURE

Before docking, it is essential to note wind direction and current relative to the dock.

The fuel dock at the marina where I spend a lot of time is perpendicular to the prevailing southwesterly wind and must be approached from the leeward. This orientation provides a lot of entertainment when boats try to come alongside the dock. About one in ten has a spring line rigged and performs the maneuver effortlessly. The rest throw the attendant the bow line and then scramble around trying to get a long enough stern line rigged to pull the boat in (see illustration next page).

If you want to look like an experienced skipper, following these cardinal rules for docking. They may spare your vessel some harm and your ego a bruising.

Cardinal Rule 3. *In almost any docking situation, the most important line to get ashore first is a spring line.*

Cardinal Rule 4. *Always put the eye of a dockline on the dock and keep the working end on board.*

Watch any commercial vessel dock. You won't be hard-pressed to

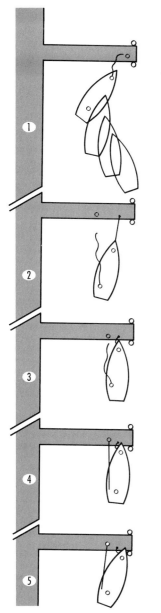

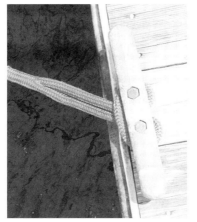

With the dockline's eye on the dock cleat, the boat's position can be adjusted on board. When strain is too great to pull by hand, forward lines can be led to the windlass capstan and aft lines to cockpit winches. It also is much easier for the skipper to communicate dockline length and placement to crew on deck rather than shouting to someone on the dock.

find somebody on the pier who doesn't know the intentions of the skipper. Loops of docklines are made fast on shore, and the skipper uses either the ship's propulsion or winches to work the vessel alongside (see photo above).

These same principles work well on pleasure boats, yet most pleasure boats keep the eye of a dockline around a deck cleat and throw the working end ashore. Fortunately,

Typical way inexperienced skippers dock to leeward of a fuel dock. 1. Skipper hollers for mate to throw bow line to attendat. 2. Boat drifts back on bow line. Skipper attempts to throw stern line into the wind and it falls short. 3. Skipper hollers to attendant to pull bow in, then throws stern line to attendant. 4. Because the boat is parallel to direction of pull, the bow comes forward as the attendant hauls the stern line. 5. The bow hits the piling supporting the outer end of the pier. (Skipper's words unprintable.)

While coiling the working end of a dockline on the dock looks "yachty," this practice identifies a skipper as having no experience with larger vessels. Only human power can adjust a dockline with the working end on the dock.

these inexperienced people generally own boats small enough to be pulled by a person, which is the only way to adjust a dockline with the working end ashore. With the working end on board, I have frequently taken a bow line to the windlass capstan and a stern line to a cockpit winch to pull a vessel closer alongside a dock. The ability to do this is critical when the wind pipes up and the boat is blown off the dock.

Spring Lines

Watching and helping people dock, I find that only about one in twenty understands the physics of docking. Fortunately, you can learn the physics while in a boring meeting or talking on the phone.

Use a sharpened pencil as a model boat. Affix a 6- to 10-inch-long piece of thread with tape or a clove hitch near the pointed end (bow), one in the middle, and one at the eraser end (stern). Hold the thread end from the bow perpendicular to the pencil and push on the eraser. As the thread tightens, the bow will come toward the finger holding the thread, and the stern will swing out. Next, try the thread in the middle of the pencil. The pencil will "dock" without either end swinging in or out. Using the stern results in a better docking than with the bow but tends to pull the stern in, forcing the bow out.

You probably noticed in each of the above tests that to cause lateral motion toward the finger holding the thread end, the pencil had to be pushed forward quite a distance. Let's try one more time. Hold the thread from the middle of the pencil about 45 degrees toward the stern. The pencil will dock evenly with less forward motion. You're now well on your way to understanding the principles of spring line use.

Spring Line Hardware

Unfortunately, most boats lack proper spring line chocks or cleats. Boatbuilders who provide spring line cleats frequently position them to fit stock lengths of toerail rather than taking into consideration the characteristics of a vessel when sprung into a dock. A pencil is nice and uniform; a boat hull is not.

If you're going to add spring line hardware, experiment with placement—the boat doesn't even have to leave the dock. Tie a loop in the middle of a line long enough to run from the bow cleat to the stern cleat on the side of your boat near the dock, preferably with some line left over at each end for ease of adjustment. Tie another line from the loop to a cleat on the dock near the stern. This is your spring line.

Loosen the bow and stern lines a little and gently put the engine in forward gear with the helm centered and the spring line snug. If the bow tends to move toward the dock, rerig the loop to which the spring line is fastened so that it's farther aft. Conversely, if the stern swings in, move the loop forward. Once a position is found that brings the vessel toward the dock in a roughly parallel orientation, try the engine in reverse with the spring line tied to a dock cleat near the bow. The chances are good that the right placement for a stern spring will be too far aft for a forward spring. This is why large yachts have multiple spring line ports. If you routinely dock bow first, a forward spring is less important.

You now know where on deck your stern spring and (if it's desired) your bow spring should lead from.

This elegant midship chock fits into a teak toerail and has rollers to reduce friction on spring lines.

Rather than installing a cleat at that point, I prefer a chock or fairlead. Then I take the stern spring line aft from the fairlead to the cockpit primary winch, making the spring line readily adjustable from the boat. That way, I don't have to rely on someone on the dock to cleat the line at just the right place and time, and it makes for much less nerve-wracking dockings.

An elegant spring line chock has rollers to reduce friction (see photo, opposite). A vessel with a robust slotted aluminum toerail can use a block affixed to a D shackle in the rail, but a better solution is a Wichard toerail pad eye, which prevents damage to the rail. If the toerail extrusion is not thick, reinforce it with aluminum plates inside and outside, through-bolted to each other. Place thin plastic (a cut-up milk jug works) between the added aluminum plates and the rail to prevent corrosion. I prefer not to use a snatch block, as load on the spring line may open the block. If a snatch block is used, be sure that the opening side is down when the block is loaded. Use shock cord to the lower lifeline to hold any block for a spring line upright until tension is taken.

Schaefer Marine has recently introduced cast stainless steel cleats on a slide that fit track on a toerail. Because the spring line will take considerable pressure, I recommend that an additional stop be placed on the track at each end of the cleat.

Docking

Let's look at how experienced skippers come alongside the fuel dock at my marina.

They all use a long spring line, and most wrap the working end around a cockpit winch. From there, the line leads forward through a midship chock (or a strong snatch block affixed to an aluminum slotted toerail or rugged pad eye). Its dock end is then taken forward on the vessel to be thrown or handed ashore on the approach to the dock (step 1). The spring line should be made fast on the dock roughly where you want the stern to end up (step 2). Powering slowly ahead against the spring line will cause the vessel to move sideways toward the dock. Belay the stern line (step 3).

In general, a spring line through a midship chock results in the bow coming in toward the dock first. If the propeller is just forward of the rudder, putting the helm over as if one were going to turn away from the dock will lessen the bow-toward-the-dock syndrome.

Departing a Dock

Using the natural tendency of a boat to pivot on secured lines can be advantageous when departing a dock.

The spring line used must be dead-ended on board, passed around a cleat or bollard on the dock, and then led back to the vessel, where it should be secured in such a manner that it can be quickly released and retrieved on board.

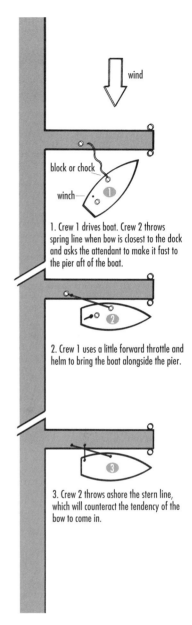

1. Crew 1 drives boat. Crew 2 throws spring line when bow is closest to the dock and asks the attendant to make it fast to the pier aft of the boat.

2. Crew 1 uses a little forward throttle and helm to bring the boat alongside the pier.

3. Crew 2 throws ashore the stern line, which will counteract the tendency of the bow to come in.

Using a spring line to dock on the leeward side. If there's a significant difference in strength between the two crew, crew 2 should be the one with greater physical strength.

Departing with Restricted Space Available Forward

Rig a line from the stern to a dock cleat about midships on your vessel. Put a fender well aft (step 1).

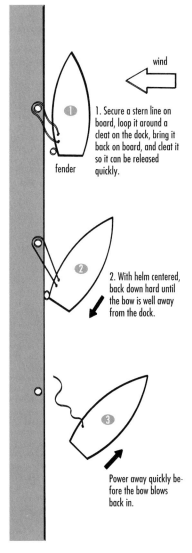

1. Secure a stern line on board, loop it around a cleat on the dock, bring it back on board, and cleat it so it can be released quickly.

fender

2. With helm centered, back down hard until the bow is well away from the dock.

Power away quickly before the bow blows back in.

Springing forward off a windward dock.

Center the helm and back down hard against the stern spring (step 2). It may take awhile, but the bow will eventually be forced away from the dock. Because Murphy's Law states that the wind will always be blowing against the dock face when you try this maneuver, and will immediately blow your bow back toward the dock when you stop, you must continue backing until the bow is at least 45 degrees from the dock before quickly freeing your spring and departing in forward gear (step 3).

Aboard *Malabar XIV* secured to the bulkhead outside Dowlings Shell in St. George's, Bermuda, I was once awakened about 3 A.M. by the metal rubrail hitting the concrete jetty. I went on deck to find a 40-knot steady wind from just aft of amidships pinning the 76-foot, 105,000-pound yacht to the dock and compressing six 12-inch-diameter fenders. I immediately started the engine and got out our strongest 1½-inch spare dockline, which I rigged around a cannon that was conveniently sunk vertically into the jetty about midships. As full reverse of the 270-horsepower turbocharged diesel began to move the bow out, the crew brought fenders aft. After five agonizing minutes, *Malabar*'s bow was about 40 degrees from the jetty, and full forward got her safely past the underwater projection of the jetty just ahead of the bow.

In the middle of the harbor we put down two 125-pound anchors, each on 400 feet of ½-inch chain. After making sure we were holding,

the crew went back to bed. When we awoke around midmorning, solid waves were washing over the jetty where we had been, and the owner apologized for being grumpy at my waking him by starting the engine in the middle of the night.

Departing a Dock by Backing Out

This works nicely if the side of the boat opposite the propeller's pull is alongside the dock. Rig a line from the bow to a dock cleat about midships (step 1). Move a fender forward. Power forward until the stern is well clear (step 2), and then back out (step 3). If the stern pulls toward the dock in reverse, be sure to get the stern out at least 45 degrees from the dock before reversing the engine.

I was working on a boat at a prestigious Oyster Bay, New York, yacht club. Boats were kept on moorings, but there was one long pier that members could tie up to for water and loading. The afternoon sou'wester had filled in, and I happened to be walking past the launch driver's office when the commodore asked for a launch to pull his boat off the windward side of the dock.

Because I wasn't a member, I felt free to ask the commodore if his engine wasn't working. He replied that his engine was fine, but his boat was being blown hard against the dock. I told him it wouldn't look good for the commodore to require outside assistance to get off the dock. So I rigged a spring line for

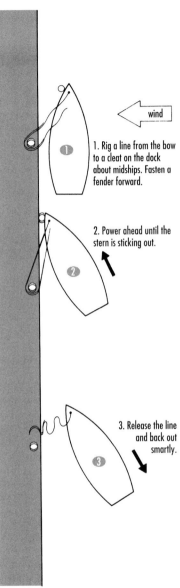

1. Rig a line from the bow to a cleat on the dock about midships. Fasten a fender forward.

wind

2. Power ahead until the stern is sticking out.

3. Release the line and back out smartly.

Springing aft from a windward dock.

him. He waved as he powered away, and I forgot the incident until a couple of days later when I was walking past one of the club's bars. The bartender asked me why I hadn't been in. I replied that the club's drinks were priced too steeply for me. The bartender laughed and told me that the commodore had passed the word that whatever I wanted, whenever I wanted it, was on him.

ABI/A&B Industries (*hardware*)
1160A Industrial Ave.
Petaluma CA 94952
707-765-6200, 800-422-1301
www.abimarine.com

ABYC (*American Boat & Yacht Council*)
3069 Solomons Island Rd.
Edgewater MD 21037
410-956-1050
www.abycinc.org

ACR Electronics (*EPIRBs*)
5757 Ravenwood Rd.
Ft. Lauderdale FL 33312
954-981-3333
www.acrelectronics.com

Airtex Products (*electric fuel pumps*)
407 West Main St.
Fairfield IL 62837
618-842-2111
wwwairtexproducts.com

Alden Yachts
1909 Alden Landing
Portsmouth RI 02871
401-683-4200
www.aldenyachts.com

All Hands Canvas (*custom sea bags*)
1 Ashurst Pl.
Newport RI 02840
401-849-1442

Ancor Marine (*tinned wire; terminals*)
531 Mercantile Dr.
Cotati CA 94931
707-792-0312, 800-424-9473
www.ancorproducts.com

Aqualarm (*cooling water flow alarm*)
1151 Bay Blvd., Suite D
Chula Vista CA 91911
888-298-6206
www.aqualarm.net

Balmar (*battery charging and monitoring equipment*)
19009 61st Ave. NE #4
Arlington WA 98223
360-435-6100
www.balmar.net

Band-It Co. (*packing bands*)
4799 Dahlia St.
Denver CO 80216
303-320-4555
www.band-it-idex.com

Beckson Marine
165 Holland Ave.
Bridgeport CT 06605
203-333-1412
www.beckson.com

Berkshire Electric Cable (*tinned wire; electrical wire*)
P.O. Box 306
Leeds MA 01053
413-584-3853

BoatU.S. (*Boat Owners Association of the United States*)
880 S. Pickett St.
Alexandria VA 22304
800-395-2628, 703-461-2878
www.boatus.com

Brinkman Turkey Farms, Inc.
16314 U.S. Rt. 68

Findlay OH 45840
419-365-5127
www.brinkmanfarms.com

Brookes & Gatehouse (*instruments*)
13191 56 Ct., Suite 106
Clearwater FL 33760
727-540-0229
E-mail: sales@bngusa.com

Caframo
RR 2, P.O. Box 70
Wiarton ON N0H 2T0
CANADA
519-534-1080, 800-567-3556
www.caframo.com

Celestaire (*Tamaya sextant*)
560 S. Oliver
Wichita KS 67218
800-727-9785, 316-686-9785
www.celestaire.com

Charles Marine Products (*step-down transformers*)
5600 Apollo Dr.
Rolling Meadows IL 60008
847-806-6300
www.charlesindustries.com

Cruising Equipment (*battery charging and monitoring equipment*)
Xantrex
5916 195th N.E.
Arlington WA 98223
206-782-8100, 360-925-5000
www.cruisingequip.com
www.xantrex.com

Davis Instruments (*plastic sextant, radar reflector*)
3465 Diablo Ave.
Hayward CA 94545
510-732-9229
www.davisnet.com

Federal Consumer Information Center
Dept. WWW
Pueblo CO 81009
888-8PUEBLO (888-878-3256)
www.pueblo.gsa.gov
E-mail: catalog.pueblo@gsa.gov

Galerider (*drogue*)
Hathaway, Reiser & Raymond
184 Selleck St.
Stamford CT 06902
203-324-9581
www.hathaways.com/galerider.htm

Galleyware
330 Water St., Suite 108
Newport DE 19804
302-996-9480
www.galleyware.com

Garhauer Marine (*hardware*)
1082 W. 9th St.
Upland CA 91786
909-985-9993
www.garhauermarine.com

Gibb
Navtec Norseman Gibb
351 New Whitfield St.
Guilford CT 06437-0388
203-458-3163
www.navtec.net

Gil Marine
140 Blaze Industrial Pkwy.
Berea OH 44017

800-624-9805
www.gilmarine.com

Guest
95 Research Pkwy.
Meriden CT 06450
203-235-4421
www.guestco.com

Hall Spars & Rigging
17 Peckham Dr.
Bristol RI 02809
401-253-4858
www.hallspars.com

Harken Yacht Equipment
1251 E. Wisconsin Ave.
Pewaukee WI 53072
262-691-3320
www.harken.com

Hehr Power Systems (*alternators*)
4616 Fairlane Ave.
Ft. Worth TX 76119
817-535-0284
www.hehrpowersystems.com

Hella Marine
201 Kelly Dr.
Peachtree City GA 30269
770-631-7500, 877-224-3552
www.hellamarine.com

IAMAT (*International Association for Medical Assistance to Travelers*)
417 Center St.
Lewiston NY 14092
716-754-4883
www.sentex.net/~iamat

Icom America (*SSB and VHF radios*)
2380 116th Ave. N.E.
Bellevue WA 98004
425-454-8155
www.icomamerica.com

IMTRA (*Henderson pumps*)
30 Samuel Barnet Blvd.
New Bedford MA 02745
508-995-7000
www.imtra.com

Jamestown Distributors
500 Wood, Bldg. #15
Bristol RI 02809
800-423-0030
www.jamestowndistributors.com

Jim Buoy (*anchor marker buoy*)
Cal-June, Inc.
P.O. Box 9551
North Hollywood CA 91609-9551
818-761-3516
www.jimbuoy.com

Jordan Series Drogue
Ace Sailmakers
Hellier Yacht Sales
128 Howard St.
New London CT 06320
860-443-5556
www.acesails.com

KVH Industries (*instruments*)
50 Enterprise Ctr.
Middletown RI 02842
401-847-3327
www.kvh.com

Kwikpoint Cards (*translation cards*)
Gaia Communications
48 S. Early St.
Alexandria VA 22304
800-KWIKPOINT (888-594-5764)
www.kwikpoint.com

Lirakis Safety Harness
18 Sheffield Ave.
Newport RI 02840
401-846-5356

Magellan (GPS)
Thales Navigation
960 Overland Ct.
San Dimas CA 91773
909-394-5000
www.magellangps.com

Magnaflux
3624 W. Lake Ave.
Glenview IL 60025
847-657-5300
www.magnaflux.com

McFeely's Square Drive Screws
1620 Wythe Rd.
P.O. Box 11169
Lynchburg VA 24506
800-443-7937
www.mcfeelys.com

McMaster-Carr
P.O. Box 740100
Atlanta GA 30374-0100
404-346-7000
www.mcmaster.com

Metal Products Engineering, Inc.
3050 Leonis Blvd.
Vernon CA 90058
800-824-0222
www.metalproductseng.com

F. W. Murphy Mfg. (oil pressure gauge)
P.O. Box 470248
Tulsa OK 74147
918-317-4100
www.fwmurphy.com

New England Ropes
848 Airport Rd.
Fall River MA 02720
508-678-8200
www.neropes.com

Northern Airborne Technology, Inc.
(EPIRBs)
5757 Ravenswood Rd.
Ft. Landerdale FL 33312
800-225-4767
www.nat-inc.com

Olsun Electrics Corp. (isolation and
step-down transformers)
10901 Commercial St.
Richmond IL 60071-0001
815-678-2421
www.olsun.com

Paneltronics (electrical distribution panels)
11960 N.W. 87th Ct.
Hialeah Gardens FL 33018
305-823-9777
www.paneltronics.com

Patagonia (clothing, foul-weather gear)
8550 White Fir St.
Reno NV 89523
800-336-9090
www.patagonia.com

Pelican Products
23215 Early Ave.
Torrance CA 90505
310-326-4700
www.pelican.com

Perko
P.O. Box 64000D
Miami FL 33164
305-621-7525
www.perko.com

Preco, Inc. (truck backup alarm)
415 N. Maple Grove
Boise ID 83704
800-453-1141
www.preco.com

Professional Mariner (battery chargers)
P.O. Box 968
Rye NH 03870
603-433-4440
www.professionalmariner.com

Quantum/Thurston Sails, Inc.
112 Tupelo St.
Bristol RI 02809
401-254-0970
www.quantumsails.com

RadioShack
100 Throckmorton St., Suite 1800
Ft. Worth TX 76102
800-843-7422
www.radioshackcorporation.com

Raymarine (Autohelm)
22 Cotton Rd., Unit H
Nashua NH 03063
603-881-5200
www.raymarine.com

RectorSeal (pipe sealant)
2601 Spenwick Dr.
Houston TX 77055
800-231-3345
www.rectorseal.com

Ross Engineering (DSC VHF)
12505 Starkey Rd., Suite E
Largo FL 33773
727-536-1226
www.rossdsc.com

Ryerson Tull Inc.
2621 W. 15th Pl.
Chicago IL 60608
773-762-2121
www.ryersontull.com

S & S Fabric Products (*polypropylene pile blankets*)
1 Maritime Dr.
Portsmouth RI 02871
401-683-5858
www.ssfabricproducts.com

Scanmar International (*Monitor steering vane*)
432 S. 1st St.
Point Richmond CA 94804
510-215-2010, 888-WINDVANE (888-946-3826)
www.selfsteer.com

Sea-Dog Line (*hardware*)
P.O. Box 479
Everett WA 98206
425-259-0194
www.sea-dog.com

SeaLand Technology (*MSDs and accessories*)
13128 State Rt. 226
P.O. Box 38
Big Prairie OH 44611
800-321-9886, 330-496-3211
www.sealandtechnology.com

Seven Seas Cruising Association
1525 South Andrews Ave, Suite 217
Ft. Lauderdale FL 33316
954-463-2431
www.ssca.org

Simrad (*instruments, radios, autopilots*)
19210 33rd Ave. W., Suite A
Lynnwood WA 98036
425-778-8821
www.simrad.com

SOSpenders (*safety equipment*)
Sporting Lives
1510 N.W. 17th St.
Fruitland ID 83619

208-452-5780
www.sospenders.com

Southworth-Milton, Inc.
100 Quarry Dr.
Milford MA 01757
508-634-3400
www.southworth-milton.com

Spartite/TCC (*mast chocking system*)
31200 Stephenson Highway
Madison Heights MI 48071
248-616-2411, 877-772-7848
www.spartite.com

Standard Horizon Marine, div. of Yaesu USA (*VHF radios*)
17210 Edwards Rd.
Cerritos CA 90703
562-404-2700
www.standardhorizon.com

Sugatsune America, Inc. (*cabinet and door hardware*)
221 Selandia Lane
Carson CA 90746
310-329-6373
www.sugatsune.com

Suncor Stainless (*anchor swivel*)
7 Riverside Dr.
Pembroke MA 02359
781-829-8899, 800-394-2222
www.suncorstainless.com

Tools on Sale, div. of Seven Corners Ace Hardware
216 West 7th St.
St. Paul MN 55102
800-328-0457, 651-224-4859
www.7cornershdwe.com

TPI
P.O. Box 60
Warren RI 02885
401-247-1050
www.tipcomp.com

Ultra Safety Systems (*bilge pump switch*)
3755 Fiscal Ct.
Riviera Beach FL 33404
800-433-2628, 561-844-8822

U.S. Sailing (*ORC rules, IMS certificates*)
15 Maritime Dr.
Portsmouth RI 02871
401-683-0800
www.ussailing.org

Vista Manufacturing Inc. (*tubular lights*)
52864 Lillian St.
Elkhart IN 46514
219-264-0711
www.vistamfg.com

West Marine (*catalog and retail stores*)
Catalog Division
P.O. Box 50070
Watsonville CA 95077-0070
800-262-8464 (U.S. and Canada)
www.westmarine.com

Woodworker's Supply
1108 N. Glenn Rd.
Casper WY 82601
800-645-9292

Woodworker's Warehouse
Trend-Lines, Inc.
Corporate Offices
126 Oxford St.
Lynn MA 01901
800-818-8652
www.woodworkerswarehouse.com

See the discussion in chapter 4 about using radios for emergency transmissions.

HAM NETS *(www.mmsn.org)*

Local Time	UTC	Frequency (kHz)	Net	Area Covered
	0030	3923	WX/TFC	North Carolina area
	0100	3935	WXFTFC	Gulf Coast of U.S. Hurricane
	0200	14334	WX/TFC	Eastern U.S. traffic
	0330	14040	Code only	Eastern U.S.
	0400	14310	TFC	Northeast Canada
	0630	14313	TFC	International Marine (frequently called Mickey Mouse Net)
	1030	3815	WX	Caribbean weather
	1100	7237	TFC	Caribbean traffic
	1100	14283	TFC	East Coast/Caribbean
	1110	3930	WX	Virgin Islands/Puerto Rico
	2200	3930	TFC	Same
	1145	14121	TFC	Eastern Canada to Caribbean
	1145	7268	TFC	U.S. East Coast/Caribbean
	1200	14040	Code	U.S. East Coast
	1230	7185	TFC	Caribbean
	1245	7268	TFC	U.S. East Coast/Caribbean
	1300	21400	TFC	Transatlantic
	1345	3968	TFC	U.S. East Coast/Caribbean
	1400	7085	TFC	East Atlantic
	1400	7292	TFC	Coast of Florida
	1800	14303	TFC	Mediterranean/Atlantic
	2130	14290	TFC	U.S. East Coast
	2230	3958	WXFTFC	Caribbean
	2230	3958	TFC	New England
	2400	14325	WX	Severe weather worldwide

Unlicensed use permitted in emergencies.
WX = Weather.
TFC = Traffic.

WLO Voice Radio Frequencies *(www.wloradio.com)*

ITU (International Telecommunication Union)	Ship Transmit (kHz)	Ship Receive (kHz)
405 #	4077.0	4369.0
		4396.0
419	4119.0	4411.0
607 #	6218.0	6519.0
824 #	8264.0	8788.0
830	8282.0	8806.0
1212 #	12263.0	13110.0
1226	12305.0	13152.0
1607	16378.0	17260.0
1641 * #	16480.0	17362.0
1807	18798.0	19773.0
2237 *	22108.0	22804.0
2503	25076.0	26151.0

* = Traffic List Channels are those on which WLO will broadcast a list of messages held for vessels. Broadcasts are every hour and half-hour.

= Guarded Channels are those on which WLO listens.

U.S. COAST GUARD HIGH SEAS FREQUENCIES
(www.navcen.uscg.gov/marcomms/cgcomms/call.htm)

ITU Channel	kHz Ship Station	kHz Coast Station	Station and Schedule (UTC) NMN	NMN/NM	NMG
424	4134	4426	2300 – 1100	2230 – 1030	24 hrs
601	6200	6501	24 hrs	24 hrs	24 hrs
816	8240	8764	24 hrs	24 hrs	24 hrs
1205	12242	13089	1100 – 2300	1030 – 2230	24 hrs
1625	16432	17314	on request	on request	on request

			NMC	NMO	NOJ
—	4125	4125	—	—	24 hrs
424	4134	4426	24 hrs	0600 – 1800	on request
601	6200	6501	24 hrs	24 hrs	24 hrs
816	8240	8764	24 hrs	24 hrs	on request
1205	12242	13089	24 hrs	1800 – 0600	on request
1625	16432	17314	on request	on request	on request

			Guam	NMN/NMA
601	6200	6501	0900 – 2100	24 hrs
1205	12242	13089	2100 – 0900	24 hrs
1625	16432	17314	—	24 hrs

U.S. Coast Guard Communication Stations

NMN	Chesapeake, Virginia
NMF	Boston, Massachusetts
NMA	Miami, Florida
NMG	New Orleans, Louisiana
NMC	Point Reyes, California
HMO	Honolulu, Hawaii
NOJ	Kodiak, Alaska

USCG COASTAL AND HIGH SEAS FORECASTS
(www.navcen.uscg.gov/marcomms/cgcomms/voice.htm)

Time (UTC)	Frequency (kHz)		
USCG Atlantic (NMN, Portsmouth Virgina)			
0330	4426	6501	8764
0500	4426	6501	8764
0930	4426	6501	8764
1130	6501	8764	13089
1600	6501	8764	13089
1730	8764	13089	17314
2200	6501	8764	13089
2330	6501	8764	13089
USCG San Francisco (NMC, Point Reyes, California)			
0430	4426	8764	13089
1030	4426	8764	13089
1630	8764	13089	17314
2230	8764	13089	17314
USCG Honolulu (NMO, Hawaii)			
0600	6501	8764	
1200	6501	8764	
1800	8764	13089	
0000	8764	13089	
USCG Marianas (Guam)			
0300	13089		
0705	2670		
0930	6501		
1530	6501		
2130	13089		
2205	2670		
USCG Kodiak (NOJ, Alaska)			
0203	6501		
1645	6501		

SOME COMMON SSB FREQUENCIES

(www.bitwrangler.com/wt/ss-ssb-freq.html)

Common Designation	ITU Channel	Simplex Frequency
4A	451	4146
4B	452	4149
4C	453	4417
6S	650	6215
6A	651	6224
68	652	6227
6C	653	6230
6D	654	6516
8S	850	8291
8A	851	8294
8B	852	8297
12S	1250	12290
12A	1251	12353
12B	1252	12356
12C	1253	12359
12D	1254	12362
12E	1255	12365
16A	1651	16528
16B	1652	16531
16C	1653	16534
22A	2251	22159
22B	2252	22162
22C	2253	22165
22D	2254	22168
22E	2255	22171

SSB Frequency Propagation

Spring and Summer

Band Propagation (miles)	4 MHz		8 MHz		12 MHz		16 MHz		22 MHz	
	Min.	Max.	Min.	Max.	Min.	Max.	Min.	Max.	Min.	Max.
Hours after sunset										
1	50	250	200	1000	500	3500	750	6000	1500	7000
2	100	600	250	1500	500	3500	750	6000		
3	100	800	250	2000	500	9500				
4	100	800	250	2500						
5	100	1000	250	2500						
6	100	1500	400	3000						
7	100	1500	500	3500						
8	250	2000	750							
9	250	2500	750	4000						
10	250	2500	750	4000						
11	100	1000	500	2500						
Hours after sunrise										
1	100	500	400	2000						
2	0	100	400	2000						
3	0	100	250	1500						
4	0	100	250	1500	500	1000				
5	0	100	250	1500	500	1500				
6	0	100	250	1500	500	2500	750	4000		
7	0	100	250	1500	500	3500	750	4000	1500	7000
8	0	100	250	1500	500	3500	750	4000	1500	7000
9	0	100	250	1500	500	3500	750	4000	1500	7000
10	0	100	250	1500	500	3500	750	4000	1500	7000
11	0	100	150	500	500	3500	750	6000	1500	7000
12	0	200	150	500	500	3500	750	6000	1500	7000
13	50	250	150	770	500	3500	750	6000	1500	7000

Fall and Winter

Band Propagation (miles)	4 MHz		8 MHz		12 MHz		16 MHz		22 MHz	
	Min.	Max.	Min.	Max.	Min.	Max.	Min.	Max.	Min.	Max.
Hours after sunset										
1	100	600	400	2000	500	3500	750	6000	1500	7000
2	100	500	400	2000	500	4000	750	6000		
3	100	1000	400	2000	500	4000				
4	100	1000	400	2500	500	4000				
5	100	1000	400	3000	500	4000				
6	100	1500	400	3500						
7	250	2000	400	4000						
8	250	250	500	4000						
9	500	3000	500	4000						
10	500	4000	500	4000						
11	500	3000	750	5000						
12	250	2500	750	5000						
13	250	1500	500	2500						
Hours after sunrise										
1	100	1000	400	2000						
2	100	500	400	2000						
3	0	100	400	2000	500	3500	750	4000		
4	0	100	400	2000	500	3500	750	4000	1500	3000
5	0	100	250	1500	500	3500	750	4000	1500	4000
6	0	100	250	1500	500	3500	750	4000	1500	5000
7	0	100	250	1500	500	4000	750	5000	1500	6000
8	0	100	250	1500	500	4000	750	5000	1500	7000
9	0	100	250	1500	500	4000	750	8000	1500	7000
10	0	100	250	1000	500	3500	750	6000	1500	7000
11	0	250	250	1500	500	3500	750	6000	1500	7000

VOICE OF AMERICA *(www.voa.gov/allsked.html)*

UTC	Frequencies
English to Europe, Middle East, and North Africa	
0000 – 0030	1260 1548
0100 – 0300	1548
0400 – 0430	792 9530 11965 15205
0430 – 0500	9530 11965 15205
0500 – 0530	792 1197 9530 11965 15205
0530 – 0600	792 9530 11965 15205
0600 – 0700	792 1197 1260 9530 9680 11805 11965 15205
0700 – 1400	1197
1400 – 1500	1197 1548 15255
1500 – 1530	1260 1548 9700 15205 15255
1530 – 1600	1197 1260 1548 9700 15205 15255
1600 – 1700	1260 1548 9700 15205 15255
1700 – 1730	9700 9760 15255
1730 – 1800	1197 9700 9760 15255
1800 – 1830	1197 9760 9770
1830 – 1900	792 9760 9770
1900 – 2000	6160 9760 9770
2000 – 2030	1197 6095 9760 9770
2030 – 2100	1197$ 6095 9760 9770
2100 – 2200	1260 1548 6040 6095 9530 9760
2200 – 2230	1548
2230 – 2400	1260 1548
English to Africa	
0300 – 0330	909 1530 5855 6080 7105 7275 7290 7340 9575 9885 17895
0330 – 0400	909 1530 5855 6080 7105 7275 7290 9575 9885 17895
0400 – 0430	909 1530 4960 5855 6080 7275 7290 9575 9885 17895
0430 – 0500	909 4960 5855 6080 7275 7290 9575 17895
0500 – 0600	909 5970 6035 6080 7195 12080 13670
0600 – 0630	909 1530 5970 6035 6080 7195 11995 12080 13670
0630 – 0700$	909 1530 5970 6035 6080 7195 11995 12080 13670
1600 – 1700	909 1530 6035 13605 13710 15225 15410
1700 – 1730	909 11920 12040 15240 15445 17895
1730 – 1800	909* 15410 15455 17895
1800 – 1830	909 6035 7415 11975 15410 15580 17895
1830 – 1900	909 6035 7415 11690$ 11975 13730$ 15410 15525$ 15580 17895
1900 – 2000	909 4950 6035 7375 7415 11975 15410 15445 15580
2000 – 2030	909 1530 4950 6035 7375 7415 11855 11975 15410 15445 15580 17745 17895
2030 – 2100	909 1530 4950$ 6035 7375 7415 11975 15410 15445 15580 17745 17895
2100 – 2200	909 1530 6035 7375 7415 11975 15410 15445 15580 17895
2200 – 2230*	909 1530 6035 7340 7375 7415 11975
English to Caribbean and Latin America	
0000 – 0100#	5995 6130 7405 9455 9775 11695 13740
0100 – 0130#	5995 6130 7405 9455 9775 13740
0130 – 0200#	5995 6130 9455
0200 – 0400	1530 1580
0400 – 0500+	1530 1580
1000 – 1100	6165 7370 9590

English to Far East Asia, South Asia, and Oceania

0000 – 0030	1575 7215 9770 11760 15185 15290 17740 17820
0100 – 0300	7115 9635 11705 11725 11820 13650 15250 17740 17820
0800 – 1000	11930 13610 15150
1000 – 1100	9770 15240 15425
1100 – 1130	1575$ 6160 9645 9760 9770 15160 15240 15425
1130 – 1200	6160 9645 9760 9770 15160 15240 15425
1200 – 1230	1143 6160 9645 9760 15160 15240 15425
1230 – 1300	6160 9645 9760 15160 15240 15425
1300 – 1400	6160 9645 9760 15160 15425
1400 – 1500	1143 6160 7125 9645 9760 15160 15425
1500 – 1600	7125 9645
1600 – 1700	6160 7125 9645 9760
1700 – 1800	1143* 1575* 5990* 6045* 6160 7125 7215* 9550* 9645 9770* 9785*
1900 – 2000	9525 11805 15180
2100 – 2200	9705 11870 15185 17740 17820
2200 – 2230	7215 9705 9770 11760 15185 15290 15305 17740 17820
2230 – 2400	1575> 7215 9705 9770 11760 15185 15290 15305 17740 17820

English – Border Crossings

1900 – 2000*	9550 9840 11780 11970 12015 13725 15235

English—Special

0030 – 0100 (Middle East and Asia)	1548 1575 7215 9770 11760 15185 15290 17740 17820
0130 – 0200# (Caribbean and Latin America)	7405 9775 13740
1500 – 1530 (Asia)	1575$ 6160 9590 9760 9845 12040 15550
1530 – 1600 (Asia)	1575 6160 9590 9760 9845 12040 15550
1600 – 1700 (Africa)	13600 15445 17895
1900 – 1930 (Middle East and Asia)	1197 7260 9680 13690
1930 – 2000 (Middle East and Asia)	1197$ 7260 9680 13690
2030 – 2100 (Europe)*	1197
2300 – 2330 (East & South Asia)	7190 7200 9545 11925 13775
2330 – 2400 (East & South Asia)	7190 7200 7225 7260 9545 11805 11925 13735 13775 15205

Frequencies are in kiloHertz (kHz). 1 MegaHertz (MHz) is equal to 1000 kHz. Conversion to meter bands: Meters = 300,000/frequency in kHz. E.g.: 17705 kHz →16.9 meters

Abbreviations: All programs/frequencies are on daily unless noted otherwise.

* Monday through Friday
# Tuesday through Saturday
> Friday and Saturday
$ Saturday and Sunday
+ Sunday and Monday

APPENDIX 9. *Metric Equivalents*

$$(°F - 32) \times 0.555 = °C$$

$$(°C \times 1.8) + 32 = °F$$

feet per second $\times$ 0.5921 = knots

feet $\times$ 0.3 = meters

inches $\times$ 2.54 = centimeters

ounces $\times$ 28.25 = grams

pounds $\times$ 0.454 = kilograms

fluid ounces $\times$ 29.6 = milliliters

cups $\times$ 2.4 = deciliters

pints $\times$ 0.47 = liters

quarts $\times$ 0.946 = liters

U.S. gallons $\times$ 3.785 = liters

cubic inches $\times$ 16.39 = cubic
    centimeters

inches (of barometric pressure)
    $\times$ 33.86 = millibars

pounds per square inch $\times$ 0.7031
    = kilograms per square centimeter

WIND STRENGTH CONVERSION

Knots	Meters per Second	Kilometers per Hour
5	2.6	9.3
10	5.1	18.5
15	7.7	27.8
20	10.3	37.0
25	12.9	46.3
30	15.4	55.6
35	18	64.8
40	20.6	74.0
45	23.2	83.3
50	25.7	92.6
60	30.9	111.1
65	33.4	120.4
70	36	129.6
80	41.2	148.2
90	46.3	166.7
100	51.5	185.2

ROPE DIAMETER EQUIVALENTS

Inches	Millimeters
1/16	1.5
1/8	3
3/16	5
1/4	6
5/16	8
3/8	9
7/16	11
1/2	12
9/16	14
5/8	16
3/4	19
7/8	22
1	25

ESTIMATING WIND STRENGTH PREDICATED ON SPACING OF ISOBARS

Weather maps generally show isobars spaced either 3 or 4 millibars apart. Measure the distance in nautical miles between isobars, then find the distance under the column that corresponds to your latitude. Read across to the left-hand column for an approximation of wind speed resultant from the isobar spacing.

	Approximate Latitude							
	30°		40°		50°		60°	
	3 mb	4 mb	3 mb	4 mb	3 mb	4 mb	3 mb	4 mb
Wind Speed in Knots	Nautical Miles between Isobars							
10	345	461	269	358	225	301	199	266
15	230	307	179	239	150	200	133	177
20	173	230	134	179	113	150	100	133
25	138	184	107	143	90	120	80	106
30	115	154	90	119	75	100	66	89
35	99	132	77	102	64	86	57	76
40	86	115	67	90	56	75	50	66
50	69	92	54	72	45	60	40	53
60	58	77	45	60	38	50	53	44

Offshore Sailing: 200 ESSENTIAL PASSAGEMAKING TIPS

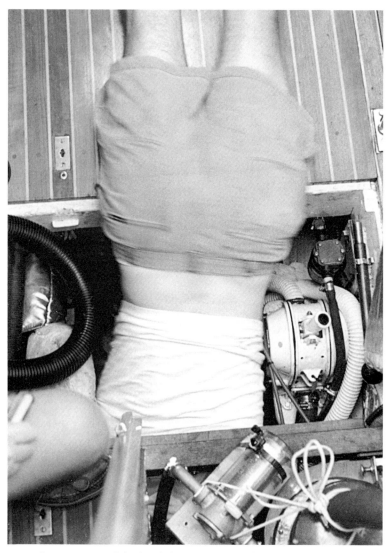

Now that you've read this book, here's some hindsight from the people who do it:

Definition of World Cruising:
Being head down, backside up
In all sorts of foreign ports
Where parts are hard to come by.

If this doesn't scare you, come do it—really, it's not a bad life!

Numbers in **bold** refer to pages with
   illustrations

water tanks
    fouled, 108–9
    ideal system, 182–83
    and tees, for flushing, **101–2**
wave heights, 17, 121
weather and navigation services. *See
    also* radio communications
    Hilgenberg's service, 140–42
    other sources, 84
    Web resources, 142–43
weight
    overall effect (sinkage), 127, 170
    of vessel (displacement), 170
weight distribution, fore and aft, 126
wheel steering, 173–74
whipping lines, **38**
winches, 177
    and securing docklines, **23**
wind angles, optimum, 170
wind indicators, **55**, 82
windlasses, waterproofing chain pipe
    in, **13**

windows
    construction and design, **186–87**
    storm shutters, **21**
wind strength
    estimating, 232
    metric equivalents, 231
wind vanes, **81**, **82**
wire
    electrical, 177
    standing rigging, 187
wiring. *See* electric wiring
wiring harness, 93
WLO voice radio frequencies, 223
wood
    interior woodwork, 184–85
    removable, 176

Y

yacht design, ideal
    deck hardware and fittings,
        175–77
    electrical system, 177–80

fuel supply, **183–84**
hull and deck construction,
    170–73, **172**
interior, 184–87
plumbing, 180–83
rig design, 187–88
stability, 169–70
steering, 173–75
yachting associations, 218–21
yachts
    naming, 84
    performance comparisons,
        169–70
    proof of ownership, 189
yellow card, 190

Z

zarpe, 189–90
zinc, 114
    deterioration, **95**, 180